Journey to the Holy Land

JOURNEY TO THE
HOLY LAND

A PILGRIM'S DIARY

AMIR AHMAD ALAWI

Translated, and with an Introduction, by
MUSHIRUL HASAN
RAKHSHANDA JALIL

OXFORD
UNIVERSITY PRESS

OXFORD

UNIVERSITY PRESS

YMCA Library Building, Jai Singh Road, New Delhi 110 001

Oxford University Press is a department of the University of Oxford. It furthers the
University's objective of excellence in research, scholarship, and education
by publishing worldwide in

Oxford   New York

Auckland   Cape Town   Dar es Salaam   Hong Kong   Karachi   Kuala Lumpur
Madrid   Melbourne   Mexico City   Nairobi   New Delhi   Shanghai   Taipei   Toronto

With offices in

Argentina   Austria   Brazil   Chile   Czech Republic   France   Greece   Guatemala
Hungary   Italy   Japan   Poland   Portugal   Singapore   South Korea   Switzerland
Thailand   Turkey   Ukraine   Vietnam

Oxford is a registered trademark of Oxford University Press
in the UK and in certain other countries

Published in India by Oxford University Press, New Delhi

© Oxford University Press 2009

First published 2009
Third impression 2010

ISBN-13: 978-0-19-806346-9
ISBN-10: 0-19-806346-6

Photographs: pp. ii–iii (On the Perilous Journey), vi–vii, viii, 88,
courtesy M.A. Mirza
Sketch: p. 258, courtesy Rasheed Ahmad

Typeset in Arno Pro 11/13
by Sai Graphic Design, New Delhi 110 055
Printed in India by Artxel, New Delhi 110 020
Published by Oxford University Press
YMCA Library Building, Jai Singh Road, New Delhi 110 001

Contents

غالبؔ ندیمِ دوست سے آتی ہے بوئے دوست

مشغولِ حق ہوں بندگیِ بو تراب میں

The Kaaba and its surroundings

Acknowledgements

We extend our heartfelt gratitude to all those who have helped in bringing out this book. Mehjabeen has helped us immensely with the Urdu text. Mohammad Javed Ansari and Shujaat Umar Khan have also been of great assistance. Nishat Zaidi and R.I. Faynan helped with the translation of Urdu and Arabic verses. R.I. Faynan spent days explaining to us the hajj terminology. We would call him at odd hours to seek clarifications to which he readily obliged. Abdul Halim translated the Persian verses for us. Amera Khatoon and H.J. Abidi were useful allies in the Dr Zakir Husain Library, Jamia Millia Islamia. Francis Robinson read the rather extended Introduction with meticulous care. M.A. Mirza from Saudi Arabia and Amera Khatoon furnished the photographs and sketches. While Mohammad Hanif Khan travelled back and forth to deliver proofs, Shujaat Sahib and Mohammad Shakir were always at hand with the Arabic and Persian dictionaries. A good part of the *sawaab* (blessing) for this venture must go to them.

A view of Medina, AD 1907 (AH 1325)

Origins, Journeys and Return
Hajj in Colonial India

Mushirul Hasan
Rakhshanda Jalil

It is the divine command for those men and women to undertake the journey once in their lives, who have sufficient resources to meet the exigencies of the road, and to maintain their families at home during their absence. Should a person be really desirous of going on the pilgrimage, and possess everything necessary for the journey, but owing to indisposition, or through fear of an enemy, be unable to proceed, if he appoint a deputy, and furnishing him with all the requisites, request him to undertake it for him in his name, and the latter putting on the pilgrim's habit, travel on his behalf, the former will obtain all the blessings attendant on the pilgrimage. Or, if a rich man or a prince, without any excuse, dispatches another person to perform the pilgrimage in his name, he earns the merit of it.[1]

Many valuable glimpses of leading writers in the nineteenth century are given in some recent writings on migration, pilgrimage and travel.[2] These we might classify as the informative, the fictional and the impressionist. By far, the greater numbers of books are on the sacred journey to Mecca, the *Ummul-Qura* (mother of all settlements), and Medina. They are from the *hajjis* themselves, who enter the Babun Nabi,

1 Jaffur Shurref (1863), *Qanoon-i Islam or The Customs of the Mussulmans of India Comprising a Full and Exact Account of their Various Rites and Ceremonies from the Moment of Birth till the Hour of Death*, translated by G.A. Herklots, Madras, p. 41.

2 For example Bushra Rahman (1999), *Urdu ke Ghair Mazhabi Safarname*, Gorakhpur; Mirza Hamid Beg (1989), *Urdu Safarnama ki Mukhtasar Tarikh*, Islamabad.; Khalid Mahmud (1995), *Urdu Safarnamon ka Tanqeedi Mutaala*, Delhi.

the gate on the north side of the Masjidul Haram, the great mosque in Mecca, with their heads held high. They offer an innocent, and perhaps an altogether useful insight into the belief system of one of the fastest growing religions in the world.

A massive collection of the hajj documents was published in ten volumes in 1993. Hajj accounts, too, have grown,[1] though they are much less regarded as worthy of serious study by the professional historian. M.N. Pearson's work lucidly analyses a heavy subject in the manner that one could wish for. Barbara Metcalf's unfinished intellectual project conjures up the picture of an authoritative and deep study. Shireen Moosvi provides the medieval background in a substantial and thoughtful essay; Sugata Bose, on the other hand, recreates the experience, atmosphere, and meanings of the hajj in the modern period. He focuses on two of Urdu's foremost writers, Khwaja Hasan Nizami (1875–1955) and Abdul Majid Daryabadi (1892–1977), who won respect and admiration for their scholarship. Both wrote history and historical biographies, which are good to read though rarely objective. Two other recent historians, Siobhan Lambert-Hurley and Subah Dayal, shed light on women's writings on hajj, an otherwise ill-chartered terrain.

Recently, Radhika Singha has uncovered the contradictory drives shaping the colonial intervention in hajj mobility. She traces how the figure of 'the Hindi' during Ottoman rule transmuted into the figure of 'the Mohammedan British Indian subject' under the British. She discusses, moreover, the image of poverty-stricken hajjis, so sedulously cultivated by some historians and colonial officials, as the product of an institutional and discursive process, 'one by which resources were stripped away from undoubtedly poor pilgrims and stigma and incapacity tagged to them.'[2]

Other admirably written short books and essays of self-examination and religious piety also exist, whereas scores of Urdu books are nothing more or less than a perfectly normal travelogue, recording an author's immediate reactions.

---

1 Ziaullah Khokar (ed.) (2004), *Faharisul Asfar*, Gujranwala.

2 'Passport, Ticket, and India-rubber Stamp: "The Problem of the Pauper Pilgrim" in Colonial India, *c.* 1882–1925', in Ashwini Tambe and Herald Fischer-Tine (eds) (2009), *The Limits of Colonial Control in South Asia, Spaces of Disorder in the Indian Ocean Region*, London.

Introduced here, for the first time, is a genuine firsthand account of a quintessentially Muslim journey. Written in a disarming prose style by an industrious scholar-journalist, its author Munshi Amir Ahmad Alawi (1879–1952) produced a *roznamcha* or daily diary, *Safar-i Sa'adat* (Propitious Journey), which is both a song of lamentation and a song of triumph. He watched, listened, and recorded with an air of confident authority. He not only focuses on the soul-stirring effects of his first hajj, but also gives 'the feel' of the period and catches the anomalies of Saudi life which tormented him, especially the malpractices, monopolies, and misdeeds that had crept in the name of commerce. In comparison to several other contemporary accounts, he displays a gay buoyancy and independence of mind and spirit. As for his co-passengers, they are different from one another, humble and arrogant, charming and sinister, righteous and satanic; yet, his dialogues with them are verbally rich because he is able to keep pace with his mind and desires. As a witness to their attributes and activities, Amir Ahmad's account has considerable posthumous significance.

This essay seeks to locate, briefly, the place of hajj in Islam, describe some of the well-known customs, rituals, and practices associated with it, and uncover, on the strength of the existing narratives, what it means when the first group of hajjis begin leaving for home, taking care to perform the *tawaf* or farewell as their final ritual act. Before the age of aeroplanes, automobiles, and airconditioners, the journey was tough, to say the least. Nonetheless, the hajjis trivialized their dangers and inconveniences in the knowledge that they would soon enter the House of God and stand before the great granite block enveloped in its black veil. Towards the end of this essay, we explore the geo-political situation of Hijaz—the strip of land hugging the eastern coast of the Red Sea containing the Holy Cities of Mecca and Medina—and the battle for political ascendancy of the House of Saud (the royal family of the Kingdom of Saudi Arabia).

What is Thy Command? I am here, O God!
What is Thy Command? I am here!
What is Thy Command? I am here!
Thou art without companion!
What is Thy Command? I am here!

Pilgrimage to the holy sites necessitated a sea voyage for the overland caravan route, which ran through inhospitable deserts and barren mountainous ranges. It is therefore a symbolic movement incorporating both bodily relocation and heightened piety. *The Encyclopaedia of Religion* identifies the classic three-stage form of a rite of passage of time: separation (the start of the journey); the liminal stage (the journey itself, the stay at the shrine, and the encounter with the sacred); and reaggregation (homecoming).[1] It is not the only factor making for cultural unity and social mobility in the Islamic world—but it is certainly an important one, perhaps the most important.[2]

The historian M.N. Pearson establishes an interesting link between the sea and maritime literature: a Muslim community developed around the shores of the Indian Ocean, linked by religion. Travelling scholars created and reinforced its commonality.[3] In earlier times, the only reason for the Muslims from the non-coastal areas to cross the Arabian Sea and the Red Sea was to travel to the holy sites. Ibn Battuta (1304–1368/9), who entered India through the north-western gateway, referred to 'the innumerable host of pilgrims' from Iraq, Khurasan, the Persian Gulf, and other eastern lands, 'so that the earth surged with them like the sea and their march resembled the movement of a high-piled cloud'. Without indicating how many people like himself had gathered in Damascus in 1326 to join the hajj caravan to Mecca, Frescobaldi, the Florentine nobleman who was in Damascus in 1384 at the start of the pilgrimage, estimated the company to number about 20,000.[4] In the sixteenth century, Haji Begum, the wife of Humayun (1508–1556), the Mughal emperor, went on the hajj during 1563–4, though it is unclear whether she went by sea via Sind or by the overland caravan route. As more ships began to ply to the Red Sea from Gujarat during Jalaluddin Mohammad Akbar's time (r. 1556–1604), Gulbadan Begum, his aunt, undertook the sea voyage during the winter monsoon of 1576. Such a large group of imperial women was never heard of again—later during Akbar's reign, or under any of his grand successors.[5] They themselves worked out the details of the journey that took place either through

1 Lindsay Jones (ed.) (2005), *The Encyclopaedia of Religion*, (2nd edition), Vol. 10, USA, p. 145.

2 Bernard Lewis, 'Hadjdj', *Encyclopaedia of Islam*, (New edition), Vol. 3, p. 37.

3 Michael Pearson (2003), *The Indian Ocean*, London, p. 62.

4 Ibn Battuta (1929), *Travels in Asia and Africa, 1325–1354*, translated and selected by H.A.R. Gibb, London, p. 78; Ross E. Dunn (1985), *The Adventures of Ibn Battuta: A Muslim Traveller of the 14th Century*, California.

5 Ruby Lal (2005), *Domesticity and Power in the Early Mughal World*, Cambridge, pp. 211–12.

Iraq or through Gujarat, across the Arabian Sea. At a time when Akbar's religious policies were under critical scrutiny in some circles, their pilgrimage may have helped reinforce the Islamic face of the empire.

Gulbadan Begum took in her charge Akbar's cousin and wife Salima Sultan Begum, two daughters of Akbar's uncle Kamran, the widow of his uncle Askari as well as others from the royal harem. Senior officers accompanied them. Their job was not merely to ensure physical safety and deter the Portuguese or any other wayfarers foolhardy enough to waylay the ladies from the Mughal harem but, equally, to quell false rumours among the pious passengers in their charge. The *Akbarnama* gives a detailed account of the party headed by Gulbadan Begum as the seniormost woman and mentions Akbar's worries that the two junks carrying the royal party, *Salimi* and *Ilahi*, might fall prey to the Portuguese who controlled the waters leading up to the Red Sea, which made him go so far as to dissuade his aunt from proceeding beyond the waters of Surat. The *Akbarnama* also mentions that Qulich Khan, governor of Surat, helped obtain passes or *qaul*, which allowed the junks to sail unmolested. The ladies were aboard the *Salimi*, whereas the male escorts were on the *Ilahi*, headed by the chief escort, a certain Sultan Khwaja, whose job was to send a detailed report of the voyage to the emperor.

Another luminous account is left by Bayazid Bayat, an official who sought leave from Akbar to go on hajj with his three sons in March-April 1578. However, permission was denied to him because the emperor did not want wealth to leave Indian shores under the pretext of the hajj. Eventually, though, Bayazid was allowed to board the *Muhammadi* in March 1580 after due inspection of all the goods he carried, whose worth was Rs 1,00,000. The ship sailed from Surat to Daman, where it paid an exorbitant 10,000 mahmudis for the Portuguese pass, a system of official blackmail so ruthlessly perfected that the Portuguese took away one of Bayazid's sons till the full amount was paid to them. His ship crossed Gulbadan Begum's ship as the latter was returning home. He himself was to return two years later, having run the gamut of adventures from being marooned on a port in southern Oman for four months, witnessing a near-mutiny on board, and the still-prevalent rite of passage of clearing his goods from custom.

As travel picked up between Surat and Aden, several Mughal nobles began to get ships built for themselves—some for solely religious reasons, others for trade. Mirza Aziz Koka, Akbar's foster brother and governor of Gujarat, had one; so did Atgah Khan and Abdur Rahim Khani-i Khanan, among several other high-ranking nobles. One of Akbar's imperial decrees instructed shipowners to send as many scholars as possible on the holy voyage. While they charged a modest sum for the fare and provisions for the journey, the passengers could not carry goods to barter or trade. Merchants who wished to take cargo on such ships could do so by paying a shipping freight, which was distributed among the needy as deemed fit by the captain of the vessel. Clearly, the pilgrim passengers were favoured over those who boarded the ships only to gain profit along the way.[1]

Even though inaccessible routes, earthly calamities, and fatigue slowed down the travel, Mecca, a barren city, achieved some degree of prosperity as a trading centre. Some months preceding hajj, it would become 'one of the largest fairs of the East, and certainly the more interesting, from the variety of nations which frequent it', wrote John Lewis Burckhardt in mid-1818.[2] The season of slave trade activity in the Red Sea area during the hajj usually coincided with the south-west monsoon (April to October) when dhows were enabled to sail northward from East Africa to Arabia. Slave brokers and their agents from the Muslim countries then swooped down on the towns of Arabia to do business with pilgrims who, on their return from Mecca, often purchased one or two slaves to take home with them.

Muslim merchants thronged the cities, mingled with the pilgrims, and traded in the big bazaars. They sold glass and metalware, cotton goods, olive oil, and dried fruits. In 1902, goods worth 10 lakh sterling were sold. While the less privileged used their merchandise to buy passage, food and accommodation, others sold rice in exchange for ornate cloth, and spices in exchange for goods infused with religious significance.[3] In the towns of Nejd, people were in want of Indian goods, drugs and articles of dress, which they procured either from Medina, or at a cheaper rate from Mecca. In Mina, the merchants arriving with the Syrian caravan,

1 The above is based on Shireen Moosvi (2008), *People, Taxation, and Trade in Mughal India*, New Delhi, pp. 244–8.

2 Adam Mez, *The Renaissance of Islam* (translated from German by Salahuddin Khuda Bakhsh and D.S. Margoliuth) (reprint 1979), Delhi, p. 500; John Lewis Burckhardt, *Travels in Arabia* (reprint 1968), London, p. 188; André Wink (1999), *Al-Hind: The Making of Indo-Islamic World*, Delhi, Vol. 1, p. 33.

3 Michael Pearson (2003), *The Indian Ocean*, London, pp. 173–5; J. L. Burckhardt, *Travels in Arabia*, pp. 189, 281.

bargained from Indian goods, and exhibited samples of the articles that they had themselves brought, and which were lying in the warehouses at Mecca.[1] Brassware from Moradabad was freely available to Nadir Ali, the hajji from Meerut. In the Bazaar-i Saweqa, wealthy merchants like Hajji Ali Khan Dehalwi had set up their business establishments and sold fabrics, condiments and swords.[2] Non-Muslims were the subsidiary beneficiaries, as in the case of the shipping companies, port authorities, and large trading conglomerates.

While the overriding impulse of that great throng of humanity was quintessentially religious, trade, politics and religion were intertwined as Mecca evolved into a merchant republic, a precursor of Venice, Pisa, and Genoa. The birth of Mohammad (570) made Mecca a city of destiny. Then, the 'descent' of the first *suras* of revelation gave this barren city of Hijaz a niche in the hall of immortals.[3] A merchant community in Southeast Asia had a saying, 'If one of them had silver, he would buy gold, but if he prospered further, he would go to Mecca.'[4] Even though some challenge the notion of correlating hajj with pan-Islamism,[5] nationalism and colonialism clashed on the high seas. Sharing and disseminating information—both worldly and religious—occurred with the buying and selling.[6] W.S. Blunt (1840–1922) observed:

The annual Haj at Mecca draws the more religious from all parts of India, and the Hajjis on their return are treated with exceptional respect and visited by their friends and neighbours, who naturally inquire about the latest news and doctrines propounded in the Holy Cities; so that for the dissemination of their views the most effective way would be for the propagandists to bring the Hajjis under their influence. I call it *effective*, because the influence of what the Hajjis say goes to the remotest villages of the Mofussil.[7]

The wider religious arena offered the opportunity to interact, to share mutual experiences, and to work out political arrangements.

---

1 J. L. Burckhardt, *Travels in Arabia*, pp. 189, 281.

2 Nadir Ali (1902), *Miratul Arab Yaani Safarnama-i Nadir*, Delhi, pp. 114, 136.

3 F.E. Peters (1994), *The Hajj: The Muslim Pilgrimage to Mecca and the Holy Places*, Princeton, N.J., pp. 180–2; M.N. Pearson (1994), *Pious Passengers: The Hajj in Earlier Times*, Delhi.

4 Michael Pearson (2003), *The Indian Ocean*, London, p. 72.

5 Subah Dayal (Forthcoming), 'Encounters of Empires: The Hajj Sojourner and Pan-Islamiam', *Third Frame*, Delhi.

6 Nadir Ali, *Miratul Arab Yaani Safarnama-i Nadir*, pp. 239–40.

7 W.S. Blunt (1882), *The Future of Islam*, London, p. 211.

Although such instances were rare, on the eve of and during the First World War, the hajjis colluded with the Germans and the Russians to overthrow British rule. Certainly, a few *ulama* of Deoband were involved in the Turco-German plots. Ubaidullah Sindhi (1887–1953), a Sikh convert to Islam, and Maulana Mahmud Hasan (1851–1920), principal of Deoband's Darul-ulum, had some part to play in the 'Silk Letter Conspiracy'.[1] Others like Abdul Majid Daryabadi discussed with the leader of the Sanusi rebellion aspects of Islam and the status of the Indian Muslim community. He compared the Sheikh with Syed Ahmad of Rae Bareli (1786–1831), the architect of an anti-British front in northwestern India. No wonder that nervous bureaucrats were haunted by the spectre of a pan-Islamic assault on the British dominions and turned to monitoring the hajj traffic. 'The most highly organized European press-propaganda sinks into insignificance compared with this gigantic dissemination of ideas', wrote a British general.'[2]

The colonial system demanded that they do so, but even a limited intervention (as compared to that of the Dutch in Indonesia) ran the risk of alienating the Indian Muslims. Thus, the Anjuman-i Khuddam-i Kaaba, founded in May 1913, addressed the immediate problem of providing help and succour to the pilgrims.[3] While in gaol, Mohamed Ali (1878–1931) exchanged views with the intelligence officer, and, on 8 July 1914, he suggested to Talat Bey (1872–1921), minister of interior, that Turkey should form an Indian-Turco-Arabian Steamship Co., to oust the English firm from the pilgrim traffic. Shaukat Ali (1873–1938) chose to become a 'Pilgrim's Broker'; Mohamed Ali wrote of his

1 M. Naeem Qureshi (1999), *Pan-Islam in British Indian Politics: A Study of the Khilafat Movement 1918–1924*, Leiden, pp. 78–81; Ayesha Jalal (2008), *Partisans of Allah: Jihad in South Asia*, Delhi, pp. 220–2. Indeed such examples of interaction and diffusion and their transmission took place in various corners of the world, except in places like Indonesia where the Dutch authorities imposed limits on the size of the pilgrims to counter anti-government activities. The government in Calcutta could not do so. Apart from the Queen's proclamation of religious neutrality in 1858, Whitehall did not like messing around with religious issues. G. R. Hawting, 'The Haj in the Second World War', in Ian Richard Nelton (ed.) (1993), *Golden Roads: Migration, Pilgrimage and Travel in Mediaeval and Modern Islam*, London; Deliar Noer (1973), *The Modernist Muslim Movement in Indonesia 1900–1942*, London, pp. 25–6. Joseph Schacht with C.E. Bosworth (eds) (1979), *The Legacy of Islam*, second edition, Oxford, p. 154.

2 Major N.N.E. Bray (1934), *Shifting Sands*, London, p. 16.

3 Francis Robinson (1974), *Separatism among Indian Muslims: The Politics of the United Provinces' Muslims, 1860–1923*, Cambridge, pp. 208–9.

brother's devotion to the hapless poor pilgrims and their plight in the so-called 'pilgrim shelters':

Here lay the most helpless mass of humanity huddled together, awaiting a favourable turn in the passage-market and in the meantime compelled to eat away in this macabre-like suspense the meager savings of half a life-time, thus reducing the very means with which it could avail itself of the long-waited-for opportunity of securing a cheap passage to the Holy Land of Islam. To the shipping Company that had gradually acquired a monopoly of this traffic, and relying on that used to commence its pilgrimage season with cheap passages and after thus luring these helpless creatures to the only port of embarkation, used to raise them when they arrived there from the remotest corners of India, and from neighbouring countries as well, my 'Broker' brother's and his 'Broker Servants' some of whom were graduates and well-to-do members of some of the best families, must have been as great a nuisance as he on his side found the Company to be. After a prolonged controversy, he came to the conclusion that the best solution of this terrible problem would be a Shipping Company for the pilgrim traffic established by the charitable Muslims themselves, beginning with Indian Muslim Princes who should contribute one or more boats according to the rank and revenue of their states; but which should be run on sound enough business lines so that losses could be avoided. Such small profits as resulted could be utilized to increase the comforts and conveniences of 'Allah's guests' and repatriate those whom some sudden misfortune during the pilgrimage had thrown upon the charity of their co-religionists.[1]

THE SEPARATION

Truly, the first House of Worship established for humankind is the one at Bakkah [Mecca], a blessing and guidance to all realms of being. In it are clear signs, such as the Place of Ibrahim, and whoever enters [the Meccan precincts] is safe. The *hajj* to the House is a duty humankind owes to God, that is, for those who are able to journey to it (Quran: 3: 96–7).

Hajj literally means an *effort*, though it is translated as pilgrimage. One of the five pillars of Islam, it is obligatory upon every Muslim to undertake it once in a lifetime. It begins on the eighth of the month of Zul Hijja, the day of setting out for Arafat, which is located some 13 miles east of Mecca. On that day in June 1927, Mohammad Habibur Rahman, the author of *Habibul Hujjaj*, noticed millions forsaking their everyday, material selves when they shed their everyday clothes and, clad in the two pieces of white unstitched cloth, united in a common purpose. The well-to-do but infirm or incapacitated send others to undertake the hajj

---

1 Mushirul Hasan (ed.) (1982), *Mohamed Ali in Indian Politics: Select Writings*, Vol. 1, Delhi, pp. 66–7, 71; Mushirul Hasan (ed.) (1999), *My Life: A Fragment, An Autobiographical Sketch of Maulana Mohamed Ali*, Delhi, pp. 88–9.

on their behalf. So do their rich compatriots. Often one man, dressed in the *ihram*, represents more than one person or even an entire village, or he may observe the rite of pilgrimage by proxy.

Mir Taqi Mir (1722–1810), the Urdu poet, had introduced a satirical note:

قصدِ حج ہے تو شیخ کو لے چل

کعبہ جانے کو یہ بھی خر ہے شرط

Qasde haj hai to shaikh ko le chal
Kaaba jaane ko ye bhi khar hai shart

You're going to make the Pilgrimage? Then take the shaikh along;
If you're to reach Kaaba, you must take an ass with you?[1]

Despite its satirical vein, this kind of poetry stimulated the reader's imagination to the pitch where he/she perceives the Reality with the freshness and wonder of new words and images. A fresh stimulus is the invocation, with its alternate kneeling, rising, and prostration towards Mecca, spoken in low tones, distinguishable at first, then blending to a whispered murmur: 'Peace be with thee and thy glory'.

During another period but in the same city—Delhi—lived Mirza Asadullah Khan Ghalib (1797–1869). The influence of Mir and Ghalib upon each other, and the nature of their influences, has been much dwelt upon. When Ghalib wrote about Mir, he recollected the sensation of a particular experience, but the mood is that of the ecstasy which informs all great poetry. Both would have had to perform the circumambulations around the Kaaba, 'the sanctuary of the free, and the threshold of the Prophet, who is God's blessing to all the worlds, is the resting place of His devotees'.[2] Indeed, it is part of the ritual to walk seven times around the Kaaba in order to show respect to the central sanctuary of Islam, acquire the apex of spiritual experience, journey through 'the enlightened history of Islam,' and recall to oneself the basic demands of Islamic life. While all other houses have fallen into ruin, the Kaaba, being the prime focus and the symbol of Islam's permanent and

---

1 The English translations of Mir's verses are from Ralph Russell and Khurshidul Islam (1992), *Three Mughal Poets: Mir, Sauda, Mir Hasan*, London, pp. 173–4.

2 Ghalib, if he will take me with him on the Pilgrimage
   His Majesty may have my share of heavenly reward.
Ralph Russell and Khurshidul Islam (1994), *Ghalib: Life and Letters*, Delhi, p. 70.

immutable character, continues to symbolize the vitality of monotheism.[1] No wonder, it attracts Muslims, quite literally, like a magnet. Ibn Battuta expressed the experience of pilgrimage thus:

Of the wondrous doings of God Most High is this, that He has created the hearts of men with an instinctive desire to seek these sublime sanctuaries, and yearning to present themselves at their illustrious sites, and has given the love of them such power over men's hearts that none alights in them but they seize his whole heart, nor quits them but with grief at separation from them.[2]

Both the colonial and the 'modern' historiography scarcely recognize that scores of Urdu poets did not image the Kaaba and the Kashi as symbols of contestation but as representations of the unity of god, his beauty, and radiance. The Baitullah[3] or the House of God denotes not a separation of minds and hearts but a common object of worship to be venerated by each and every lover of Allah. Consequently, while relegating the symbolism of a mosque or a temple to second place, Mir Taqi Mir underlined the uppermost aspect of one's faith being the contact with God, the access to the summits of Divine Majesty, and the idea of God's radiant beauty—one that neither the Sheikh nor the Brahmin comprehends.

It is an article of literary faith for innumerable writers that Mir Taqi Mir was, in some ways, ahead of his time in articulating heterodox ideas and an inclusive vision in his poetry. Without taking recourse to the trivialities and ephemeralities of Urdu poetry, his intricate and subtle mind reflected on symbols of unity and common worship. The largeness and penetration of Mir's vision is illustrated by the following lines:

کس کو کہتے ہیں نہیں میں جانتا اسلام و کفر

دیر ہو یا کعبہ مطلب مجھ کو تیرے در سے ہے

Kis ko kehte hain nahin main jaanta islam-o-kufr,
dair ho ya kaaba matlab mujh ko tere dar se hai.

1 Captain Sir Richard Burton (1913), *Personal Narrative of a Pilgrimage to Al Madinah and Meccah*, Vol. 1, London.

2 Annemarie Schimmel (1982), *As Through a Veil: Mystical Poetry in Islam*, New York, p. 197; Battuta quoted in Albert Hourani (1991), *A History of the Arab Peoples*, London, p. 151.

3 It is spoken of in the Quran as Al-masjid. It is a structure and the focal point of identification for the Muslim with Allah, namely the Kaaba. All Muslims face this house when they pray and are obliged to make a proper pilgrimage to it at least once in their lifetime if they can afford it.

What does it mean to me? Call me believer, call me infidel.
I seek His threshold, be it in the temple or the mosque.

مقصود درد دل ہے نہ اسلام ہے نہ کفر

پھر ہر گلے میں سبّحہ و زُنّار کیوں نہ ہو

Maqsood dard e-dil hai na islam hai na kufr
phir har gale me sabha-o-zunnar kyon na ho.

The bond of love is all—Islam and unbelief are nothing:
Take rosary and sacred cord and wear them on your neck.

شرکت شیخ و برہمن سے میر

کعبہ و دیر سے بھی جائے گا

اپنی ڈیڑھ اینٹ کی جدی مسجد

کسی ویرانے میں بنائے گا

Shirkato shaikh-o-birahman se meer
kaaba-o-dair se bhi jaaiga.
Apni derh eent ki jaddi masjid,
kisi weeraane me banaiye ga.

Mir, quit the company of Shaikh and Brahmin
And mosque and temple too—leave them behind.
Lay one stone on another in the desert:
Worship your Love at your own humble shrine.

اس کے فروغ حسن سے جھمکے ہے سب میں نور

شمع حرم ہو یا کہ دیا سومنات کا

Uske faroghe husn se jhamke hai sab me noor,
sham-e-haram ho ya ke diya somnaat ka.

It is the power of *His* beauty that fills the world with light,
Be it the Kaaba's candle or the lamp that lights Somnath.

Chronology matters little, but still when we come to Mohammad
Iqbal (1876–1938) we have, in vivid colours, a description of the Kaaba
in the *masnawi, Rumuz-i Bekhudi*. To him, the Baitullah bears with it
all the influence of centuries of associations carrying his back to the

cradle of his faith and reminding him of the worship of the One God. The Kaaba, moreover, reminds him that all his brethren worship in that direction, that he is one of the great company of believers, united by one faith, filled with the same hopes, reverencing the same thing, worshipping the same Allah. According to Iqbal, 'the centre of the Islamic nation is the House of God where all Muslims are brethren.' His own role is that of a caravan bell, which helps guide the travellers to the central sanctuary in Mecca, as the title of the Urdu collection of poetry, *Bang-i Dara* indicates.[1] He connects Mecca with different locations in diverse continents—to the flowing river in Punjab, to the antecedents of Islam in the supreme sacrifice of Ismail, the eldest son of Abraham, to Imam Husain, the martyr of Karbala (strange and simple and colourful is the story of Kaaba; its end is Husain, its beginning Ismail), and to the glory of Andalusia. Such is his emotional response that he envisaged a Muslim fraternity as a series of concentric circles with a shared centre in Mecca.[2] With his emphasis on the unity and egalitarian ethos promoted by the sacred journey, Iqbal's arguments find a resonance in the notion of 'communitas'. Victor Turner defined communitas as the spontaneous and joyful commonsense of feeling, liable to strike pilgrims at some stage during the pilgrimage process.[3]

It is said of Rudyard Kipling (1865–1936) that he could write for any national occasion of national concern, not perfunctorily or as 'a job' but because he was profoundly stirred by such events and could immerse himself in them as other poets immerse themselves in eternal issues. Iqbal's poems, which were sometimes interspersed and welded with his letters and lectures, reflect this skill. No wonder that he sensitively portrayed the Hijaz as Islam's spiritual and material centre and the Prophet's Mosque in Medina (in full, *Madinat al-Nabi*, the city of the Prophet) as one of the two sanctuaries of Islam, the other being in Mecca. 'One prayer in this my Mosque is more efficacious than a thousand in other places, save only the Masjidul Haram,' the Prophet is reported to have said. Therefore, his followers must pray all five times a day and spend as much time as possible in these two places, apart from

1 Annemarie Schimmel (1963), *Gabriel's Wing, A Study into the Religious Ideas of Sir Muhammad Iqbal*, Leiden, p. 47; Annemarie Schimmel (1982), *As Through a Veil: Mystical Poetry in Islam*, New York, p. 208.

2 Javed Majeed (2009), *Muhammad Iqbal, Islam, Aesthetics and Postcolonialism*, London, p. 63.

3 Victor Turner (1979), *Process, Performance and Pilgrimage*, New Delhi.

the time spent in the hajj rituals. 'In this fulfilment,' wrote Muhammad Asad, a convert to Islam who performed hajj five times, 'man strides along in all his God-given splendour; his stride is joy, and his knowledge is freedom, and his world a sphere within bounds ...'[1]

THE LIMINAL STAGE

Labbaik, Allahumma, labbaik
For Thee I am ready, O God, for Thee I am ready!

If the fatigues, privations and difficulties of the pilgrimage to Mecca be considered, the distance of Hindustan must render the hajj a formidable undertaking; fulfilling the injunction of the law-givers, and at the same time, gratifying their laudable feelings of sympathy and curiosity—their sympathy as regards the religious veneration for the places and its purposes; their curiosity, to witness with their own eyes those places rendered sacred by the words of the Quran in one instance, and also for the deposits contained in the several tombs of the prophets, whom they have been taught to revere and respect as the servants of God.[2]

Indian ships ferried back and forth carrying pilgrims to Mecca.[3] Often, their passengers stayed on. Muzaffar Shams (d. 1400), an immigrant from Balkh, taught *hadith* for four years.[4] Abdul Haqq Dehlawi performed the hajj rites, studied in Mecca to perform his 'secondary goal', and upon his return set up a madrasa in Delhi for the Sharia disciplines. He criticized the various religious movements during Akbar's reign.[5]

The stay of Shah Waliullah (1703–1763) of Delhi in April 1731 coincided with the education of Mohammad bin Abdul Wahhab (1703–1787), the architect of a new fundamentalist ideology. A pupil of Shaikh Abdul Tahir Mohammad bin Ibrahim of Medina and Shaikh Tajuddin Qali, Mecca's mufti, he experienced in his dreams and revelations the Prophet inspiring him to assume his community's religious and political

---

1 Muhammad Asad, *Road to Mecca* (reprint 2000), London, pp. 174–5.

2 Meer Hasan Ali (1974), *Observations on the Mussulmans of India* (reprint of 1832 edition), Delhi, pp. 112–13.

3 Suraiya Faroqhi (1994), *Pilgrims and Sultans: The Hajj under the Ottomans*, London, p. 159. For records of periodic rich donations to Mecca and Medina, Muzaffar Alam (2004), *The Languages of Political Islam in India, c. 1200–1800*, Delhi, p. 78.

4 Richard M. Eaton (1997), *The Rise of Islam and the Bengal Frontier, 1204–1760*, Delhi, pp. 86–7.

5 Scott Kugle (2008), 'Abd al-Haqq Dihlawi, 'An Accidental Revivalist: Knowledge and Power in the Passage from Delhi to Macca', *Journal of Islamic Studies*, Vol. 19, No. 2, May.

leadership.[1] Mir Ghulam Ali Azad Bilgrami (1704–1786), Waliullah's contemporary, accomplished the hajj and followed up with his study of *ahadith*.[2] In East Bengal, Hajji Shariat Allah (1781–1840) acted in accordance with the faith when he was only eighteen years of age; he spent nineteen years in the Hijaz and performed a second pilgrimage.

Syed Ahmad, the mujahidin leader, insisted that the hajj had fallen into abeyance owing to political disorder and Hindu/Shia influences.[3] He, therefore, set out with 400 followers, including women and children, and spent a year and 10 months travelling from May 1824 to 17 January 1826. The caravan stopped at Dalmau on the banks of the Ganges before reaching Calcutta in November 1821 via Allahabad, Banaras, and Azimabad (Patna). By the time their ship set sail, the Syed had 693 persons on board. With them, he discussed matters of faith, appointed *khalifas*, and secured the allegiance of others.[4] Piety, devotion, and benevolence moved his devotees.[5]

John Lewis Burckhardt, who entered Jiddah in mid-July 1814 disguised as a beggar, estimated the number of persons assembled at Arafat at about 70,000. This was confirmed by Lieutenant Richard F. Burton of the Bombay Army, one of the five prominent British writers known to have visited Mecca in 1853.[6] How did they arrive at these estimates is hard to tell! Meer Hasan Ali, the English lady who lived mostly in Lucknow from 1816 to 1828, reported caravans from north India travelling overland to Bombay and others making Calcutta their place of embarkation. The Arab ships carried cargoes of coffee, Arabian fruits, and drugs.[7] Indeed, of the total Muslim population, only a small percentage could at any time afford to pay for travel, food, lodging, and various services. However, with sea voyages becoming a little cheaper and a little more accessible with steam-powered ships sailing across the

1 Saiyid Athar Abbas Rizvi (1980), *Shah Wali-Allah and his Times*, Canberra, pp. 215–16.

2 Barbara Daly Metcalf (1982), *Islamic Revival in British India: Deoband, 1860–1900*, Delhi, pp. 44, 68.

3 Ibid., p. 61.

4 Qeyamuddin Ahmad (1994), *The Wahhabi Movement in India*, Delhi, p. 46; Barbara Daly Metcalf, *Islamic Revival in British India*, p. 61.

5 Mohiuddin Ahmad (1975), *Saiyid Ahmad Shahid: His Life and Mission*, Lucknow, Chapter 6.

6 John Sabini (1981), *Armies in the Sand: The Struggle for Mecca and Medina*, London, p. 209; J. L. Burckhardt, *Travels in Arabia*, p. 269.

7 Meer Hasan Ali, *Observations on the Mussalmans of India*, p. 114.

Arabian Sea, a marked increase in the hajj traffic took place.[1] In the early 1880s, Blunt noticed a massive congregation—93,250—at Arafat, a figure which 'afford[s] us as an index not without value of the degree of religious vitality existing in the various Mussulman countries.'[2] Of these, 15,000 were Indians (Table 1). In 1885, Mirza Mohammad Hosayan Farahani's *safarnama* mentioned 5,000 to 25,000 Indian pilgrims going to Mecca.[3] By the late nineteenth century, a total of at least 1,00,000 fulfilled their religious obligation; some 30,000 travelled by sea.[4] On 19 September 1920, a report from Istanbul stated that the caravans for Medina had left Mecca with 1,200 Indians.[5] From 1919 to 1928, on an average, 19,464 pilgrims sailed annually from the Indian ports.[6] International health records placed the figures at 55,000 in 1933, at 60,000 in 1934, at 80,000 in 1935, and at 10,000 in 1937. Of these, about half arrived by sea, mainly from India, Indonesia, and Malaysia.[7]

The numbers varied from year to year, depending on political and economic conditions at home, the weather, and the safety and security of the route. The decline, as and when it occurred, was due to poor harvesting and the consequent shortfall in incomes (Table 2). On the other hand, the increase, as in 1927 (Table 3), was due to the under-cutting of rates by the two rival shipping companies—the Mogul Line, owned by Messrs Turner Morrison and Company, and their new rivals, the Scindia Navigation Company (also known as the Hajj Line), owned mostly by some Hindu merchants. A decade later, the number of hajjis increased by 50 per cent (Table 4); most belonged to Bengal, Assam, Punjab, Sind, Baluchistan, and the North-West Frontier Province (NWFP). This was, again, owing to the rivalry between the shipping

1 From Indonesia, where it took three years for the journey alone in the first half of the nineteenth century, 7,300 persons performed the hajj from 1899 to 1909.

2 W.S. Blunt, *The Future of Islam*, p. 9.

3 Mirza Mohammad Hosayn Farahani (1990), *A Shiite Pilgrimage to Mecca 1885–1886*, London, p. 187.

4 UP Government Records (Political) 1894, File no. 89; 1913, File no. 142, Uttar Pradesh State Archives, Lucknow; Michael Pearson, *Indian Ocean*, p. 243; Barbara Daly Metcalf, *Islamic Revival*, p. 359; Sugata Bose (2006), *A Hundred Horizons: The Indian Ocean in the Age of Global Empire*, Delhi, pp. 204–5.

5 Bilal N. Simsir (ed.) (1973), *Ingliz Belgelerinde Ataturk* (British Documents on Ataturk), Ankara, Vol. 2, p. 343.

6 J.A. Rahim, Report of the Special Hajj Enquiry in Home Public and Judicial Department, File No. 8/758, British Library, London.

7 Mirza Mohammad Hosayn Farahani, *A Shiite Pilgrimage to Mecca*, p. xxii.

TABLE 1: Mecca pilgrimage, 1880

Nationality of pilgrims	Arriving by sea	Arriving by land	Total of Muslim population represented
Ottoman subjects including pilgrims from Syria and Iraq, but not from Egypt or Arabia proper	8,500	1,000	22,000,000
Egyptians	5,000	1,000	5,000,000
Mogrebbins (people of the West) that is to say Arabic-speaking Muslims from the Barbary States, Tripoli, Tunis, Algiers, and Morocco. These are always classed together and are not easily distinguishable from each other.	6,000	...	18,000,000
Arabs from Yemen	3,000	...	2,500,000
Arabs from Oman and Hadramaut	3,000	...	3,000,000
Arabs from Nejd, Assir, and Hasa, most of them Wahhabites	...	5,000	4,000,000
Arabs from Hijaz, of these perhaps 10,000 Meccans	...	22,000	2,000,000
Negroes from Sudan	2,000	...	(?)10,000,000
Negroes from Zanzibar	1,000	...	1,500,000
Malabaris from the Cape of Good Hope	150	...	
Persians	6,000	2,500	8,000,000
Indians (British subjects)	15,000	...	40,000,000
Malays, chiefly from Java and Dutch subjects	12,000	...	30,000,000
Chinese	100	...	15,000,000
Mongols from the Khanates, included in the Ottoman hajjis	...	...	6,000,000
Lazis, Circassians, Tartars, etc. (Russian subjects), included in the Ottoman hajjis	...	...	5,000,000
Independent Afghans and Beluchis, included in the Indian and Persian hajjis	...	...	3,000,000
Total of pilgrims present at Arafat	93,250		
	Total Census of Islam		175,000,000

Source: W.S. Blunt, *The Future of Islam,* p. 10.

TABLE 2: Number of pilgrims who sailed from British India
to the Hijaz, 1907–15

1907–08	1908–09	1909–10	1910–11	1911–12	1912–13	1913–14	1914–15
21,648	15,947	20,901	17,884	22,995	15,555	15,186	13,336

Source: Statistical Abstract for British India, 1916–17 (Calcutta, 1919), Vol. 4, p. 129.

TABLE 3: Number of pilgrims, 1927–29[1]

Seasons	OUTWARD			INWARD		
	No. of pilgrim ships	No. of other ships	No. of pilgrims	No. of pilgrim ships	No. of other ships	No. of pilgrims
1927	23	2	21,285	20	1	15,503
1928	19	Nil	10,640	16	2	7,542
1929	13	2	11,379	18	1	7,940

Source: Hajj Inquiry (Clayton) Committee, 1929, IOR/v/26/844/6, British Library.

giants, which led to competitive prices. In the first half of January 1938, therefore, one could purchase a return ticket from Karachi for just 25 or 30 rupees. The pattern was the same in other countries: in 1938, the profits accruing from the high rubber prices in Java and Malaya led to a 50 per cent rise in the number of pilgrims.

No discussion of numbers, however, would be complete without mentioning that the rite of pilgrimage involves and affects more people than those who physically perform it. It is often a collective activity, especially when the family, the village, or the city quarter deputes a person on their behalf and, in such cases, they participate by proxy.

When Nadir Ali 'Wakil' travelled from Hoogly in Calcutta on 10 January 1902, he came across a cross-section of society: educated and illiterate, rich and poor, well-placed and socially and economically

1 The substantial difference between the outward and inward figures is because some pilgrims died or stayed back in the Hijaz or returned to their homes in other countries without passing through India or even returned to India by routes other than via Bombay. Till the system of mandatory buying of return tickets was instituted, the discrepancy between outward and inward passage remained high.

TABLE 4: Number of pilgrims from each province of India and Ceylon, classified according to ports of embarkation

Province	Total number of pilgrims in 1937	In 1938			
		Bombay	Karachi	Calcutta	Total
Bengal and Assam	1,776	2,737	123	956	3,816
Punjab	2,211	154	3,743	...	3,897
Bombay Presidency	1,770	1,404	105	...	1,509
United Provinces	1,126	943	541	...	1,484
Madras Presidency	245	376	12	...	388
Sind Province	913	...	2,340	...	2,340
Behar and Orissa	254	230	19	2	251
Central Provinces	521	78	...	...	78
Baluchistan	359	29	699	...	728
North-West Frontier Province	256	51	456	...	507
Hyderabad (Deccan)	281	262	1	...	263
Delhi	158	31	180	...	211
Burma	131	74	2	41	117
Ceylon	40	32	1	...	33
French India	...	2	...	...	2
Portuguese India	...	2	...	...	2
Mauritius	...	...	...	...	...
Rajputana States	...	128	131	...	259
Central India Agency	...	127	16	...	143
Miscellaneous	...	4	6	...	10
	10,041	6,664	8,375	999	16,038

Source: Hajj Inquiry (Clayton) Committee, 1929, IOR/v/26/844/6, British Library.

disadvantaged. Indeed, ships carried *pirs, maulvis*, teachers, newspaper-editors, engineers, pleaders, doctors, *subedar*-majors, landlords, merchants, petty clerks, and colonial officials, among others. For many of them, this was a first outing—often from the village or town, sometimes from the province, and almost always the first voyage outside the country. Except for the common goal of the hajj, they had more differences than commonalities among them.

The hajjis were divided into rank and status in terms of power and wealth. Nawab Mir Usman Ali Khan (1886–1967) of Hyderabad and his predecessors, Nawab Sultan Jahan Begum of Bhopal (1858–1930) and the Nawabs of Rampur, Jaora, and Tonk, travelled with a retinue of servants and *musahib* (hangers-on), and spent lavishly on their comfort: they followed the great imperial tradition of members of the royal Ottoman and Mughal families.[1] But they also adopted Akbar's practice of subsidizing the poor pilgrims. Taking a cue from him and the latter-day Mughal nobles, whose lifetysle they tried to emulate, they built graveyards, hotels, houses, baths, mosques, and *serai* or *rebats*. W.H. Sleeman (1788–1856) reported that, when Ghaziuddin Haider succeeded his father in 1814, he spent about 50 lakh rupees in charity at the shrines of the Prophet and his companions, and constructed works of utility.[2] Gradually, however, such properties were seized or transferred illegally, and, instead of being utilized for the purpose for which they were established, they were dealt with as the private property of those who happened to be in possession of these properties.

As with pilgrimages the world over, the educated and relatively well-to-do had a different experience than the poor and the illiterate. While the rich, having brought a few articles for sale which they disposed of without trouble, paid several pounds for 'a flacon of perfume, pour it all out on their heads and walk off', the poor were at the mercy of the sun and the sand, lived in the barren and untidy cities, and encountered the rustic and backward Bedouins. In 1885, Indian pilgrims were found begging in the streets and alleys in the daytime, and sleeping in the open at night. An Iranian pilgrim observed in 1910–11 that some had barely the wherewithal to stay alive. Passers-by offered them something to eat, and occasionally some generous persons took them to Mecca on their camels.[3] Many died from exposure, thirst, flash floods, epidemic, or an attack by local nomads. The following story is, however, of the type that kept the morale high and stimulated enthusiasm:

1 Suraiya Faroqhi, *Pilgrims and Sultans: The Hajj under the Ottomans*, p. 129.

2 W.H. Sleeman (1858), *Journey Through the Kingdom of Oude in 1849–1850*, London, Vol. 2, pp. 9–10.

3 Mirza Mohammad Hosayn Farahani (1990), *A Shiite Pilgrimage to Mecca*, p. 187; F.E. Peters, *The Hajj*, p. 275.

A dervish had gone for the hajj. When he had completed the hajj, he saw that every one was offering some sacrifice; a camel, a sheep or whatever a person had taken, he was sacrificing in the way of the Lord. The dervish stood at the place and said, 'O God, Thou knowest I have not much to offer. I shall sacrifice myself for Thy sake. If my hajj has been acceptable to Thee, accept my sacrifice also.' He said this and ran his forefinger across his throat. His head was severed from his body.[1]

The pilgrims came with exalted hopes. But, from the moment of their landing in Jiddah, officials fleeced some of them, religious touts befooled them, and highway robbers robbed them openly. At every step, they were in danger of being waylaid, tricked, and ill-treated.[2] The *taqrir* system, whereby one *mutawwif* monopolized the supervision of pilgrims from one district or those belonging to one community, added to their humiliation. It applied mostly to the Memons from western India.[3] In Assam and Chittagong, East Bengal's main seaport and the main hub of revolutionary activities during the period 1920–40, vested interests sought similar monopolistic rights over pilgrims from other districts of India. Whether in Jiddah or Bombay, the mutawwifs indulged in speculation, extortion, overcharge, and the fixing of an artificial rate of exchange.

Indian hajjis were unhappy with the *muallims*.[4] Known to be wily and sweet-talking, they descended in droves upon towns and hamlets in search of prey. On 8 July 1909, Arab brokers, purporting to represent the ulama of Mecca, visited village mosques and Sufi shrines in Bengal and Assam, preaching the imperative of the hajj to Muslim cultivators. In the absence of a full knowledge of the actual precepts of Islam, they were induced to blindly follow the official guides. The uneducated, poor Muslims did not have sufficient means to provide for the sacred journey.

1 Mohammad Mujeeb (1967), *The Indian Muslims*, London, p. 122.
2 File No. 4436, 1936, L/E/7/1168, British Library, London.
3 See July 1931–June 1940, L/PJ/8/774, British Library, London.
4 The hajj cannot be performed on one's own. Pilgrims are, therefore, allotted to the muallims in accordance with their respective districts or provinces, and once they are so allotted, the Hijaz authorities allow no change. July 1930–October 1944, see L/PJ/8/775, British Library, London. As Amir Ahmad discovered:
   'Unfortunately, the muallim who has once been appointed for you cannot be changed once you reach here, and you can do nothing without the permission of your muallim. Forget Medina, you can not even go to Arafat without the approval of your muallim! This great respect is not accorded to the muallims because of their high birth but simply because the government gets its fee through them. And so it was found to be necessary to stretch the rights of the muallim.'

They were, therefore, compelled to unwisely encumber or dispose of their valuable properties for a trifle, generally to Hindu moneylenders.

Many of these so-called Arabs were Bengalis by birth; having settled in the Hijaz, they spoke Bangla fluently, and learnt local customs to better ingratiate themselves with the pilgrims, who fell under their spell with alacrity for two reasons—(a) they were from the Holy Land and were to be venerated for that simple reason; and (b) they promised to facilitate a journey that all Muslims dreamt of. However, once the trophy had been bagged—or the prey netted—the muallim dumped unsuspecting, often poor, clients leaving them at the mercy of their rapacious and inconsiderate employees and sub-contractors. They transferred to their own pockets much money belonging to the pilgrims by way of charging unwarrantable commission and illegal fees. Ultimately, many of their victims passed the remainder of their lives in a penniless condition.

Scores of pilgrims waited for a week or ten days before boarding the ship for an Indian port. The poorer ones made for themselves such shelters as they could on the desert bordering the town; some even lay down on the streets without such shelters.[1] Once on board an overcrowded ship, they had to bear with the poor quality of food and inadequate medical facilities. In 1937, the steamship *Khusrou* carried 1,402 pilgrims though it had sanction for only 1,396; the steamship *Rehmani* carried 1,651 pilgrims when it was licensed for 1,402; and the steamships *Akbar*, *Rizwani* and *Islami* carried 10, 23, and 49 extra pilgrims, respectively.

---

1 Lieutenant J.R. Wellsted, an Indian Navy officer engaged in surveying the Red Sea in 1835, commented:

'Attached to the caravans, and at the various stations, are a number of wretched beings, for the most part in the last stage of disease, and safely dependent on the precarious charity of their fellow travelers for the means of visiting and returning from the holy cities. To prevent their accumulation at the different ports, where they would probably engender disease, they are portioned out into separate parties by the governors, who compel the different boats and ships to furnish them with provisions, and convey them, free of expense, to the various ports whither they may be proceeding. To evade this burden, the honest captains do not scruple to use every artifice, and the poor wretches are frequently enticed out of the vessel and left at the first place she may touch at. If that is near any port having a competent authority, he places them on board the next vessel; but if, as more commonly happens, they are landed on some unfrequented shore, a miserable death by thirst and starvation awaits them.' Quoted in F.E. Peters, *The Hajj*, p. 275.

Remarkably, however, as the pilgrims rolled their prayer mats and headed back to their homelands, 'haggard wayfarers became celebrants, uplifted and renewed, and the whole dusty company was transformed into a joyous, white-robed procession.'[1] According to Burckhardt:

The freedom and oblivion of care which accompany traveling, render it a period of enjoyment among the people of the East as many Europeans; and the same kind of happiness results from their residence at Mekka, where reading the Koran, smoking in the streets or coffee-houses, praying or conversing in the mosque, are added to the indulgence of their pride in being near the holy house, and to the anticipation of the honours attached to the title of the hadjy [sic] for the remainder of their lives; besides the gratification of religious feelings, and the hopes of futurity, which influence many of the pilgrims.[2]

On the morning of the tenth day of the month of Zul Hijja, when the pilgrims assemble at Mina for the start of the Feast of Sacrifice (Idul Azha), they are so consumed with the thought of being in the Holy Land that they only speak of the fulfilment of a religious mission. As Jaffur Shurref wrote in 1832, 'many live for years in the joyful anticipation of being one day able to perform the pilgrimage. Nay, very many never have the idea of it out of their minds.'[3] Mohammad Ilyas of Baran (Bulandshahar) sat cross-legged on the ground and stared fixedly towards the east, in the direction of Mecca, the cradle of Islam. He had just returned to Mina for two or three nights. As he got ready to throw pebbles (which he had picked up along the road from Arafat) at all three of the devil-pillars each day, sacrifice additional animals, and socialize with friends and countrymen, there was a faraway peace on his face. On his return, he offered *fateha* at the shrines of Khwaja Muinuddin Chishti (1142–1236) in Ajmer and Nizamuddin Auliya (1238–1325), the Chishti saint in Delhi.[4] In 1902, Nadir Ali, the barrister from Meerut, stood at Muzdalifa, a point three miles back along the road to Mina. As he reflected on the places of spiritual retreat and ascetic exercise, the following thought came to his mind:

---

1 Ross E. Dunn, *The Adventures of Ibn Battuta*, p. 69.
2 J.L. Burckhardt, *Travels in Arabia*, p. 261.
3 Jaffur Shurref (1863), *Qanoon-i Islam*, translated by G.A. Herklots, Madras, p. 48.
4 Mohammad Ilyas Barani (1928), *Sirat-al Hameed, yaani Safarnama-i Maqamat, Sham, Phalastin wa Hijaz*, Aligarh; Mohammad Hamidullah Khan (1914), *Safarnama-i Medina-i Munawarra*, Lucknow.

The shock and grief at the time of leaving the Baitullah can only be understood by those who have, themselves, stayed in that House of the Beloved, and from whence they have perforce been sent away. Upon reaching their home and hearth they find their hearts brimming over with joy because they know God has granted them salvation and mercy. They know they have been endowed with His munificence for he hath called upon them to His home, showered them with His blessings and the gift of His hospitality. He has, finally, and with all due care and concern, ensured their safety to their homes and families.[1]

Hajj Narratives[2]

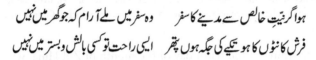

Ho gar neeyate khaalis se madine ka safar
woh safar me mile aaraam ke jo ghar me nahin,
farsh kaaton ka ho takiye ki jagah hon patthar,
aisi raahat to kisi baalish-o-bistar me nahin.

When the journey to Medina is taken up with intent pure
The travails of travel turn into the comfort of home for sure
The floor covered with thorns, stones in place of cushions
Yet solace such as no other couch or cushion may ensure.

Choudhry Mohammad Ali (1882–1959) lived in Rudauli. A Shia *taluqdar*, he was a beneficiary of the Nawabs of Awadh, who surfaced in the wake of the decline of the Mughal Empire. He was not quite a devout Muslim, but his wife's resolve to perform the hajj on her own drew him to Bombay and, by sheer coincidence, he secured a berth on the same ship which sailed with his wife on board. In the Hijaz, he met Abdul Majid Daryabadi and Amir Ahmad. His conversational gifts made him welcome in literary society and led to some continuing interest in his book *Mera Mazhab*, which covers the hajj journey in two chapters. They are seriously purposive and designed to convey some lesson of instruction and delight. There are good things in them—humour specially, and a lively sense of the ridiculous. The description of Arafat is dramatic and poignant.[3]

---

1 Nadir Ali, *Mir'aatul-Arab Yaani Safarnama-i Nadir*, p. 241.
2 We have used hajj narratives as a literary label to cover many diverse writers, artists and works.
3 Masoodul Haq (ed.) (2005), *Kulliyat Choudhry Mohammad Ali*, Delhi, Vol. 2, pp. 48, 54.

Shaikh Mohammad Zakariya, at the other end of the social scale, lived in Machhlishahar, in Awadh's Jaunpur district. Situated on the metalled road to Allahabad, this predominantly Muslim town was once noted for its salt and cloth manufactures. Soon, though, decline set in. By the end of the nineteenth century, Machhlishahar presented the appearance of a quiet agricultural centre whose prosperity had gone by.[1] While there were some landholdings, it was mostly occupied by professional families, who earned enough to afford the travel to Mecca and Medina. Zakariya was one of them. He set out on 8 August 1911, reached Bombay on 20 August (24th Sha'baan), sailed for Aden on 28 August, and reached Jiddah on 8 September. His other companions in the first class salon were Hakim Latafat Ali of Nahtore, an old *qasba* in Bijnor district, and Abdul Ahad Khan of Pilibhit, a small town in the Terai. Next to them were Syed Ali Hasan Shah and Hafiz Bashir Taali of Machhlishahar. They travelled second class.

For the next six months, the sound of the caravan bell guided them to Mecca, where the Beloved dwelt. The bell went silent at the destination, for no words could possibly describe the perfect union. They saw the many thousands from all over the Muslim world making the hajj at the same time; together they went round the Kaaba, stood at Arafat, stoned the Devil and sacrificed their animals. That moment ushered in the 'Feast of Sacrifice' (Bakr Id). In the ritual sacrifice of the Pilgrimage, it is not the blood or the flesh of the animals, it is the piety which rises towards God. With his heart full of joy, Shaikh Mohammad Zakariya returned home on 31 December 1911.[2]

'When you see a pilgrim,' the Prophet stated, 'salute and embrace him, and request him to ask pardon of God for you, for his own sins have been forgiven and his supplications will be accepted.' Accordingly, the mohalla and the wider world of the qasba shared Zakariya's joy and excitement, the exhilaration, and the enlightenment and wonder. They

---

1 W.W. Hunter (1886), *Imperial Gazetteer of India*, London, Vol. 8, p. 534.

2 Another exciting occurrence shortly after Baqr Id (in Banaras) is the return of hajjis. Only the well-off can thus become hajji, but ordinary people participate indirectly in the event by visiting them, listening to their accounts, looking at the souvenirs they bring back, tasting the holy water from Mecca and talking about it all. Weavers, whose masters, employers or rich neighbours go off, meet them at the railway station on their return and help in organizing welcoming receptions for them. See Nita Kumar (1988), *The Artisans of Banaras: Popular Culture and Identity, 1880–1986*, Delhi, p. 172.

brought garlands, sweets, and paan[1], and took part in *nazr-o niyaz*; poets recited poems and musicians sang qawwalis. Brides sought blessings for a happy married life; the sick expected to be cured by the hajji's touch. Piety and religiosity filled the air until the first of Muharram, the month of mourning. Meanwhile, Zakariya offered prayers in the local mosque urging Allah to grant that his pilgrimage would not be his last. He rejoiced at the great favour bestowed upon him, praising Allah for allowing him easy access to the Holy Places.[2] He, then, began to unpack his bags to distribute dates, rosaries, and prayer mats.

This is how most pilgrimage narratives read. Writing on the novel experience was as difficult as composing hymns in praise of the Almighty or composing *naat*s in praise of the Prophet, warned Maulana Syed Abul Hasan Ali Nadwi. These skills demanded refined taste and sophistication, love and faith, the opening up of one's heart, and the unbridled expression of one's emotions. The scholar at Lucknow's Nadwatul Ulama attributed creative writings only to those who combined love and reverence with etiquette and propriety.[3] Not all conformed to the standard set by him, but some did. Syed Jalaluddin Haider (b. 1872), a graduate in government employment, was one of them. His safarnama is a studied performance in prose; his style is more austere than opulent.[4]

When was the first hajj narrative produced in South Asia? Pearson claims that Safi bin Wali Qazvini wrote one around 1687. One of the earliest texts documenting the voyage and the sights was by Abdul Haq Muhaddis Dehlawi, Princess Zaibunnisa's tutor. It was dedicated to Aurangzeb (r. 1658–1707). Maulana Rafiuddin Moradabadi, Shah Waliullah's disciple, authored an authoritative text, whereas Shah Waliullah's *Fuyud al-Haramain* in Arabic (1733), is in the form of 'visions' or extremely personal experiences that the narrator-recorder had during his stay in the holy places. Besides, he compiled a biographical account (*Al-insan al-ayn fi mashaikh al-Haramain*) of the Sufis and scholars in Mecca and Medina.

---

1 Betel leaf, usually folded into the shape of a triangle package and filled with spices for eating. It is commonly offered to guests and visitors as a sign of hospitality and also eaten at cultural events.

2 Deoband (n.d.), *Rehlatul-Nasik alal-bait wal-manasik*.

3 Sulaiman Salik (1978), *Qatra: Samandar Me*, Delhi, p. 5.

4 Haji Syed Jalaluddin Haider (2002), *Khudnawisht Sawanahumari*, Lucknow.

The literate people belonging to the *shurafa* or holding government jobs showed a marked propensity to jot down their experiences. Their narratives are a seamless blend of the secular and religious, at once travelogues and religious treatises.[1] To this category belonged Siddiq Hasan Khan of Bhopal (1870), Sikandar Begum of Bhopal, the Nawab of Rampur (1872), and Jalaluddin Haider (1894), a graduate from Aligarh who rose to become the Chief Justice of the Lahore High Court.[2] Shibli Nomani (1857–1914), professor of Arabic at M.A.O. College and later at the Nadwatul Ulama, concentrated on historical biographies which make for good reading; he also wrote *Safarnama-i Rum-o Misr*. It is humourless in its general tone, despite containing excellent passages of insight and information. One of the better-known works is by Nuruddin, the successor of the Ahmadi leader, Ghulam Ahmad.[3] Scores of other writings have little claim to attention, but they are part of the soil from which most hajj literature grew.

There was a sudden proliferation of magazines and journals connected with hajj. Shaukat Ali edited the *Khuddam al-Kaaba* first published in June 1914. The Madrasa Saulatiya[4] in Delhi published a magazine called *Nida-i Haram* (January 1945). A number of other Urdu magazines brought out special issues on hajj. One of the earliest roznamchas is *Safarnama-i Hijaz* (Lucknow, 1894) by Mirza Irfan Ali Beg, Deputy Collector in Basti district. He left Gonda on 9 April 1894, performed the hajj, and returned to India on 9 July 1894. *Mir'aatul Arab* by Nadir Ali, as mentioned earlier, records the journey of a barrister from Meerut in 1902. It is a big book, containing 241 pages, with information on the Arab tribes (pp. 107–8), Arab geography, trade (pp. 102–3) agriculture, and flora and fauna (pp. 95–8, 101), and an analysis of Arab society.

Safarnama Khwaja Hasan Nizami: Babat Siyahati, Phalastine, Sham-o Hijaz (Delhi, 1923) belongs to the same genre. A *sajjadanashin* belonging

---

1 Mohammad Hamid Allah Khan (1914), *Safarnama-i Medina Munawarrah*, Lucknow; Ahmad Said Malihabadi (1972), *Allah ke Ghar Me*, Calcutta.

2 Barbara Daly Metcalf, *Islamic Revival in British India*, p. 296.

3 Yohanan Friedmann (1989), *Prophecy Continuous: Aspects of Ahmadi Religious Thought and its Medieval Background*, Berkeley, p. 14.

4 This madrasa was founded by Maulana Rahmatullah Kairanvi at Mecca in AH 1290. Under British rule, he realized the need for an Islamic centre there which became famous as Darul Ulum Haram Saulatiya, for imparting education to Muslim students from all parts of the world.

to an unbroken line of caretakers of the *dargah* of Nizamuddin Auliya,[1] Khwaja Hasan Nizami wrote his diary with the intention of adding to his already formidable list of publications, which included treatises in simple homespun Urdu, pamphlets, and collections of aphorisms. Known for his audacious disregard of convention and an expansive capacity for melodramatic self-dramatization, he unravelled the amazing complexity of the entire pilgrimage experience. Useful though his book is, it is hampered by the author's inability to let himself come through freely. He is held in check by his experience-ridden sardonic view of the world.[2]

While many of the twentieth-century travelogues are pathologically self-centred, inflated, and largely barren of content, the *Safarnama-i Shaikhul Hind* is a political-religious document of immense significance. It relates the experiences of Maulana Mahmud Hasan (1889–1920), the Principal of Deoband's seminary. This book has such a ring of sincerity that one is reluctant to raise a note of discord. Journalism had equipped another well-known writer, Abdul Majid Daryabadi, to produce excellent descriptive passages. An ardent pan-Islamist under Mohamed Ali's influence, his *Safar-i Hijaz* is studded here and there with brilliant passages.[3] It illustrates the range and depth of his erudition.

Women are not permitted to go unaccompanied or in the company of those male members of the immediate family other than the ones classified as *mehram*. They must be accompanied by a relative with whom they need not observe the purdah; husbands, brothers and sons constitute the mehram. This explains in part why the professional women author of travelogues arrived only tardily. The versatile Sikandar Begum (1816–1868), Bhopal's ruler, took earnestly to a literary occupation. This is evident from her travelogue. In 1863, she found Jiddah 'a desolate-looking city, very dirty, and pervaded with unsavoury odour.'[4] She was told, moreover, that the local people considered it a meritorious act to oppress the Indians—'just as a heretic considered it a meritorious act

1 Khwaja Hasan Nizami (1913), *Roznama-i Bit-taswir*, Meerut.

2 For an analysis of his roznamcha, see Sugata Bose, *A Hundred Horizons*, pp. 195–202.

3 For Daryabadi's work, see Sugata Bose, ibid., pp. 221–30.

4 Nawab Sikandar Begum (2007), *A Princess's Pilgrimage*, edited, introduced and with an afterword by Siobhan Lambert-Hurley, Delhi.

to persecute the true believer.' She compared their manners to those of the Gonds, who lived by rapine and deeds of violence.[1]

Even though saturated by a peculiar blend of religious zeal and social conservatism, Nishatul Nisa (1885–1937), wife of the Urdu poet-journalist, Hasrat Mohani (1878–1951), broke into the literary world during the anti-colonial struggle in the early 1920s with her two travelogues—*Safarnama-i Iraq* and *Safarnama-i Hijaz*—published in 1937. These are of lasting interest and merit as literature.[2] She was accompanied by her husband, who made the pilgrimage at least eleven, and possibly thirteen, times with the last occasion being in 1950, the year before his death.

A distinct individuality is bestowed upon some other personal impressions and observations, adventures and misadventures. They provide a panorama of Muslim lands and societies, depict certain stages en route, and pay attention to shrines, routes, weather, and the ease and safety of the journey.[3] Thus, Hyderabad's Nawab Bahadur Yar Jung described the cities and countries he passed through on his return journey, including Turkey and Afghanistan.[4] Individuals like him loved and understood the people about whom they wrote, and since they understood the latter, they did not falsify them with trappings of make-believe.

Some of north India's publishers, notably Nawal Kishore Press, set Urdu travelogue writers on a new track in which the situation, atmosphere, and characters share some of the characteristics of a short story or a novel. Some of these books often turned into thinly-coated tracts for the time.[5] In Lucknow, the Nazir Book Agency stocked the following books:

1 Nawab Sikandar Begum, *A Princess's Pilgrimage*, pp. 29, 30.

2 Atiq Siddiqi (1981), *Begum Hasrat Mohani aur Unke Khutut*, Delhi; Bushra Rahman (1999), *Urdu ke Ghair Mazhabi Safarname*, Gorakhpur. In 1937, Hasrat travelled from Basra and Baghdad to Kazmain, visiting the tomb of Imam Husain. He performed the hajj thereafter. See Khalid Hasan Qadiri (1985), *Hasrat Mohani*, Delhi, p. 266; Waheeda Naseem (1980), *Hadis-i Dil: Safarnama-i Hijaz*, Karachi.

3 For example, Habibur Rahmat Qadri (1927), *Safarnama-i Hijaz Muqaddas*, in two parts, Hazaribagh.

4 Shahid Husain Razzaqi (ed.) (1988), *Siyahati Mamalik-i Islamia Bahadur Yar Jung ka Roznamcha*, Karachi. He travelled from 29 March to 2 November 1931.

5 The Maarif Press in Azamgarh, the Nizami Press in Budaun, and Bijnore's Medina Press printed *Kaleed Babul Hajj* by Munshi Ahmad Ali (1871) and Irfan Ali Beg's *Safarnama-i Hijaz* (1895); the Nizami Press published *Khamkhani-i Hijaz* by Hafiz

1. *Zubdatul Manasik* by Maulana Shaheed Ahmad Gangohvi, a booklet for those planning to go on a pilgrimage. It contains details about the duties to be performed, necessary instructions, and things of general use during the pilgrimage.
2. *Kitabul Haj-o-Ziyarat* by Maulana Munawaruddin Sahib Dehlavi on hajj and *ziyarat*.
3. *Sirat-ul-Hameed* by Maulvi Iliyas Barni. He taught economics at Osmania University, Hyderabad, and visited Iraq, Palestine, Syria, and Hijaz in 1937.
4. *Safarnama-e-Haramain Sharifain* by Maulvi Mohiuddin Hasan about the decorum of ziyarat, about the city of Medina, its famous and holy places, the society and culture of its people, its *madaris*, toilets and bathrooms, vegetables and fruits, dresses, weights and measures, currency, and the cordiality and behaviour of the people of Medina, as also the modalities of performing the hajj (in 1322 Hijri).
5. *Aain-e-Haj* by Haji Syed Fazal Mahmud (B.A., Former Deputy Inspector of Schools, Punjab) put together the necessary information on hajj and ziyarat.[1]
6. *Zaadus-Sabil ala Darul Khalil* by Maulvi Sadullah Sahib outlined the importance and merits of hajj and *umrah*, the occasions and methods of putting on *ihram*, dos and don'ts, the timings for ihram, methods and rites of hajj and umrah, and details of impurities, and information about ziyarat of Mecca and Medina.
7. The *Safar-i Hijaz* (there are several books bearing the same name) record not merely the narrators' own experiences but also the experiences of others whom the author had known or known of. For the historian, they are invaluable because they: (a) trace the 'genealogy' of a variety of hajjis and provide several sites for cross-referencing; (b) place on record the oral narratives passed

---

Khaliluddin Hasan (not dated), and the Medina Press brought out Mohammad Habibul Rahman's *Habibul-Hujjaj* (1929).

1 There is an essential difference between hajj and umrah or ziyarat, namely, that while the hajj is one of the five *arkan* or pillars of Islam, umrah is considered as meritorious but not obligatory action. Thus, the pilgrim to Medina and the other holy sites is called a *zair*, but the visitor to Mecca, the Prophet's birthplace and the site of the Kaaba, is called a hajji. And, while the ihram or pilgrim's dress of unstitched white cloth is a hajj prerequisite, it is not mandatory for ziyarat, not even of the Masjid al-Nabawi. Umrah and ziyarat or visitation can be performed at any time.

on among the families of different members of the extended family, who had been on the hajj at different points in time; and (c) record the experiences of people from the village or the qasba and the province (in this case UP, since such safarnamas were written in Urdu) and by so doing, provide a larger cultural map to locate the hajj experience.

Amir Ahmad's Antecedents

In the fifteenth century, two branches of the Hashemite clan—a term commonly applied in the eighth–ninth centuries to members of the Abbasis house and occasionally to their followers and supporters— migrated to India and settled in Kakori, a qasba situated 14 kilometres north of Lucknow, and once a thoroughfare for the traffic between Lucknow and Kanpur. They were Alawis and Abbasis. Amir Ahmad belonged to the family of the Alawis, who arrived in Kakori around 1512–13. Tracing their lineage to Ali, the Prophet's son-in-law, through his son Mohammad bin Hanafia with his wife Khaula Al-Hanafia, the Alawis rendered useful service as scholars and soldiers to the Mughals, the Nawabs of Awadh, and the East India Company. They prospered, moreover, in the princely states.

Thanks to the inner, mystical dimension of Islam, the Sufi movement spanned several continents and cultures. In this respect, Kakori occupied a unique position. The famous shrine of Takiya Sharif itself drew followers from all over the country.[1] To the south of the town lay the *khanqah*[2] of Hazrat Shah Muhammad Kazim (AD 1806), a Sufi and an eminent poet of Brij Bhasha and Punjabi. He was followed by a long line of sajjadanashins.

Kakori was unmatched for its cognoscenti, its men of letters and good taste, its love for literature, the sheer eclecticism of its spirit, and the easy and seamless coexistence of religion, politics, and literature on its intellectual firmament. These elements spilled out and influenced people, events, movements in South Asia. Translators such as Nadir Kakorwi brought the best of Western, secular influences and enriched

---

1 Claudia Liebeskind (1998), *Piety on its Knees: Three Sufi Traditions in South Asia in Modern Times*, New Delhi, pp. 58–61.

2 Traditionally, a building designed specifically for gatherings of a Sufi brotherhood, or *tariqa*, and is a place for spiritual retreat and character reformation. Khanqahs adjoined to dargahs (shrines of sufi saints), mosques and madrasas (Islamic schools) are very often found especially in Iran, Central Asia and South Asia.

Urdu's literary traditions. Others such as the Alawi family, while taking their own illustrious lineage further with every new generation producing a fresh crop of cultural elite, contributed to the making of a creative, broad-minded, open-hearted, and generous environment. Thus, unlike other qasbas, Kakori, instead of becoming an island or oasis of excellence breeding insular, narrow-minded, chauvinistic, inward-looking people, managed to do just the opposite. It imbibed from the world and gave back in generous measure, too. According to Sleeman:

The little town of Kakori, about ten or twelve miles from Lucknow, has, I believe, more educated men, filling high and lucrative offices in our civil establishments, than any other town in India except Calcutta. They owe the greater security which they there enjoy, compared with other small towns in Oude, chiefly to the respect in which they are held by the British Government and its officers, and to the influence of their friends and relatives who hold office about the Court of Lucknow.[1]

The life and times of Amir Ahmad represent, in many ways, the best and brightest aspects of the *qasbati shurafa*. Born into a family that epitomized the aspirations of the Muslim gentry, Amir Ahmad was part of a long line of illustrious men of letters who combined *duniyavi tehzeeb* (worldly manners), *deeni ilm* (religious education), and *nayi taleem* (new education). Culture, religion, and knowledge merged seamlessly to produce men who lived and worked in distant parts of colonial India but, upon retirement, retuned home to roost. Having travelled and seen something of the world and its ways, they found that it was invariably their *watan* or homeland that afforded them the best that life had to offer.

Sukhanwaran-i Kakori, a collection of essays on the illustrious sons of Kakori, provides several valuable nuggets of information on Amir Ahmad and his family's contribution. His father, Munshi Zakiuddin, a pious and well-regarded gentleman, practised law in Etawah. Amir Ahmad was born in 1870 in the home of his maternal grandfather, the famous poet and elegist Mohsin Kakorwi, who had been tutored by some of the leading contemporary Urdu poets (including Nasiq and Atish). Amir Ahmad received his early education in Persian and Arabic from his maternal uncle, Nurul Hasan. In order to enable him to acquire an English-medium education, he was sent to the M.A.O. College,

1 W.H. Sleeman, *Journey through the Kingdom of Oude*, p. 10, cited in Claudia Liebeskind, *Piety on its Knees*, p. 60. See also Farman Ali Makhmoor Kakorwi (1977), *Dar Kakorwi Hayat*, Delhi; Masud Alawi Kakorwi (1977), *Kawakib*, Lucknow; Masud Anwar Ali Kakorwi (1983), *Maqalat-i Anwar*, Lucknow.

Aligarh, from where he obtained his B.A. degree. In Aligarh, he made a lasting friendship with the firebrand Hasrat Mohani. In later years, when Hasrat was incarcerated for political reasons, Amir Ahmad, despite serving the British government, would send a large portion of his salary to Hasrat's wife. During his active career as a government servant, Amir Ahmad served as *tehsildar* and deputy collector in Banaras, Allahabad, and Kanpur, among other places. He also served as District Magistrate in distant Neemuch.[1] He took retirement in 1939 and spent the rest of his years in Kakori till his death in 1952.

Like many young men of his generation in Lucknow and its neighbouring qasbas, Amir Ahmad read poetry. By all accounts, he did not write any poetry, though almost all his prose writing has a lyrical quality. He wrote a history of Urdu poetry, biographies, and the history of Indore and Malwa. Some of his noteworthy publications include a treatise on *naatiya adab*, with a special focus on his grandfather's elegiac poetry, a biographical account of the legendary *marsiya* writer called *Yadgar-e Anis*, a eulogy to the homeland called *Yaad-e Watan*, another on the last Mughal emperor Bahadur Shah Zafar called *Tazkira-e Hind*, and even a drama called *Khwab-e-Pareshan* (Anxious Dreams).[2]

In short, our narrator is not just a man of education, he is also a gentleman of some means. He was one of four Indian passengers travelling first class on the *Rehmani*, and carried sufficient money with him in the form of a *hundi*[3] as well as a letter of credit made out in the name of the Netherland Trading Company. Thus, while observing and recording the plight of the third class passengers and later the travails of the poorer, ill-equipped, illiterate pilgrims, especially from Afghanistan and Bengal, he was cushioned from the unpleasantness around him.

Like his father Zaki Kakori and grandfather Mohsin Kakori, Amir Ahmad was consumed with a burning desire to see the two holiest shrines of the Muslim world, the *Baitul Muqaddas*, the Holiest of

1 Neemuch (Nimach) is a town in the Malwa region in the Indian state of Madhya Pradesh. It shares its north-eastern border with Rajasthan. Formerly it was a large British cantonment of the Gwalior princely state. In 1857, Neemuch was the most southerly place to which the Mutiny extended.

2 Biographical information is based on Hakim Nisar Ahmad Alawi (1978), *Sukhanwaran-i Kakori*, Karachi, pp. 105–6.

3 Also known as *hawala*. This is an informal currency transfer system based on the performance and honour of a huge network of money brokers, who are primarily located in the Middle East, Africa and Asia.

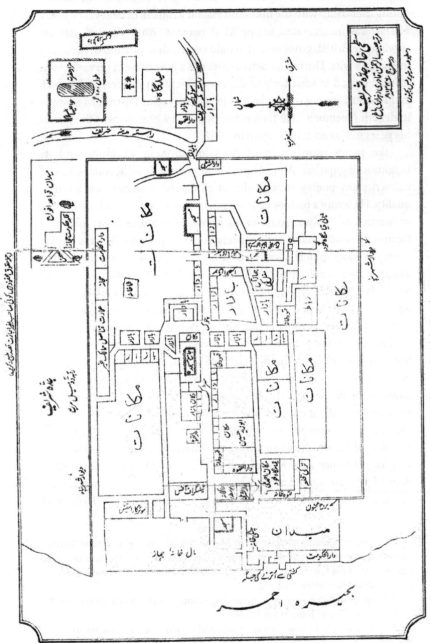

Sketch of Jiddah Sharif in 1929.
Mohammad Habibur Rahman, *Habibul Al-Hujjaj* (Bijnor, 1929), p. 65.

Homes, and the *Haram Sharif*. Like Believers the world over, he believed that the hajj was not merely one of the five pillars of Islam and the duty of every Muslim, man and woman, to perform at least once in their lifetime, but that it also led to spiritual regeneration and salvation. Therefore, in the late winter of the year 1929 (AH 1347) in the month of Sha'baan,[1] he embarked upon a journey of faith that would take him out of the small, protected world he had known, across the seas to another world, which he had only dreamt of visiting some day. He would have carried with him many memories, of his childhood, his growing up, his education, as also the political turbulence in his small qasba. The most significant of these was, of course, the event of 9 August 1925, when ten revolutionaries stopped a train near Kakori and looted the government treasury travelling in it.

With every nautical mile covered by the ship, Amir Ahmad's excitement grows—not because the arduous voyage would be nearing its end but because the vessel that had set sail would bring him closer to the land of his dreams. So many distinguished men of letters from Kakori had undertook this journey.[2] Now, he thanked Allah for being blessed with the sight of the land of Arabia: '...the fragrance of faith blows in from Yemen. By the grace of the Merciful God, may this fragrance bring comfort to my heart!' His ardour to see the Holiest of Homes, the Cupola of Islam, increased with every step he took in the direction of the *qibla*. The Jiddah–Mecca road remained in its pristine state, but Amir Ahmad barely controlled his excitement till he finally sighted the journey's end: By about 12 midnight, he saw the lights of Mecca from a distance. First the driver, then he and his fellow-travellers shouted *Labbaika* loudly! Their hearts jumped with joy: 'Like moths to a flame, we raced towards that light with abandon. The tongue and the pen cannot describe the state of our mind[s] at that instant.'

In the Baitul Muqaddas, the Holiest of Homes, Amir Ahmad found himself to be a small speck in a vast ocean of humanity. People from every corner of the world converged here—from the Indian subcontinent, Java, Burma, Cape Town, Shiraz (Iran), Anatolia, Chinese Kyrghystan, Turkey, Egypt, Afghanistan, and the deepest, darkest corner of Africa.[3]

1 Eighth month of the Muslim calendar.

2 See Mohammad Ali Haider (1927), *Tazkira-i Mashahiri Kakori*, Patna.

3 See, for example, C. Bawa Yamba (1995), *Permanent Pilgrims: The Role of Pilgrimage in the Lives of West African Muslims in Sudan*, Edinburgh.

At about the time he set out, Islam was beginning to make inroads into the Depression-era ghettos and the mean streets of America. However, it would be a long time before the American hajjis would arrive in sizeable numbers. Wali Akram, an Imam from Cleveland, was among the first African Americans to be awarded a visa to Mecca. He wrote *From the Cotton Fields of the South to the Sandy Deserts of Arabia*, wherein he talked of travelling by rail, bus, camel, donkey, and rickshaw through Europe, Turkey, Syria, Saudi Arabia, Egypt, the Sudan, Pakistan, Afghanistan, and India, canvassing and observing the people in these countries and remembering the conditions and misunderstandings that prevailed in America: discrimination, segregation, prejudice, and envy. Wali Akram, a born-again Muslim and new convert to Islam, concluded that the task ahead required honest dedication and direction.[1]

From the day Amir Ahmad left home, he began writing a travelogue in the form of a daily diary: the pilgrimage was in many ways the central event of his whole lifetime. It would appear that he wrote for himself, at best perhaps he wanted to share his experiences with friends and relatives. But, on his return to Kakori, friends prevailed upon him to publish his dairy. In July 1932, he completed the draft in Daryabad (Barabanki). In May 1933, Al-Nazir Press in Lucknow published *Safar-i Sa'adat* (Propitious Journey).

M.N. Pearson suspects that the accounts of returning hajjis are programmed as to what to *feel*.[2] From the perspective of an intellectual and keen observer, *Safar-i Sa'adat* is an intimate account of not just what an individual saw and heard in the course of his travels—first by train to Bombay, and then by ship till Jiddah, and from thereon sometimes in a swaying contraption made of wood and leather, called *shaqdaf* (double-slung litters balanced precariously atop a camel) or a bumpy motor lorry on potholed roads as well as his stay in Arabia—but is also, far more significantly, a candid record of the author's feelings and observations at different points in this voyage. His narrative gains merit through his sensitive and keen commentaries on the social, economic, and political conditions of the places he passed through. At the same time, it merits attention as a fluent account of a rite of passage—both of the spirit and of the world. Readers can, thus, experience this from the vantage of the pilgrim and from the long-term perspective of history.

---

1 Robert Dannin (2002), *Black Pilgrimage to Islam*, New York, p. 112.
2 M.N. Pearson, *Pious Passengers*, p. 5.

Safar-i Sa'adat offers a clue to understanding, at least superficially, some elements of the qasbati culture. The qasba is, after all, Amir Ahmad's beautiful and artfully fashioned universe. His agile wit, impudent humour, and purposive mind do not leave him even on the high sea. He also reveals, in a colonial milieu, the management, administration, and regulation of the hajj by the government. Lastly, he sheds light on the role of the hajj—a visible expression of the unity of the *umma*—in providing an impetus to the then fledgling idea of pan-Islamism.

C. Poenson, a nineteenth-century missionary in Central Java, had pointed out that Arabia not only constituted the uniting centre for pilgrims, but also offered the site for their leaders to meet, worship, and discuss political interests and plans. The returning pilgrims, in turn, received tracts for religious stimulation and conversion.[1] The Dutch experience with the *paderi* in the Minangkabau in the 1820s and 1830s, whose leaders began the spread of their teaching, particularly after their return from Mecca, was sometimes repeated in the subcontinent. Those who returned with a heightened sense of religiosity set about 'purifying' or 'cleansing' of 'impure' practices and customs. Indeed, they endeavoured to rid Indian Islam of 'deviant' practices and branded many local rites and customs as *bid'at* or improvisations that were 'sinful'. Hajji Shariat Allah, having been exposed to Wahhabism, resolved to purge Islam of Hindu and Shia accretions. According to his tombstone, he was 'a defender of religion against the menace of the Shias and the disbelievers and against all misguidance.' Maulana Ahmad Riza Khan, founder of the Ahl-i Sunnat wa Jamaat, performed the hajj twice, at a twenty-year interval. He was infused with the desire to engage in *tajdid* or renewal of faith.[2] In 1891, the ethnographer H.H. Risley had written, '...even the distant Mecca has been brought, by means of Messrs Cook's steamers and return-tickets, within reach of the faithful in India; and the influence of Mahomeddan missionaries and return pilgrims has made itself felt in a quiet but steady revival of orthodox usage in eastern Bengal.'[3] In early twentieth century, Sultan Jahan Begum of Bhopal

---

1 Deliar Noer, *The Modernist Muslim Movement in Indonesia, 1900–1942*, p. 25.

2 Usha Sanyal (1996), *Devotional Islam and Politics in British India: Ahmad Riza Khan Barelvi and his Movement, 1870–1920*, Delhi, p. 6.

3 H.H. Risley (1981), *Tribes and Castes of Bengal* (reprint Firma Mukhopadhyay, 1981, Calcutta) p. 1: xxx, quoted in Richard M. Eaton , *The Rise of Islam*, p. 284.

(1858–1930) returned from hajj as 'a much more ardent follower of the Prophet', and 'much more zealous in her own religion.'[1]

Amir Ahmad is uncharacteristically modest about his writing skills; yet, the informative purpose of his text takes precedence over its literary pretensions. He profiled people and described his exchanges in an easy-flowing writing style and plain language. He included quality Urdu verses, an illustration of his great burst of concentrated poetic energy, and kept his story alive through his talent for ridicule and his skill in handling comic scenes. Tinged with self-pity and spiced by self-ridicule, he incorporated a good deal of biting satire, especially in its reference to the colonial officials for whom he had nothing but contempt. This is not surprising: word-play was a recurrent preoccupation with the Lakhnavis. They excelled in it and were often besotted by it.

The Qasba Background

Knowledge and acceptance of one's proper station in life was a basic, or even *the* basic, element in the qasba, a unique cultural entity in pre-Partition India. Notwithstanding the social divide, the economic disparities and the hierarchy of authorities, the qasba life avoided clinging to the doctrine of laissez-faire, which advocated the barest minimum of interference from the urban classes. It had, moreover, all the qualities attributed to the English country—clouds and sky, woodlands and streams, grass and orchards, birds and fishes, sounds, and even silences. At once a microcosm and self-contained, yet open and uncloistered, the qasba was a living-breathing embodiment of a plural, composite culture. Often described as stereotypical at best and elitist at worst, its cultural ethos opened a window into a certain way of life and a way of looking at life.[2] There is no denying that it bred a certain type of individual—aware, literate, multi-dimensional, and above all supremely confident of himself and his place in the world. We see these qualities in Amir Ahmad. It is, therefore, worth examining the culture and ethos that produced such a fine embodiment of moderation, rationality and good sense.

The glimpses of *sharif* culture in a great many Urdu accounts leaven some of the hajj narratives written by well-to-do gentlemen from the

---

1 Sultan Jahan Begum, *Safarnama*, p. lxi.

2 See Mushirul Hasan (2004), *From Pluralism to Separatism: Qasbas in Colonial Awadh*, Delhi, for a detailed study of the qasba and the qasbati culture.

qasbas and their neighbourhoods with a subtle extra flavour. While the hajj rituals remain, at all times, the central experience, the author-narrator-recorder's own distinctly qasbati identity becomes a lodestar, as it were, to navigate the new terrain and, in a sense, calibrate or measure his own range of new experiences and adventures. Thus, while the record or memoir becomes a *bildungsroman*, the author moves from innocence to wisdom by gaining knowledge (in this case, both secular knowledge of the ways of the world and 'divine' or spiritual knowledge accompanied by an upliftment of one's mind and morals). And the voyage becomes an extended metaphor for a rite of passage, a crossing-over not just across the seas but also from innocence to maturity, and a journey accompanied by a commensurate moral, psychological, and intellectual development.

Not all in the qasbas were equally placed. A qasba, typically, had three main constituents. The *ashraf*, the gentry or high-born families, included soldiers, administrators, scholars, theologians and Sufis. Then, the leisured class of the landed aristocracy, who had inherited rent-free lands. The lowest tier was occupied by a large mass loosely called the *ajlaf* or the low-born. These included cultivators, landless labourers, and a motley bunch of service providers such as *dhobis* (washermen), *bhishtis* (water drawers and water carriers), *nais* or *hajjams* (barbers), *rangrez* (dyers), *julahe* (weavers), *kunjar* (greengrocers), *kasai* (butcher), *ghosi* (milkmen), *dhuniyas* (cotton carders), *manihars* (bangle-makers) and several craftsmen, petty traders, shopkeepers, and professional singers, among a host of others. It was these, the lowest of the low, who constituted the bulk of the pilgrim traffic year after year. These class distinctions reflected the social profile of the hajjis, which were sometimes even magnified during the interactions on board and occasionally in the streets of Mecca and Medina.

Judging the hajj narratives is difficult, but the ones in Urdu share a quality of brevity and pay attention to details at the expense of history or sociology. There is the carefully guarded statement and there is also the carefree verdict of the observer. Again, in the latter classification, we observe the tendency to mildly criticize or praise. Generally speaking, criticism is diplomatic and under-emphasis the dominant strain. However, Amir Ahmad did not worry as to whether he gave offence to either the Indian or the Saudi establishment. He entered the country with the substance of an independent outlook. While Hasan Nizami made a virtue of not discussing politics in his roznamcha and recommended instead, in his *Nataij-o-Hidayate Zaruri* (Essential Conclusions and Instructions), the hajj accounts of Khwaja Ghulamus Saqlain, an Aligarh 'Old Boy' and editor of *Asr-i Jadid*, and Munshi Mahbub Alam,[1] editor of *Paisa Akhbar*, Amir Ahmad did not eschew political discussions. Like Choudhry Mohammad Ali,[2] he did not hide his scorn of the Nejdis.[3] The qasbati culture endowed him with an urbane, sophisticated and singularly self-assured worldview. Unlike Hasan Nizami, who adopted a 'neutral' posture, he took sides and candidly admitted doing so. 'Do not, for a minute, think that the author of this diary went about with his eyes closed', remarked Abdul Majid Daryabadi in his foreword to the *Safar-i Sa'adat*. 'Or that he returned with no more than a few homely observations studded in his notebook. Few ever noticed what he observed. Fewer still are able to articulate as well as he does.' Daryabadi cited these lines as evidence of the forthright manner of Amir Ahmad's writing style:

I am a native of India, weak of faith, timorous of belief, and oblivious of the intricacies of dogma. A man like me, though dazzled by the splendid celebrations in this citadel of Islam, is also distressed by a few things. You have heard my paeans of praise; listen now to my tale of woe.

The *Safar-i Sa'adat* thus provides material for comment or discussion, as well as the assertion of a point of view. It is not just a straightforward travelogue, but a series of sketches on people, places, pastimes, and customs prevailing in and around those places. Its author Amir Ahmad was a man of exceptional moral courage, who spoke his mind without fear of the colonial authorities and others, irrespective of their rank or influence. Incensed by the rude behaviour of a British Sergeant supervising the boarding of passengers at the Bombay dock, he remarked: 'Every lash of that tyrant's cane bled my heart and roused my anger.' At the same time, he bemoaned that the Bengali Muslims,

---

1 Munshi Mahbub Alam (1908), *Safarnama-e Europe*, Lahore; Khwaja Hasan Nizami (1913), *Roznama-i Biltasveer*, Meerut, p. 199; Khalid Mahmud, *Urdu Safarnamon ka Tanqeedi Mutaala*, pp.159–64.

2 He was distressed by the desecration of graves in the Jannat-ul Baqi. This sight turned him against the Wahhabis. Masoodul Haq (ed.) (2005) *Kulliyat Choudhry Mohammad Ali*, Delhi, p. 57.

3 'Just as the Muslim victors had defaced the idols by slashing their noses and ears, so too the Nejdis have made the monuments of Koh-i Uhad lame and maimed ... The man giving the sermon was a Nejdi. He delivered a provocative speech and termed all those who say *Assalamo Alaika Ya Rasool Allah* as polytheists and sinners.'

who were victims of his harsh treatment, were either insensitive to their humiliation or the prospect of hajj made them impervious to pain (14 February). Moreover, Amir Ahmad espoused causes that he believed were just, however unpopular they might be with his own friends or superiors. This had something to do with the *timing* of his voyage, which marked a transition in the Arabian Peninsula. This requires elaboration.

The late 1920s were a tumultuous time, with some changes likely to have a lasting impact on power-lines across the world. The two holy shrines, having been historically controlled by the Ottomans,[1] had by now fallen under the sway of the Nejdis.[2] This was the time when the army of Wahhabi warriors was beginning to lay down the laws of what was proper and what was not—in both Islamic practice and doctrine. While appreciating some of the initiatives taken by the fledgling Hijaz government, Amir Ahmad criticized the rapacious pilgrims' guides and brokers, and the Nejdis, who inflicted their version of Islam on those who flocked to the holy sites from different parts of the world, bringing with them their own versions of Islam. Used to observing certain rituals such as raising one's hands in *dua* after *namaz*, he felt deeply affronted at being sternly rebuked by the Nejdi custodians of the holy places, while doing so.

The H.B. Clayton Hajj Inquiry Committee observed: 'The Nejdis are reactionary and intolerant in matters of religion and are at pains to interfere with certain observances and practices, which have been customary as part of the pilgrimage among Indian and other pilgrims'. Oriented towards a qasba version of liberal Islam, Amir Ahmad felt uncomfortable with the Wahhabi regime, which was established after the surrender of Mecca and the capitulation of Jiddah. He saw them as self-appointed guardians of Islam bent upon erasing all traces of Islam's tolerant, pluralistic past. For example, he felt indignant that a grave in Jiddah, said to be of Eve, was razed by the order of Abdul Aziz ibn Saud (1879–1953), who followed the treatise of Wahhabism

---

1 The Ottomans are regarded as the heirs to both Roman and Islamic traditions. The Ottoman empire or Ottoman Khilafat (1299 to 1922) was at the centre of interactions between the Eastern and Western worlds for six centuries. At the height of its power, the empire contained 29 provinces with Istanbul as its capital.

2 Nejd or Najd (literally 'highland') is the central region of the Arabian Peninsula. It is also one of the main regions comprising the modern Saudi capital, Riyadh. The Saudi royal family, the Al Saud, belong to Nejd.

by Abdul Wahhab (*Book of God's Unity*), which affirmed that one must explicitly deny any other object of worship. Similarly, Amir Ahmad did not approve of the guards posted on the Cave of Hira, and of the fact that the faithful were not allowed to pay their respects at this historical spot where the Prophet had prayed for a long time and where the first verses of the Holy Book were revealed. Here is what he stated about the wilful desecration of the graves of the *Ahl-i Bait* (the Prophet, his daughter Fatima, Ali, Hasan and Husain):

We had studied in the history of the Great Roman Empire that when the Vandals and Goths had attacked Rome, they had vanquished it and destroyed its ancient monuments and razed centuries-old art and architecture to the ground. The state of Jannat-ul Baqi[1] under the Nejdis is similar to the ruin and havoc unleashed by those barbarians.

Amir Ahmad was, furthermore, outraged by the tendency to crush certain practices such as facing the Haram Sharif while making a dua, or offering salaam[2] at the Prophet's grave:

The Bani Umayya tied horses in the Masjid-e Nabawi. The Abbasids slaughtered the Sadaat. The Qaramita destroyed Medina with their atrocities and cruelties. The traitor Hussein laid siege upon the city of Medina for three years and vanquished its people. The Nejdis rained canon balls over the city and traumatized its citizens. And today from the *mimbar* of the Prophet, a *fatwa* of infidelity or *kufr* is being issued to those who sit facing the Kaaba.

...

It is also ordered that after the salaam, the dua should be made with one's back to the Prophet's grave because it is considered *shirk* [polytheism] and bid'at [innovation] to make a dua while facing the auspicious window that overlooks the grave. *Nauzu-billahe* ...

Close to the Masjid-e Quba is the mosque of Syedna Ali. It is not permitted to pray here; in fact, the Nejdis have posted a police force here. In Lucknow when an old mosque had been turned into a dispensary the Muslims had been angry. Here, it ought to inflame much worse passions to see the Nejdis occupying Hazrat Ali's mosque. Close to this mosque, there were once several smaller mosques but they have all been destroyed by the Nejdis. Now all you see are heaps of broken stones and no one is allowed to go there. I never used to speak ill of the Saudis before this hajj travel but now it has become impossible to keep one's tongue silent after having witnessed their barbaric actions. May Allah give them better counsel!

1 There is an interesting description of the graves of certain prominent figures, including Fatima's, the daughter of the Prophet, in Nadir Ali's *Mir-aatul-Arab yaani Safarnama-i Nadir*, pp. 78–9.

2 The word 'salaam' is used in a variety of expressions and contexts in Arabic and Islamic speech and writing. *As-Salamu Alaykum* literally means 'Peace be upon you'.

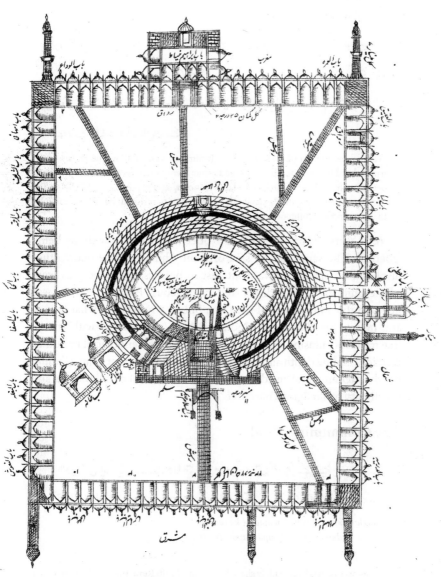

A beautiful and detailed view of Bab-e-Ibrahim.
Munshi Mohammad S. Anwar Ali, *Kaleed Baab-ul Hajj*
(Munshi Nawal Kishore: Lucknow, n.d.), p. 70

On Amir Ahmad's distress over the desecration and levelling of the graves and shrines of the pious, which he himself shared, Abdul Majid Daryabadi remarked, 'You will find the expression of his aching heart inscribed within these pages.'[1]

کیا قبورِ مسلمین کی تو ہیں، چہ جائیکہ قبورِ صالحین وصدیقین کی اہانت، کا حکم بھی کہیں وارد ہوا ہے؟ حکم نہ سہی، کسی امام نے اس کی اجازت بھی دی ہے؟ نجدیوں نے قبے گرا دیئے، درست، قبریں بھی تمام تر کچی بنا دی گئی ہوتیں، تو حکومت کا ہاتھ پکڑنے والا کوئی نہ تھا، لیکن یہ کیا قیامت ہے، کہ مقبرہ صالحین کو گرے ہوئے مکانات کا ملبہ بنا دیا جائے۔

Has the desecration of even ordinary Muslims' graves, let alone the graves of the truthful and the virtuous, been decreed somewhere? If not decreed, has it ever been permitted by an Imam? Nejdis razed down domes, alright. Nobody would blame the government even if entirely clay-built graves has been restored. But what a calamity that the tombs of righteous ones are reduced to rubble.

W.B. Yeats (1865–1939) was a poet in his prose, without being 'poetical'. The same can be said of Amir Ahmad. While many other displayed no strong outward interest in politics, his reflections were wholesome, confident, direct and courageous. Political animus was heavy in the atmosphere of the time, but he wrote about what he saw and he saw his characters—Indian, British, and Arabs—with an eye free from rosy illusion. He dealt with the ugly matter of racial prejudice candidly, adding depth and clarity to his narrative. So that *Safar-i Sa'adat* has the excitement of an adventure story, the interest of a chronicle, and the dignity of a religious narrative.

The Communing Mind

آنکھوں میں چھا گیا ہے مدینے کا راستا   ہر ہر قدم میں ہیں جھونپڑے اپنے پڑے ہوئے

سمجھے کہ راہِ طیبہ میں موتی پڑے ملے   دیکھے جو ہم نے پاوں میں چھالے پڑے ہوئے

Aankhon me chha gaya hai madine ka raasta
har har qadam me hain jhonpare apne pare hue.

---

1 This distress has been widely shared over time. Mufti Reza Ansari of Firangi Mahal, for example, bemoaned that the grave of Amir Hamza and other martyrs of the Battle of Uhud were razed to the ground four decades ago. See Mohammad Reza Ansari (1966), *Hajj ka Safar*, Lucknow, p. 341.

Samjhe keh raah-e-tayyaba me moti pare mile
dekhe jo hum ne paaon me chhaale pare hue.

The Path to Medina gleams in my vision
At each and every step, our thatched huts abound
When I look at blisters of my feet
Pearls they seem in the path of Taiba.

The English poet Percy Bysshe Shelley (1792–1822) claimed in *A Defence of Poetry* (1821) that, 'poets are the acknowledged legislators of the world.' If so, then the profusion of writing and publishing activity discussed above had an interesting literary and cultural fallout, one that has been seldom commented upon: it spawned a great deal of popular poetry in the form of naat, *paidaish, munajat, manqabat,* dua, *durood,* salaam; these were essentially different sub-genres within the bigger genre of panegyric poetry in praise of the Prophet. This coincided with the increasing popularity of *maulud* or the celebration of the Prophet's birthday, on the twelfth day of the month of Rabi-ul Awwal. Coloured by Sufism and influenced by the fast-gaining popularity of Awadh's *sozkhwani* (chanting of dirges) and *marsiyakhwani* (reciting of elegies), such forms of poetry were recited, and they evolved and flourished from the nineteenth-century onwards in homes and literary clubs all across north India reaching as far east as Bengal.[1] It is said that Ahmad Riza Khan read a poem for maulud from a mosque's pulpit at the age of four. Abdul Halim Sharar (1860–1926) tells us that Maulvi Ghulam Ahmad Shahid wrote his celebrated *Maulud-i Sharif* in Lucknow and that it conformed to such a high degree with contemporary literary taste that everyone was pleased with it.[2] He added:

The Maulud Sharif assemblies of the Sunnis, which commemorate the nativity of the Prophet, are conducted in much the same way as the Shia assemblies. One difference is that Sunnis have no pulpit and instead the maulvi or reciter sits on a small *takhat* covered with a *farsh* in some prominent place. Traditionally a maulvi recounts the circumstances of the nativity and when he reaches the moment of the Prophet's birth, all those present stand up in respect. The narrator also recites a poem to express joy at the event and rosewater is sprinkled all around the audience. If no maulvi is available, a well-respected man reads out from the pages of *Maulud-e-Sharif*, 'The Exalted Birth',

---

1 Amit Dey (2006), *The Image of the Prophet in Bengali Muslim Piety, 1850–1947,* Kolkata, pp. 28–39; Ali Jawad Zaidi (1993), *A History of Urdu Literature,* Delhi, pp. 173–4, 200.

2 Abdul Halim Sharar (1975), *Lucknow: The Last Phase of an Oriental Culture,* (translated and edited by E.S. Harcourt and Fakhir Hussain), London, p. 89.

by Maulvi Ghulam Imam Shaheed. But the public seems to be no longer satisfied with this form of recital and has replaced it by a new type which imitates sozkhwani. As in sozkhwani, the reciter is accompanied by two persons who maintain the melody. He sits between them chanting the circumstances of the nativity and at intervals, when he comes to verses and *qasidas* in honour of the Prophet, they join in. But whereas the sozkhwans have given vitality to music, these people who sing about the nativity remain amateurs.[1]

The first-hand published hajj accounts provided the poets, many of whom had not undertaken the journey themselves, with the landscape of a distant land, which was dearly beloved because of its association with the Prophet whom they eulogized for his piety and devotion, warmth and kindliness, the strength of mind and his abounding common sense. Ghulam Imam Shahid, an Urdu poet of the early nineteenth century, put it best when he announced:

Friends, before all of us is the journey into non-existence—
But when one has words of the naat, then one has provisions for the road!

While every naat-poet down the ages expressed his inability to convey the Prophet's true greatness, they struggled nonetheless to find the right words. 'Tender', 'loving', 'colourful', 'rustic', 'sophisticated', 'subtle', 'grandiloquent'—the terms and images vary but what did not (and does not) vary is admiration for the manifold qualities that the Prophet embodied.

عاشق نبی کے دیکھیے کیا دیکھیں بعدِ مرگ   ہیں زندگی میں جینے کے لالے پڑے ہوئے

طفلی میں تھے ہمارے نبی۔فخرِ انبیاء   چھوٹی سی عمر میں وہ بڑوں سے بڑے ہوئے

وہ پیشوا ملا جو سراپا ہے صلحِ کل   حقّا کہ ہیں نصیب ہمارے لڑے ہوئے

Aashiqe nabi ke dekhiye kya dekhen baad-e marg,
hain zindagi me jeene ke laale pare hue.
Tifli me the hamaare nabi pakh-e-anbiya,
chhoti si umar me woh baron se bare hue.
Woh peshwa mila jo saraapa hai sulhe kul,
haqqa ke hain naseeb hamaare lare hue.

Let's see what awaits the Prophet's followers after death
Their lives are nothing but beds of thorns
Even as a child our Prophet was the best

1 Abdul Halim Sharar, *Lucknow*, p. 217.

In tender age his wisdom surpassed the wisest.
We have found a leader who epitomizes peace
The truth is that our destinies are tied together.

A plethora of songs celebrate the *Mard-i Kamil,* the Perfect Man, the exemplar and model for every believing Muslim, whose every action and habit, no matter how seemingly trivial, were written about not just in Urdu but in many dialects such as *khari boli, bhojpuri* and *dehati.* In naat after naat, the Prophet appears before his listeners as an archetype for all forms of human beauty, or he becomes: 'Beauty from Head to toe, Love embodied'. Fashioned first on Arab models such as the *burda* and later on the Persian masnawi, the Indian versions of these panegyrics wove in many indigenous elements. 'Unexcelled in grandeur of style as in devotional fervour' and remarkable for its frequent references to Hindu mythological allusions, Mohsin Kakorwi (1827–1905) hoped his naat would intercede, as it were, on the Day of Judgement. A lawyer of repute, he did not extend his creative talent beyond writing naat and qasida in praise of the Prophet. It was only through naat that such great passions, such ecstasy, such quickened and multiplied consciousness, could be experienced. One of his long poems, reproduced below, is moving and dignified.

In the rows of resurrection your panegyrist will be with you
In his hand he has this enthusiastic *ghazal,* this qasida
And Gabriel will say with a hint: Now in the name of God recite:
From the direction of Benares went a cloud towards Mathura
With lightning, carrying the sacred Ganga waters on their shoulders
The news is flashed across to Mathura
That the clouds are heading (for the city) on pilgrimage;
For miles, the dark clouds are spread before us. ...
It has rained a full fortnight, Tuesday to Tuesday,
Raining non-stop all this while.
How shall we have an audience with Shri Krishna?
The hearts of Gopis are tense with suspense.
Let the Brahmins come out with amber
To propitiate the rain god to stop awhile.
(For it is Saluno, first day of full moon in the month of Sawan).
The clouds seem to be steering westward:
Emerging from the Indian tavern and the temple of Braj
The clouds have unrolled their prayer mat in front of Kaaba.

Religious hearts swelled to the stanzas of Ghalib's masnawi called *Abr-e-gauharbar* or 'The Jewel-Carrying Cloud', wherein he compared the Prophet to the rain cloud which brought blessings in the form of life-giving rain, and was in keeping with his role as *rahmat lil-aalamin*. The masnawi is descriptive, passionate and evocative.[1]

In his mingling of faith, religion and worldly matters, Iqbal saw Mohammad as the political leader who guides people towards their destinies even in this world: 'With the key of religion he opened the door of this world', and 'On his forehead is written the destiny of nations.' Writing with a deliberately reformatory intention, Iqbal likened the Prophet to the leader of a caravan. In *Asrar-i Khudi*, he wrote:

We are like a rose with many petals, but with one perfume
He is the soul of the society, and he is one.

'Miraj' or the Prophet's ascension to the celestial regions—*Sidratul Muntaha* (the Highest Point)—is one of the most significant events of Iqbal's life.

Miley hey nukta yeh Miraj-e Mustafa se mujhe
Keh alam-e bashariyat ki zad mein hain gardoon.

The ascension of Mustafa has revealed to me that the heavens are within man's reach.

With time, *milad mehfils* acquired a certain set pattern. Beginning with poems celebrating the Prophet's birth, the naat goes on to relate anecdotes about his life, and express joy at his many sayings, or the longing to visit Medina. They dwell, in great ecstasy, on the motif of Medina, imploring its Prince to intercede on their behalf. In the course of a milad, the naats are interspersed, at every few intervals, with prose passages narrating specific instances from the Prophet's life, his views, on say, education, on women, or any other subject chosen by the *zakir* or the narrator. Those who have not been able to visit the holy places have written some incredible verses, describing the arduous journey, each according to their imagination in ever-new imagery. So you have naats such as *Saani tera kaunain ke kishwar me nahin hai*, or

Azal tu, abad tu, ahad tu samad tu
Is Akbar ki goya zaban tu hi tu.

Thou art the Beginning
Thou art the End.
The Only One,
The self- contained.
Thou art Akbar's eloquence.

1 Annemarie Schimmel (1982), *As Through a Veil: Mystical Poetry in Islam*, New York, pp. 209, 210. Also, references to Iqbal below.

Or,

Haqqa ke teri yaad se abaad hai zamana[1]

The world thrives by Thy presence.

In large public gatherings, a renowned scholar or maulvi performs the *zikr*. In private gatherings, it can be performed by any well-respected man or woman. The audience is encouraged to recite durood sharif and send salaam, greetings, to the Prophet. Rosewater is sprinkled, or *itr*[2] is applied on the wrists of all those present. The entire congregation gets to its feet when the salaam is read. One of the most popular salaams, found in a compilation called *Milad-i Akbar*, one that is read with solemn and sonorous dignity by the entire congregation, is:

يا نبی سلام علیک

يا رسول سلام علیک

يا حبیب سلام علیک

صَلوٰۃ اللہ علیک

Ya nabi salaam alaika ya rasool salaam alaika
Ya habib salaam alaika, salawatullah alaika

Greetings to thee O Prophet!
O Messenger of Lord! Greetings to thee
Greetings to thee, O God's friend,
May Lord's benevolence be upon thee!

Other salaams—*Salaam ae Aamina ke laal, ae Mehboob-i Subhani*— send similar salutations to Amina's son and Beloved of God. The *mehfil* or congregation ends with a dua or munajat. Some of the most popular ones, which quicken the imagination and satisfy the spirit, are: *Momino'n waqt-i rehmat-i rab hai, ab woh maango jo dil ka maqsad hai;* unconventional choices would be Iqbal's *Ya rab dil-i Muslim ko woh zinda tamanna de, jo rooh ko tadpa de jo qalb ko garma de,* or Altaf Husain Hali's *Wo nabion men rehmat laqab pane wala; Muraden gharibon ki bar lane wala; Musibat men ghairon ke kam ane wala; Woh apne parae ka gham*

---

1 Khwaja Mohammad Akbar Warsi (n.d.), *Milad-i Akbar*, Delhi.
2 Itr is an Indian perfume, usually made of jasmine, rose or sandal. This perfume evolved during the time of Mughals, Nizams and other princely states of India.

khane wala; Faqiron ka malja zaifon ka mava; Yatimon ka wali ghulamon ka maula.[1] Sweets are distributed before the congregation disperses.

The Perilous Journey

On the one hand, the British sought to control all religious congregations, *melas* and pilgrimages included, because they recognized the latter's potential to act as powerful conduits of disease as well as of news, rumours, sedition and eventually pan-Islamism,[2] and on the other hand, their over-riding prejudice against indigenous religious and cultural institutions caused them to exclude well-informed people from the process of consultation and to pay scant attention to improve the organization of pilgrimages and local hygiene.[3]

This may well explain the government's 'culpable negligence' of the interests of the pilgrims.[4] Blunt, who made this observation in 1882, urged the government to resist 'such influences as the propagandists might bring to bear upon the hajjis with a view to animate them with hostility to the British supremacy in India.' He referred to Britain's 'Asiatic interests' in the 'humaner thought' of Islam in India, Egypt, and elsewhere and wanted his country to occupy the position 'marked out for her by Providence of leading the Mohammedan world in its advance towards better things.'[5] In 1907, he touched on much the same theme, though his chief concern was to defend and promote the idea of benevolence associated with British colonialism. He, therefore, remarked that the Muslims looked to the government under which they lived as a fountain of authority, and that they expected the imperial authority to organize the shipment of pilgrims and afford protection to them while they were travelling. This was made more than ever necessary by the growing abuses connected with the quarantine and other vexatious regulations at Jiddah. 'Indifference with them is tantamount to neglect of duty,' observed Blunt.[6]

1 See translation in Christopher Shacke and Javed Majeed (eds) (1997), *Hali's Musaddas: The Flow and Ebb of Islam*, Delhi, p. 14.

2 Kama Maclean (2008), *Pilgrimage and Power: The Kumbh Mela in Allahabad, 1765–1954*, Delhi.

3 C.A. Bayly (1999), *Empire and Information: Intelligence Gathering and Social Communication in India, 1780–1870*, Cambridge, p. 339.

4 W.S. Blunt, *The Future of Islam*, p. 29.

5 Ibid., p. 212.

6 W.S. Blunt (1909), *India under Ripon*, London, pp. 296, 297.

Hajj records do illustrate the importance attached to the pilgrimage by the colonial government. This is reflected in the efforts to control the spread of diseases through quarantine and fumigation; the setting up of Hajj Inquiry Committees (especially the H.B. Clayton Committee constituted in 1929); and their recommendations and the reasons for the failure to execute most of them. All these measures were initiated not because of altruistic reasons but because the government anxiously wanted to avoid adverse publicity, which could cause disaffection in the colonies and raise eyebrows in the parliament. Soon, it also began to respond to pressure groups. One of them was of the Muslim businessmen in Bombay, who retained, despite the presence of the British shipping cartels till the First World War, a small slice of the business. Speculators, too, pooled their capital to charter a ship for the season, or refurbished an old steamship to get it licensed for pilgrim traffic.[1] Added to them were the publicists, who began to use, especially in early twentieth century, the hajj traffic to gain leverage as community spokesmen. Besides Shaukat Ali, Seth Jan Mohammad Chotani (1883–1932), Hajji Abdullah Haroon (1872–1942) and Maulvi Shafi Daudi (1879–1946) belonged to this group. Their efforts bore fruit. Chotani set up, with Turkish aid, a wholly Muslim shipping company to break into the European monopoly. Indeed, he did much to improve the conditions of the pilgrims.[2] There were, besides these motivated individuals, the hajj brokers, who amassed large sums of money through the colonial officials, muallim[3] and employees of the shipping company. Their nexus of corruption went far beyond the confines of the Bombay and Karachi ports.

The pilgrim's journey was perilous for a variety of reasons, but the problems faced by the officials and the shipping companies were a lot more complex. First, it was something of a challenge to 'encourage' people from one part of the country to board ship from 'their' port,

---

1 This information is based on Radhika Singha, 'Passport, Ticket, and India-rubber Stamp'.

2 Francis Robinson, *Separatism among Indian Muslims*, pp. 210–11.

3 The muallims were carefully supervised and made responsible for the safety of the pilgrims in their charge. New regulations were issued from time to time to prevent them from stealing the property of pilgrims who died while in their charge. A list of the authorized charges and fees was drawn up every year and published, and, though the scale of fees largely increased and the amount taken by the government was exorbitant, the publication of such a list of charges prevented extortion.

that is, the English masters were convinced that if the Bengalis could be persuaded to board from Calcutta only, the problem of feeding them, at the very least, could be taken care of by the Bengal Hajj Committee. Second, the pilgrims came from different parts of the subcontinent, and different social and economic backgrounds, unlike say those from Java where Muslims had a far more homogeneous profile. Consequently, the shipping authorities had to cater to their vastly different needs, especially their food preferences. The eating houses, for example, found it difficult to cater to their varied tastes and hugely different paying capacities.

Pilgrims were prohibited from cooking on the ship. Thus, the experiment of the hotel system was resorted to. While they were subsidized, the poorer pilgrims still found the costs prohibitively high and spent the sea voyage subsisting on whatever they had taken along from their homes, whatever, that is, had survived the rigours of the fumigation and the long days at sea. In this regard, the Javanese pilgrims were better off. In their case, the master of the pilgrim ship was required to supply each pilgrim the prescribed allowance of good food and pure water. The Indian Merchant Shipping Act, on the other hand, still required extensive legislative changes before it could match the provisions afforded to the Javanese pilgrims.

The government, on its part, hoped that the Muslims would themselves remedy the faults in the system, but clearly this was not to be. While the poorer and illiterate pilgrims stayed silent about the many hardships suffered by them (some believing that the more they suffered during the journey and in the course of their stay in the Holy Cities, the greater would be the reward of the pilgrimage), others aired their grievances publicly. Little of any consequence emerged from this public chest beating. By the early twentieth century, however, the government conceded that the problems encountered by the pilgrims were sufficiently serious to merit special legislation.

Already, a number of legislations were in place. As early as 1873, the Merchant Shipping Act provided that those ships plying between Bombay and the Hijaz must comply with the 'boat capacity' required by the Act when it came to carrying coolies, hajjis, etc. Five years later, the government deputed, for the first time, an Assistant Surgeon to observe and report on the sanitary conditions.[1] The Bombay Pilgrim

---

1 See William R. Roff (1982), 'Sanitation and Security: The Imperial Powers and the Nineteenth Century Hajj', *Arabian Studies*, VI, p. 147. Quoted in Usha Sanyal,

Act (1887), the oldest piece of legislation, which dealt with India in a rudimentary way, laid down laws to control shipping lines and appoint pilgrim protectors. In 1895, the Pilgrim Ships Act was passed to regulate ships and ensure the health and comfort of the pilgrims. It provided the template for similar legislation in other parts of the world. A Special Calcutta Act, modelled on the Bombay Act, was passed in 1896. There had already been in circulation for some time then an Urdu handbook entitled *Bab-i Mecca*, which gave useful tips on how to prepare baggage for medical inspection at the ports, how to reach the docks from the pilgrims' guest houses, how to negotiate around the disinfected sheds, how to label boxes and bundles with the owners' names and such other handy details. There is a record of the *Bab-i Mecca* as early as 1909 but with most pilgrims being poor and illiterate, clearly it would be a long time before the many useful suggestions listed in it percolated down through word of mouth.

These legislations dealt with: (a) the increasing cost of repatriation of those who had overstayed or did not have the means to return; (b) the death of destitute pilgrims either during hajj or in the course of their extended stay, often without the means for paying for their burial; and (c) the frequent outbreak of smallpox and other infectious diseases in overcrowded shelters and makeshift camps. Over the years, it had been the practice for pilgrims to get vaccinated for smallpox and cholera, when they applied for pilgrim passes. At the time of applying for passes, they were expected to get these inoculations and obtain certificates from any registered medical practitioners counter-signed by the Civil Surgeon of the district. But these procedures were not followed at the district level; consequently, pilgrims poured into Bombay and Karachi either without vaccinations or with certificates of dubious authenticity. Even though health authorities could deny them embarkation, they could not authenticate the certificates of foreign nationals from Afghanistan, Iran, Uzbekistan and Chinese Turkmenistan.

Pilgrims heading directly to the ports stayed in *musafirkhanas* or camps, thus imposing further strains on the already stretched resources. As one irate Health Officer for Bombay noted in July 1930: 'Port Health Authorities have enough to do inspecting and controlling the pilgrims without having to perform immunization operations and issue certificates—though I admit that to do these things oneself

_____

Devotional Islam and Politics in British India, fn 38.9, p. 60.

would be more satisfactory from other points of view.' This implied that, while from the point of view of Bombay's safety and in order to prevent the pilgrims from shacking up for weeks, properly safeguarded immunization ought to have been done before the pilgrims' reaching the ports, but in view of the malpractices at the district level, it had to be done before they boarded the ship. In effect, many of them ended up getting re-vaccinated before they were allowed to buy their tickets. Moreover, the government could not control disease and infections.

A government report listed the following main features of the 1929 'season':

1. The outbreak of disturbances in Afghanistan due to which Afghans boarded from Bombay. According to the Report, Bombay's Commissioner of Police had to accommodate for over a week 250 Pathans in the Carnac Road musafirkhana and 150 in the Wadi Bunder musafirkhana for shelter. The temporary 'Pilgrim Police' in fact had its work cut out in stopping the Pathans from 'mixing with the pilgrims and creating trouble';[1]
2. Riots in Bombay in February just before the beginning of the hajj season;
3. Appointment of the Hajj Inquiry Committee; and
4. Opening of eating houses on board ships.

The Report is informative; for instance, it mentions that at the time of the sailing of the S.S. Rehmani when Bombay was affected by the riots, owing to the difficulty of obtaining labour-carts to convey pilgrims' luggage from the musafirkhanas to the docks, the authorities engaged a few motor lorries. With 1,500 pilgrims, all the musafirkhanas were full. The Report also provides another useful nugget of information: that the official minimum expenditure incurred by a hajji was the same as that in the previous year and pilgrims were advised to carry not less than 600 rupees, a return ticket, and if they preferred to travel to the Hijaz by motor car, a further 100 rupees. It mentions that the Central Khilafat Committee had established a Pilgrim Welfare Department in Bombay to

1 The presence of this unusually large contingent of Afghans is also borne out by Amir Ahmad's account and the mention of the wild Pathans who commandeered the deck, thereby blocking the free passage of other passengers on board.

look after the pilgrims from distant parts of the country, many of whom were stepping out of their villages for the first time even though for the sake of safety, they would be travelling with several others from their neighbourhood, village, or province in the form of a *kafila* or caravan.

Three main shipping lines monopolized the pilgrim traffic; these were Messrs Turner Morrison and Company Ltd, A. Nemazee and Company and Hajji Sultanali Shushtary and Company. The *Rehmani*, which carried Amir Ahmad in 1929 and was owned by Messrs Turner Morrison and Company, was previously owned by the Bombay and Persia Steam Navigation Company Ltd. During previous years, many attempts had been made to charter ships during the season. One such attempt, made as early as 1876, ended up in a court of law when it was found that certain pilgrim brokers who had chartered a steamer had duped over 300 pilgrims. During the 1929 season, the Nemazee line of steamers was run by M.K. Khaleeli. Again, to quote Pearson:

There was also a political dimension to the hajj. Control of the Holy Cities passed in the sixteenth century from the Mamluk dynasty in Egypt, which had only a vestigial control over the hereditary sheikhs of the cities, to the Ottoman Empire. The sultans took very seriously their role as Guardians of the Holy Places, did public works in the two cities, provided food to the inhabitants, and financed the vast pilgrim caravans from Cairo and Damascus to the Hijaz. Muslim Indian rulers similarly patronized those wanting to go on the hajj.

However, the Indian rulers were content to 'sponsor' a certain number of pilgrims, establish inns or lodges for their citizens, and send medical assistance; Richard Burton identified a well built by an Indian at Bir el-Hindi, a favourite halting place. It was the British who stepped in in an organized and forceful fashion. While some part of their 'assistance' was motivated more by the famous Anglo-Saxon instinct for control and surveillance, the formidable organizational abilities and managerial skills of the British bureaucrats were put to good use. In effect they did far more to streamline the entire annual exercise and invest some degree of order in the otherwise chaotic spill of pilgrims during the previous decades. Clearly, though, as far as the arrangements for the hajj were concerned, the Indian Muslims wanted more. To end with an observation from Blunt's account:

Of the pilgrimage, I will only say that the need of organization in the shipment of pilgrims is still strongly demanded, and of protection while on their journey. Something has been, indeed, done in the last three years, but exceedingly little; and the Indian Mohammedans regard such protection as a duty of the Imperial Government, made more than ever necessary by the growing abuses connected with the quarantine and other vexatious regulations at Jiddah.[1]

By the early 1920s, the government had begun to take a serious view of the complications that could arise from mismanagement on the part of the authorities—both in the Hijaz and in the countries of origin— and the misinformation among the pilgrims. Impelled no doubt by political considerations and the fear of subversion among its Muslim populace, it began a concerted move which was propelled by the twin engines of surveillance and control. Its concerns and directions were spelt out in a pamphlet, *General Instructions for Pilgrims to the Hedjaz and a Manual for the Guidance of Officers and Others Concerned in the Sea Pilgrim Traffic* (1922).

Innocence and Experience

Nearly two decades after Blunt's plea for a humane disposition towards the hajj traffic, Amir Ahmad noticed the tide of official policies moving against Islam, and the journey of faith becoming more and more hazardous. He found the conduct of the Bombay Hajj Committee unsatisfactory. Often, he noticed the ships plying the Bombay–Jiddah route loading their bellies with coal, wheat, cotton and commercial goods, and, in the process, squeezing the pilgrims into smaller and smaller spaces as the journey progressed. One night, he found 1,000 out of 1,400 hajjis being inconvenienced all night.

Had Muslims been owners of ships, they would never have put innocent hajjis to such hardship, and for the sake of a few extra rupees they would never have troubled hapless pilgrims in this manner. The *Rehmani*, on which I am travelling, belongs to the Mogul Line; ships belonging to this line are considered superior. But since the British own them, the revenue earned through profit from transporting goods is given greater premium than the comfort of pilgrims.

Amir Ahmad noted the lack of drinking water on the ship,[2] the shoddy treatment meted out to passengers travelling third class, the longer

1 W.S. Blunt, *India under Ripon*, p. 296.
2 A latter-day description is as follows: 'How they crouched on the deck planks, in tight groups, men, women and children, and with difficulty managed their household chores (for no food was provided by the company); how they always struggled to and fro with tin cans and canvas canteens, every movement a torture in this press of humanity; how they assembled five times a day around the water taps—of which there were too few for so many people—in order to perform their ablutions before prayer;

waiting periods—whether they were for boarding or disembarking or in the fumigation and custom sheds—the gross insensitivity towards the passengers' comfort and basic needs on the part of the shipping authorities. He expressed his anguish at the state of affairs:

O *Qadir e Zuljalal,* have pity on the state of the Muslims! Steeped in their passion to see your Exalted House, they are willing to undergo every manner of humiliation and not a word of protest escapes from their lips. They are treated no better than goats and sheep in a slaughterhouse; yet they do not pollute their tongue with grievance or complaint.

Later, Amir Ahmad described the stepmotherly treatment meted out to those who could not afford the same small luxuries that he was able to procure, such as hiring his own steamboat to take him from the ship to the shore to avoid waiting in queues, hiring motor cars, mostly Ford cars,[1] instead of walking, sitting in the relative comfort of the litters called shaqdaf tied atop camels and being able to take reasonably well-appointed rooms on rent for both his extended stays in Mecca and Medina as well as the shorter spells in Arafat[2] and Muzdalifa. Similarly, he hired a chair with mosquito netting on a daily charge of one qarsh. Everywhere, there were small indications of how money well spent could make life simpler. Equally, he was aware that others who were not so fortunate were making do without these conveniences and were, therefore, battling not just with the journey's fatigue but with various big and small hardships and deprivations, not to mention the unwarranted humiliations meted out by the authorities.

Officials of the Immigration Department handling the incoming tide of hajjis were, in many ways, no better; apart from being callous, they were also corrupt. One of them commented:

I had heard that passengers who came by sea were subjected to a severe search of their belongings; now the roughness of the Indian port authorities seemed nothing when

---

how they suffered in the stifling air of the deep holds, two stories below the deck, where at other times only bales and cases of goods traveled: whoever saw this had recognized the power of faith which was in these pilgrims.' Muhammad Asad, *Road to Mecca,* p. 357.

1 Automobiles were introduced in 1926. By 1938, the year for which information is available, the total number of pilgrims using Ford cars had increased by 10,000.

2 A granite hill, situated 12 miles/19 kilometers east of Mecca. It is also known as the 'Mountain of Mercy' (*Jabal-e Rehmat*). The hill is the place where Mohammad delivered the Farewell Sermon to the Muslims, who had accompanied him for the hajj towards the end of his life. During hajj, pilgrims perform the main rite called *wuquf* or 'the standing'.

compared to the Immigration Department of Jiddah. Every suitcase was opened up. Every article of clothing was closely inspected. Pillows were stripped of their cases and torn open to see if they hid valuable bolts of cloth. Books were impounded. My cigar box was taken away. Muhammad Yusuf Sahab and I had two or three electric lamps and a couple of spare batteries which we had kept, fearing that these might be difficult to find in Arabia. The lamps were returned to us after due inspection but the government servants carefully pocketed our batteries. We had a couple of bottles of English candy. Some of these too found their way into their pockets. We stood still and silent, patient and praise-giving, supine in following God's will. Had they stuffed all our belongings into their pockets, what right did we have to complain? Each box and bedding was stamped after inspection and after much mishandling we were finally allowed to take away our damaged and diminished belongings. I was told that my cigar box would be handed over to me after I had paid the toll tax. About the books, I was told that nothing could be said at this point; there was no knowing whether they would be allowed to go beyond the port or not. Grateful to have our lives intact and believing that what we had lost was a small recompense, we came out of the station...

Approximately 1,900 passengers stepped off the *Rehmani* ship with Amir Ahmad on 1 March 1929. Of these, only four, including Amir Ahmad, travelled first class. The rest were third or inter class passengers, and they were treated a lot worse than the relatively better-off first class passengers. However, certain laws governed all; for instance, the passports and return tickets of all hajjis had to be deposited with the British Consul in Jiddah,[1] to be returned only after hajj. In this, Amir Ahmad saw a larger design, a conspiracy against Islam:

Their real design is that the number of pilgrims should go down and all the wealth of the world should not reach the *Jaziratul Arab* [the Island of the Arabs] to be expended. But this secret can never be revealed in clear words; instead, expediency is resorted to and attempts are made to inflict inconveniences so that, frustrated, the hajjis might drop out of the journey to Hijaz. Forcing the poor pilgrims to deposit their tickets at the British Consul's office and, on this pretext, making them come several times to bow subserviently before the embassy staff is obviously a ploy meant to benefit the locals.

Abdul Qadir Sikandar, Amir Ahmad's muallim, did not receive him in Jiddah. In his place, a lawyer named Abdur Razzaq appeared. In Mecca, he expected to do his first tawaf under a muallim's supervision; instead,

1 The British Consul at Jiddah was the diplomatic representative of the King of Hijaz, and, as such, responsible for the welfare of the pilgrims not only from India but from the Malay States and other British possessions. But the Consul's activities were, to some extent, curtailed by the restrictions placed upon non-Muslims in the Hijaz. A non-Muslim Consul cannot visit Mecca and Medina, or indeed travel more than a few miles beyond Jiddah. Some of the other nations who are represented in Jiddah, either regularly or occasionally, appoint Muslims in that capacity.

he found himself up against an Arab who knew no English or Hindustani and got embroiled in an undignified dispute over the amount to be paid to the Arab for this 'service'.

The needless unpleasantness with the Arab had cast a shadow over me. Also, there was the sorrow that here I was doing my first tawaf with a person who was not learned or versed in the correct way of doing the tawaf. Maybe, if I had held my head and postponed the decision of choosing the muallim till we had reached Jiddah, this entire unfortunate episode could have been avoided ... When I return to India I shall surely tell friends and acquaintances to beware of falling into the deceiving traps of the muallims who come to India to ensnare unwary pilgrims, and that they should not sell their freedom to any muallim till they have reached Jiddah. My muallim, Abdul Qadir Sikandar, is having a good time in Lucknow. His son hunts for prey among the hajjis at Bombay. Yusuf, his employee who received me at the ship, is ignorant about the correct way of performing the tawaf and *saii*. Such muallims have no right to charge a fee of Rs 25–30 from their clients.

In Turkish times, no tax was levied on the hajjis. The Nejdi government, however, realized almost 10 pounds from them, extracted through a network of muallims. The chief grievance of pilgrims was the enormous increase made since the War in those heads of taxation, which affected them. The amount paid as steamer fare doubled after 1913; the amount paid to the Hijaz Government in the form of direct and indirect taxes—Rs 15 per head—quadrupled. In other directions, too, the taxes increased the cost of the pilgrimage considerably. The motor car fares were so fixed that practically half of what was paid by the pilgrim went to the State and, as the cost of a seat in a car from Jiddah to Medina and back was about £15, this form of tax produced much profit. The State similarly realized a large percentage of the fares charged for camel hire. Even the poorest pilgrim, who did not travel by motor car, paid at least Rs 100 in taxation, while richer pilgrims paid not less than twice that amount. In effect, the Hijaz Government raised taxation to a figure so high as to discourage the pilgrimage and so 'kill the goose that lays the golden eggs', Amir Ahmad remarked:

One can, thus, calculate how much the royal treasury makes from the hajjis in a year. Earlier this money was used in the welfare of the people of Mecca; now it is used to buy goods according to the latest English fashion in Nejd and Mecca. The people of Mecca are in dire straits. Poverty makes them commit such acts of omission that are the necessary consequences of being penniless. But the Nejdis can't care less. They know and are well aware that their rule over Mecca is temporary and it shall not last for more than a few years. Therefore, they want to amass as much wealth as they can from here. The son of Sultan Ibn Saud, who is the Crown Prince of Hijaz, lives in Mecca. Every Friday, he comes to the Haram Sharif but no one looks at him with affection. Whether he will gain the permanent rule over this land or the Nejdis will retain control over Mecca is known only to God. One can only pray that the Malik-ul Mulk keeps this holy land free from the rule of the infidels and except for this anything else is tolerable.

However, the present government is praised, grudgingly, for maintaining law and order on the roads:

It used to be a two-day journey from Jiddah to Mecca. It entailed traversing waterless deserts and mountains. There was the fear of dacoits and Beduoins. But now, thanks to the motor cars, the journey can be made in two hours. Along the way, there are four or five halts where tea is ready and waiting to be served. Policemen are stationed who keep a watchful eye on the motors to make sure they don't carry more than the prescribed number of passengers. One can walk alone on this road at midnight and no robber can dare waylay you. These days, because of Ramazan, most passengers prefer to travel during the night but there are no incidents of looting. My motor broke down near the mountains at 10.00 in the night and we had to get off. For nearly half an hour, we stood by the road while the driver tried to change the wheel. But there was no cause for fear. We saw several pilgrims walking alone. They looked fearless.

Amir Ahmad's sympathies would probably have rested with the proponents of the Khilafat movement; he seems to be a status quoist as far as the Ottoman Empire is concerned. This became evident when he first spotted a small contingent of pilgrims from Anatolia.[1] He wrote:

I am struck with amazement when I see their faces. Once upon a time they were the rulers over this land and now no one bothers about them. The bigger part of the present building of the Masjidul Haram is a memorial to Sultan Selim and Suleiman the Great. Every nook and corner of Mecca is buried under the weight of the benevolence and determination of Turkish sultans. In actual fact, the Islamic world can never disregard the great service rendered by the Turks to Haramain Sharifain. On the one hand, they have protected the Islamic sultanate with their blood and, on the other, enriched Mecca with their gold and jewels and their fabulous wealth. It is heart-rending to watch the poverty of the small Turkish contingent as it goes about performing the tawaf. May Allah bless them for their piety and may He restore them to their former glory so they can once again serve Islam.

While praising the Ottomans for all the gold and valuables they had poured into the two Holy Cities, Amir Ahmad was filled with sorrow at the poverty all around: '...the poverty here is such and the beggars swarm around in such numbers that it is unsafe to carry cash in one's pockets. May Allah remove the poverty of the inhabitants of Mecca!' And elsewhere, 'a matter of great shame that causes pain even to write', is to see women embracing pilgrims to seek alms.

1 A geographic region bound by the Black Sea, the Caucasus to the northeast, the Aegean Sea to the west, the Mediterranean Sea to the south, and the Iranian plateau to the east and southeast.

REAGGREGATION

Finally, let us look at the geo-political situation in Hijaz in 1929. An irregular parallelogram, about 250 miles in length, Hijaz has always been a prized trophy. While a greater part of this strip of land was independent, the rule of Pax Brittanica was very much in evidence—as also the control exercised by the British Consul in Jiddah. The economy was almost totally controlled by the British with the shops and markets flooded with English goods. Here is what Amir Ahmad has to say:

English sweets and biscuits are found in all the shops. Tea and cigarettes are a way of life. Bullets and ammunition come from abroad. Postal stamps are printed abroad. Riyal and qarsh are minted in London. Cloth comes from English mills. And this valley has always been inhospitable for the cultivation of wheat. The only native produce is watermelon and the water of the sacred spring of zumzum. Camels were once a source of livelihood. According to Sharif Hussein, the former ruler of Hijaz, a camel would support 140 families. The coming of the automobile put an end to this.

...

This was the state of the economy; now let us look at politics. Although Sultan Ibn Saud rules over Jiddah, the real power is wielded by the British. Ibn Saud's slaves run away and take refuge in the British embassy where the Consul General puts them on ships and transports them to safe havens abroad. And the King can do nothing. No caravan can cross from Jiddah to Medina or Nejd without the Consul's permission. The King has no say. The embassy has warned the Afghans that they must submit their return tickets to the Vice-Consul or else they will not be allowed to travel to Mecca. And the self-proclaimed sovereign Arab King dare not say a word.

Mecca and Medina are in God's protection but the British Consul can, in a matter of minutes, occupy it if he so wishes. The Nejd soldiers who are stationed here are not even properly armed. When I saw them on *Jumatul-Wada* and earlier today in a procession, some wore boots, some slippers, others walked barefoot with guns on their shoulders. Belts of cartridges are looped about their waist; no one knows if they are full or empty. But, as everyone can see, the guns are broken and rusted. In India, the troops of Hyderabad, Gwalior, and Indore are far better organized and equipped than this 'royal' force. One machine gun is enough to make mincemeat out of this entire force. These soldiers cannot face an organized army for more than five minutes. And on top of that the people of Mecca are weary of the Sultan. I have been here for ten days and I have yet to meet a person who is not critical of the Nejdis or condemns Ibn Saud. The inhabitants are beholden to the Turks. Sharif Hussein betrayed the people and unleashed barbaric cruelties upon the Turkish soldiers because the elite of Mecca had begun to hate him and had begun to furtively fawn upon the Nejdis merely to humiliate him.

After defeating Sharif the Nejdis unleashed mass mayhem and slaughter in Taif. When the population went out of sight, they made a declaration of peace. Many innocents were beguiled by this and appeared in public. Then they reneged on their promise of mercy and people were ruthlessly put under the sword. Thousands of innocents were killed. This aggression and brutality shook the Meccans. The rich and poor alike silently paid allegiance to the ruler of Nejd. Today every Meccan—May God be with him—is an inveterate enemy of the Nejdi and is biding the time when he can shake off the yoke of tyranny. The tragedy is that the Nejdi have managed to defeat the Bedouin. Thousands of Bedouin—innocent and blameless—were slaughtered. Peace was restored after this terrible bloodbath. The roads became safe once again. Today, if one were to throw gold all the way from the shores of Jiddah to Amman there would be not the slightest looting. But consider the price that has been paid for this peace. The soldiers who were stationed to defend Haramain Sharif too were killed. Now the field is clear for an enemy to attack. May Allah save all from evil times!

Separated by thousands of miles from the Indian subcontinent, reached either through an arduous sea voyage or an equally taxing overland journey through inhospitable terrain, the Hijaz was, for Indian Muslims, a classic instance of the adage: 'So near yet so far'. Religious sentiment made the Muslims of the East not just look and bow Westward but also imitate and name their own holy places after the shrines and sites of the Hijaz. As early as 1567, an inscription on a congregational mosque in Malda compared it with the holy shrine in Mecca, calling it the 'second Kaaba' (*thani Kaaba*).[1] Throughout the length and breadth of India, small mosques, khanqahs, dargahs and *imambaras* housed relics brought back from the Hijaz. Nobility, in many old families, was determined in direct proportion to the time when one's ancestors had migrated eastwards from Arabia. The title 'hajji' was affixed by the Muslim ashraf with pride, for it denoted a man of not just faith but also of sufficient means and enterprise to have undertaken the long voyage to the West. The affinity to the holy places in the Hijaz was assiduously maintained through generations and the links, no matter how tenuous, kept fresh and alive through repeated assertions of loyalty to the custodians of the holy shrines—be they Arab or Turk.

Only a small number of those performing the hajj and a fraction of those who maintained or published accounts of their travels criticized the authorities. This, they felt, was not in keeping with the spirit of the pilgrimage and any criticism directed at the custodians of the holy places was tantamount to sacrilege. Moreover, many even believed that being Allah's guests, those who die in the Holiest of Homes, were assured a straight passage to heaven. They, therefore, not only made light of any

---

1 Such a practice, according to Richard Eaton, served to 'mitigate the great distance separating Bengal from Islam's holiest shrines in Arabia, tenuously linked to the delta by a long and dangerous sea voyage.' See Richard M. Eaton, *The Rise of Islam*, p. 100.

inconveniences or misfortunes but even considered it a rare privilege to die and be buried in the soil of the holy sites. The few who did note the grislier side of the entire proceedings chose to concentrate on the unsanitary conditions, especially after the ritual sacrifice of an animal at Mina, some 3 miles/5 kilometres to the east of Mecca.[1]

In 1893, of the 2,00,000 pilgrims undertaking the hajj, 33,000 perished. An Indian physician, Qasim Izzedine, describes the scene at Mina thus:

Along the streets...you could see pilgrims being carried away. Those assigned to wash the corpses could no longer carry on their duties. Several of them had died and the survivors found themselves worn out by fatigue.... The cadavers of (sacrificed) sheep... lay exposed to the sun and putrefying.... The corpses on the streets were far more numerous than yesterday. Everywhere one could see the ill tied to the backs of camels ... The pilgrims were pensive and serious. No one cried out. The 13th of *Dhu al-Hijja* [29 June 1893], the fourth day of the (pilgrimage) festival, the situation became more frightful. On that day the death toll reached ... the dead were no longer buried; they were simply left in the streets. Some streets were choked with dead bodies...But the pilgrims continued calmly to perform their devotions without complaint.

The health hazards increased manifold because the great majority of those who flocked to the Holy Cities were either poor or enfeebled by age. Cholera, for long a scourge in India, appeared in the Hijaz in 1831. From then on till the early twentieth century, it continued to rage and claim thousands of pious victims. The Ottomans and later the Nejdis tried their best to contain it, but by 1865 a major cholera epidemic originated in Java and was carried to Mecca by pilgrims, one-third of whom perished during the pilgrimage. By June, the disease raged in Alexandria. And later that same month, it reached Marseilles and thence most of the cities of Europe. In November 1865, cholera was reported in New York City.

Once the threat of this annual epidemic ravaging western non-endemic, non-Islamic nations became real, quarantine stations were set up. Port authorities—at both the points of embarkation and disembarkation—stepped up vigilance. The fumigation of pilgrims' luggage was made compulsory. The opening of the Suez Canal in 1869, lauded as a great victory for European hegemonic interests, was suddenly

---

1 This and the following references to the cholera epidemic are drawn from F.E. Peters, *The Hajj*, pp. 301, 302, 308, 309. In the valley of Mina is the Jamarat Bridge, the location of the Stoning of the Devil ritual, performed between sunrise and sunset on the last day of the hajj.

seen as a portal of death and destruction. Fear replaced greed for the first time in the history of the West's interaction with the Middle East. This fear was overlaid with self-preservation. The threat of devastating cholera epidemics invading Europe united rival European powers in a concerted *politique sanitaire*; its objective was to regulate the life of Western Arabia and, no less, of the most sacred ritual of Islam. As one French physician put it after the 1865 epidemic, 'Europe realized that it could not remain like this, every year, at the mercy of the pilgrimage to Mecca.'

The last of the great cholera epidemics in the Hijaz was reported in 1912, thus ending one chapter in the intertwined story of public health and politics as played out against the backdrop of pilgrimage. Other hazards, however, continued. The congregation of pilgrims at Arafat, the ritual slaughtering of an animal at Mina and the stoning of Satan at Mecca continued to be problem areas where stampedes would routinely occur. Fires broke out in the pilgrims' tents, and instances of robberies were reported on the highways. The fleecing of the pilgrims by the locals over rents of camels, lorries, litters, rooms, small daily amenities such as mosquito nets, as well as the sale of everyday food items and toiletries continued unchecked.

The First World War brought many changes—not just in the geopolitics of the Hijaz but also in the way the pilgrimages began to be conducted. Sharif Hussein[1] proclaimed himself to be the 'king' of the Hijaz on 10 June 1916. He mulcted the pilgrim trade for all it was worth: he extorted a 'landing fee' from all those who got off the ship(s) at Jiddah; charged baggage and customs fee (up to 600 per cent of the retail value of goods), floated an artificially high exchange rate for currency, and worst of all, even introduced customs dues on the personal effects of the pilgrims such as food rations, silks, ornaments, perfumes, etc. He also enjoyed a virtual monopoly over all forms of transport—both inland and through steamers plying the waters of the Red Sea. He made some basic improvements in the conditions of the hajj; for instance, he provided a roof over the stretch between the hillocks of Safa and Marwa

---

1 Sharif Hussein bin Ali (1854–1931) revolted against the Ottoman empire, occupied Mecca, and beseiged Medina, beginning in 1916 and lasting till January 1919. He ruled Hijaz until 1924 when he was defeated by Abdul Aziz Al-Saud.

(where the pilgrims had to make seven trips) and installed electricity in 1923.[1]

Given the 'support' extended to Sharif Hussein by the British Government and given the large numbers of hajjis from the British colonies, the post-war British Foreign Office decided to examine th nature and extent of its intervention in an exercise that was frankly none of its business. While these measures were ostensibly 'for the protection of the pilgrims both from the point of view of defence and sanitation', it would be an added bonus if 'no handle be given to pro-Turkish and anti-Sharif propaganda'.[2] Any investment in quarantine or sanitary arrangements was, therefore, considered for the larger good of British interests in the region. The rail link had already penetrated as far as Medina in 1908. By the 1920s, motorable roads were in place, and motor cars and lorries began to ply along with the camel caravans. While efforts were made to provide medical facilities, many countries preferred sending their own medical envoys. The British Government, for instance, appointed Indian doctors at the Consulate in Jiddah. But when Egypt tried sending medical assistance in 1923, it led to a full-fledged diplomatic row. Hussein saw it as a reflection on his administration. Soon, however, many countries developed a vested interest in ensuring a safe and reasonably comfortable passage to Jiddah for their citizens.

In the autumn of 1924, Ibn Saud invaded the Hijaz and expelled Sharif Hussein, his old rival and adversary. In India, a close affinity existed between Wahhabism and the Ahl-i Hadith movement. As is known, in addition to the primacy attached to Prophetic traditions, their desire to revive Ibn Taymiyya's teachings, and their call to eliminate visits to saints' tombs and intercessionary prayers, the Ahl-i Hadith also concurred with the Wahhabis in regarding Sufis and Shias as unbelievers and in being intolerant of other Muslims.[3] No wonder then that, they, along with the Nadwatul Ulama, supported Ibn Saud. But the Sufis and the ulama of

1 Safa and Marwa are two small hills near the Kaaba. Pilgrims go back and forth between these hills seven times to re-enact Hajira's search for water for her baby, Ismail (Ishmael).

2 F. E. Peters, *The Hajj*, p. 336; Radhika Singha, 'Passport, Ticket, and India-rubber Stamp'.

3 David Commins (2006), *The Wahhabi Mission and Saudi Arabia*, London. For general accounts, see Major N. N. E. Bray, *Shifting Sands*; J. B. Philby (1922), *The Heart of Arabia: Record of Travel and Exploration*, London.

Firangi Mahal and Bareilly thought differently. The Ali brothers backed Ibn Saud, but by 1925, they had changed their stand owing to Ibn Saud's dealings with Britain. In the end, the antagonism between the two factions led to the disintegration of the Khilafat Party.[1] Hindu-Muslim tensions developed, almost simultaneously. They dimmed the future of an enduring Congress-Muslim alliance in politics.[2]

One begins to understand Amir Ahmad's disenchantment only in the light of the bitter struggle for power waged by the Nejdis and the ruthlessness with which they laid down the sternest, most austere principles of Unitarian Islam. He arrived in Hijaz with devotion in his heart and stars in his eyes, and returned from the Holy Land a wiser, albeit sadder, man.

Homebound

'It is in the road to God, by Him cometh our reward.' Thus prepared, the faithful sets out on his duty, with faith in its efficacy, and reliance on the goodness of Divine Providence to make him/her prosper in the arduous undertaking.[3] The hajj marks the fufilment of an extraordinary covenant with Allah and the reiteration of *tauhid*, the quintessential feature of Islam. Every step taken at the Kaaba means that a sin is blotted, and that thereafter the person will be highly exalted. Should anyone die, he/she will be ranked as a martyr, and on the Day of Judgement he/she will rise with the martyrs.

Numerous other blessings attend the performance of the hajj. Amir Ahmad shares with us his joy and frustration, his small victories and defeats, his exhilaration and exhaustion, and his humour and frustration. He returned to Kakori suffused with the *barakat*, blessing, of the Prophet whom he loved more dearly than ever, his faith strengthened, his worldview enlarged, his belief in pluralism bolstered, and his distaste for Unitarianism more marked. There are moving, lyrical passages in his text, which describe his invigorated faith. Amir Ahmad was no exception. From the earliest times, those returning from the Hijaz brought back with them the beliefs and practices then current in the Arab heartland.

1 M. Naeem Qureshi, *Pan-Islam in British Indian Politics*, pp. 396–400.

2 Gail Minault (1982), *The Khilafat Movement: Religious Symbolism and Political Mobilization in India*, New York; Francis Robinson, *Separatism among Indian Muslims*; Mushirul Hasan (1991), *Nationalism and Communal Politics in India 1885–1930*, Delhi.

3 Meer Hasan Ali, *Observations*, p. 114.

Some even set out, zealously and industriously, to integrate those beliefs and practices that they had seen and experienced first-hand into their own religious-cultural identities as Muslims. For example, they would grow beards and urge others to do so, or discourage their women from dressing in a certain way. In an extreme case, a Bengali Muslim returned from the hajj and urged fellow-villagers to eat grasshoppers on the ground that Arabs ate locusts.[1]

Amir Ahmad does not reconsider or re-engage with a lost or diminishing faith. The long voyage from Kakori to Baitul Muqaddas is a journey of faith from start to finish. Amir Ahmad sets out as a Muslim, a believer, and remains one. His disaffection, mostly clear and unequivocal, is with the Nejdi rulers and bureaucrats, and not with the message of Islam. As in the case of two recent writers in South Africa, the hajj inspired in him a new spirituality, a new humanness, a new understanding of morality and of the greatness of the human spirit. He learned many things, and returned to find that the process would continue as the faithful move forward in life.[2]

This is not all. Muslims travelling in the Islamic world expected to be enveloped by a sense of Muslim solidarity; yet, as often, their 'consciousness of locality and difference' heightened.[3] In Amir Ahmad's case, he celebrated the ideal of an *ummat*, a global community bound by the Islamic tenets. At the same time, he diligently recorded the fissures in the Muslim countries. The qasba or *watan*, with its mosques, ghats, melas, shrines and imambaras, mattered more than pan-Islamic solidarity.[4] He seemed to regard his era as the last age of taste and style before rampant urbanization and industrialism negated all aesthetic standards. Sleeman, whose career in India extended over a period of four decades and who was Resident at Lucknow from 1849 to 1856, had placed in perspective the attitude of the qasba elites, as follows:

---

1 Richard M. Eaton, *The Rise of Islam*, fn. 46, p. 282,

2 Naeem Jeenah and Shamina Shaikh (2000), *Journey of Discovery: A South African Hajj*, South Africa, p. 133.

3 D.F. Eickelman and James Piscatori (eds) (1990), *Muslim Travellers: Pilgrimage, Migration, and the Religious Imagination*, London, pp. xii–xv; Tim Youngs (ed.) (2006), *Travel Writing in the Nineteenth Century: Filling the Black Spaces*, London, p. 108.

4 Reaching Kakori at the end of his journey, he felt exultant: 'My homeland's breeze gladdened my heart. Such happiness surged deep within my heart that the journey's troubles and toils disappeared, as though by magic.'

Some few Hindoo and Mohammedan gentlemen, when they have lost their places and favour at the Oude Court, go and reside at Cawnpoor, and some few other places in the British territory for greater security; but generally it may be said, that in spite of all disadvantages Mohammedan gentlemen from Oude, in whatever country they may serve, like to leave their families in Oude, and to return and spend what they acquire among them. They find better society there than in our own territories, or society more to their tastes; better means for educating their sons; more splendid processions, festivals, and other inviting sights, in which they and their families can participate without cost; more consideration for rank and learning, and more attractive places for worship and religious observances.[1]

The steady increase in the number of hajjis illustrates a corporate religious life being formed, though not necessarily in opposition to other religious groups. The 'pluralistic' or 'syncretic' traditions remained intact in cities, qasbas and the rural hinterland. The Tamil poet Umaru Pulavar (d. 1703) described Mecca, beginning with a number of Tamil/cosmological details. He also used established tropes of classical literature and managed to incorporate the Prophet into a Tamil world that is shared by both Muslims and Hindus.[2] Diwan Raja Ram Prashad, Bhagwant Rai 'Rahat', Chedi Lal 'Tamanna', Raj Bahadur 'Zakhmi', Mukund Lal 'Johari', Mangli Lal 'Wafa', Hiralal 'Sarshar' and Jaswant Rai were as much part of Kakori's social and cultural landscape as Amir Ahmad.[3]

The roznamcha does not provide a model for succeeding travel writers, but it constitutes, all in all, a part of a unique collection of pilgrimage narratives. Abdul Majid Daryabadi, a recognized judge of quality writing, described Safar-i Sa'adat as 'singularly unique'. He writes:

The writer addresses himself or, at best, friends and relatives in the pleasure its reading affords. He also mentions people like me who have been on hajj. He could have embellished his narrative and made it more colourful and weighty, but he has eschewed doing so. As a result, his simple and unadorned text appeals to the reader. You may dress up to the nines and go for a walk outdoors but it will not give you as much pleasure as lounging about at home.

To conclude, the hajj narratives belong to the territory of quasi-religious writings. They reveal, for that very reason, important dimensions of Islam as a modern religion, of modes of self-representation,

1 W.H. Sleeman, *Journey through the Kingdom of Oude*, Vol. 2, p. 10.

2 Richard M. Eaton (ed.) (2003), *India's Islamic Traditions, 711–1750*, Delhi, pp. 402–3.

3 Haider Alawi (1941), *Tazkira Mashair-i Alawi*, Lucknow, pp. 487–91; Hakim Nisar Ahmad Alawi (1978), *Sukhanwaran-i Alawi*, Karachi, pp. 544–58.

and of Muslim social and corporate life as recounted in distinctive individual lives.[1] With a lingering element of melancholy they combine autobiographical candour carried to the point of conscious posturing and self-dramatization. They are accounts of journeys that are at once inner and outer; and they guide us, both to changing patterns of religious sensibilities and to a world in technological, social and political transition.'[2]

Amir Ahmad's book is of equal interest to the armchair traveller who 'lounges about at home', as it is to the student of literature and the historian who wish to examine how the momentousness of a religious journey lives on in the people's memories, as it shaped social and religious lives and perspectives, and perhaps even politics. We have, therefore, not merely translated the roznamcha and provided annotation but also written this somewhat extended introduction. We have done so in the belief that one good turn deserves another. Amir Ahmad did a great job of jotting down his thoughts and experiences in 1929; exactly eighty years later, we have re-traced his journey and introduced him to a larger audience—one far removed from his Urdu-speaking, largely qasbati milieu.

---

1 Barbara Daly Metcalf (2004), *Islamic Contestations: Essays on Muslims in India and Pakistan*, Delhi, p. 295.
   2 Ibid.

Many thanks to thee O Almighty!
My caravan has set off for Hijaz
Salutes from that Omnipresent Lord
To the benefactor of bounties on worlds all
May our Lord bestow His benevolence
Upon our Prophet's companions and progeny
May God's Grace be upon us
That we may discern between Good and Bad
Move us into Action O Lord!
Thy benign presence can cherish even dust
May we guide others to goodness
And abstain forever from vices
May Habeeb never fail to remember Thee
May success embrace him by Thy grace.[1]

---

1 Mohammad Habibur Rahman (1929), *Habibul Hujjaj*, Vol. 2, Bijnor, p. 1.

My Experience of the Hajj of 1916[1]

J.S. Kadri

War and the Hajj

The world-disturbing war had practically stopped the emigration of Muslim pilgrims to Mecca for the last two years and it was thought improbable that the hajj would be open to Indians this year. But the ways of God are inscrutable and He does what man can never divine. A sudden change came over Hijaz and the attitude of the Sherif of Mecca in declaring his independence of the Turkish rule, and his friendship with the British Government made it possible for Indian Mussulmans to go to Mecca to perform one of their most cherished and fundamental duties of faith.

On account of the difficulty of booking a passage for Jiddah direct from Aden, I had to undertake a roundabout voyage to go there via Port Soudan, which was reached after three days of pleasant sailing. Port Soudan is a rising port of Africa on the western coast of the Red Sea, almost opposite Jiddah on the east. It has a splendid harbour and a railway connecting it with Khartoum and Omdurman in the interior.

1 Aden, 8 November 1916. This report and the following tables were accessed at the British Library, London. We do not know about J.S. Kadri, except that he was a Muslim officer from Bombay who was asked to submit his report for the hajj in 1916. We have retained his spellings of place-names.

The town is planned on modern principles with wide roads and electric light, and it bids fair to grow in population and prosperity in the course of time.

Although very hot, expensive, and deficient in good water supply, Port Soudan appears to be a healthy place, and my flying visit to it was more than repaid by the change and the natural scenery I enjoyed there. After three days' halt at Port Soudan, I left for Jiddah by a Khedivial mail steamer and reached there the next day at noon. On board the ship, we had a few Soudanese pilgrims from Khartoum and its neighbourhood, bound for Mecca.

Jiddah from the Sea

The view of Jiddah from the sea is very picturesque. As the ship approached nearer, the multi-storeyed buildings of the town towering high above the sea with the hills beyond and the harbour bristling with the masts of the native craft became clearly visible. A man-of-war was lying in anchor on the sea. As the harbour is shallow and the sea near the coast full of shoals and rocks, big ships have to anchor at a distance of about three miles from the coast. The boatmen of Jiddah are rapacious. They press for *bakhshish* before hire and would have it before taking passengers or their effects. From Jiddah onward, the whole atmosphere resounds with the echo of 'bakhshish' (tip money) desired by all and sundry for service or no service rendered.

The Town and its People

The outside of the town appears fine and attractive but the inside is not so. The outskirts of the town are open and airy but the interior is over-crowded and dirty. The roads are narrow and not properly paved, while the streets and bye-lanes are nasty and filthy. The main market, which is long and narrow, is crowded, closed, and dark. The market routes with a continuous planked roof overhead never see the light of the sun.

The hotels and coffee-shops are neither neat nor pleasant, and are chiefly resorted to by idlers. The sanitary and conservancy arrangements of the town are far from satisfactory. The natural water supply of the town is scanty and precarious. Well water is brackish. The rainwater is stored up in subterranean tanks and used for drinking and other purposes. At some distance from the town, there is a fountain of fresh water but its supply is precarious and insufficient. The city is fortunate in having a condenser and an ice factory.

Trade and Commerce of Jiddah

The population of Jiddah, estimated at about 20,000 souls, consists chiefly of Arabs, with a sprinkling of Persians, Egyptians, Javanese, Sudanese, Abyssinians, and Indians. Jiddah is a port of great commercial importance. It is the gateway of Hijaz and an emporium of import and export for a considerable part of Arabia. Its traders and merchants are reported to be generally well off, though they have suffered heavily during the last two years on account of the war and the stoppage of pilgrim traffic. The town can hardly boast of any indigenous arts and industries worth mentioning.

The people felt much gratified and thankful at the port being freed by the British Government from the restrictions of a prohibited port and being allowed to receive foodstuffs and other provisions from India. Mecca shared the benefit of the revival of trade in Jiddah.

Indian Pilgrims in Jiddah and the Government

The facilities afforded to pilgrims by the Government enabled about 2,500 Muslims from India to go to Mecca for hajj this year. Three steamers brought them to Jiddah from Bombay. Among the pilgrims was noticed a universal sense of heartfelt satisfaction and gratitude for the care taken by the Government for their welfare and the attention they received from Colonel Wilson, the British Agent at Jiddah, who is a very kind and sympathetic officer. The Bombay Government has sent a special Mohammedan Police Officer to Jiddah to look after the needs and comforts of Indian pilgrims.

Inspection of Pilgrims

At Jiddah, there was no medical inspection of pilgrims either on board the ship or at the landing pier. The passports were demanded at the quarantine office from the pilgrims who were asked to pay a fee of Rs 2–4–0 per head and allowed to go. No customs dues were charged.

The Vakils or Agents of Mecca Mutawwifs

The muallims or *vakils*, as they are called in Jiddah, are the agents of the mutawwifs (the religious guides and instructors) to whom the pilgrims would go first in Mecca and through whom they would perform all the rites and formalities relating to hajj. Many of these agents and mutawwifs are not very scrupulous folks and they often play the role of friendly despots. They take charge of the pilgrims' person and property, and often try to fleece poor hajjis of their money in various ways. There seems to be little or no healthy check on the grabbing tendencies of these touting agents of the hajjis.

From Jiddah to Mecca

A number of pilgrims had assembled in Jiddah. On the day previous to my arrival, 636 pilgrims had landed in the *S.S. Sardar* from Bombay. A day or two earlier, a *wafd* or deputation consisting of some high Arab officials and leading men of Tripoli dispatched by the French Government to congratulate the Sherif had arrived and was given a fitting reception at the harbour. On the day prescribed, the whole kafila of about 700 or 800 men was ready and we started for Mecca in the morning. The caravan halted at a small village called Behra en-route for the night. Behra is a place notorious for bad water and few conveniences. Mecca was reached on the early morning of the third day. The caravan did not meet with any accident or mishap on the way. Bedouin raids were dreaded but the road was clear of the Bedouins and there was a mounted escort of the Sherif's men accompanying the caravan. The only trouble that the hajjis experienced on the way was at the hands of the Bedouin camel-drivers who bored their protégés for food and bakhshish and harassed them, if they were not satisfied.

The Condition of Mecca

The city had passed through a period of stress and strain on account of the stoppage of pilgrims for the last two years. The people were, therefore, jubilant and welcomed the influx of hajjis into their city as a sign of their reviving trade and prosperity. The whole business activity of Mecca is more or less confined to the hajj season during which roaring business is done and fat profits are earned, sufficient to last till the next season. Formerly, pilgrims from Persia, Syria, Constantinople, and other countries used to bring with them various articles of merchandise, which found easy sale in Mecca. The people of Java and Egypt are considered as the most welcome pilgrims in Mecca, as they are reported to be very liberal and luxurious. This year, there were a few hundreds and they were mostly military men.

Health and Sanitation

Mecca is situated amidst hills like Aden. It is a big city with a population of more than a lakh souls of various countries. The chief element is Arab. Many Indian Mohammedans have been domiciled there and have adopted Arab dress and customs. Many Javanese, Egyptians, Syrians, and a few Persians are also to be found there. There was no trade of the Turks in the city.

Mecca is, on the whole, a healthy place and its climate fairly good. It enjoys the benefit of a copious supply of fresh water from the Zobeida canal, which runs underground. The famous well of Zumzum situated within the limits of the Harem is also a perennial source of excellent water, which is considered by pious Mohammedans as a tonic for the body and soul. Fresh and dry fruits are abundant and cheap in Mecca. Grapes, pomegranates, quince, watermelons, dates, almonds, and so on are daily imported from Taif and its neighbourhood.

The sanitary arrangements in Mecca are far better than those in Jiddah.

The Arrival of Mistri 'Mahmal' in Mecca

A few days before the hajj, the Egyptian Mahmal, escorted by a large number of mounted and foot soldiers under the command of a Pasha, arrived with great pomp at Mecca and was accorded due honour. The Sherif and his eldest son, attended by their retinue, went out to welcome the party, which brought the *kisiva* or the black embroidered covering for the holy Kaaba, and presents for the Sherif and other people connected with the service of 'Baitullah'—the House of God.

There are large state endowments in Egypt dedicated to *Haramain-ul-Sharifain* (the holy places, viz. Mecca and Medina) and every year, presents in the shape of cash, clothing, and corn are sent to these places from their income. This year, a large quantity of wheat was sent from Egypt for distribution among the Meccans and it proved a veritable boon in the time of need.

The Day of Hajj

The hajj actually took place on Saturday, the 9th of *Zil Hajj* (7 October 1916), though it was eagerly anticipated to be an Akbari hajj, falling on Friday, a day earlier. The appearance of the new moon was in doubt and no testimony was received by the Sherif to fix the hajj for Friday. When, however, Saturday was announced as the hajj day by a *khutba* (sermon) preached in the Haram on the seventh day of the month, a thrill of deep disappointment and sorrow passed through the ranks of the congregation. Many people were not quite satisfied about the accuracy of the lunar calculation and to be on the safe side, went to Arafat or Jabel-i-Rehmat (the hill of Mercy sanctified for hajj) on Friday, so that they may reap the blessings of Akbari hajj, if that day happened to be the real hajj day.

How the Hajj Passed Off

The hajj passed off quite smoothly and happily. The Sherif, accompanied by his eldest son and retinue of armed Bedouins and retainers, had as usual come for the hajj and was encamped in tents near the hill of Arafat. The Egyptian *Mahmal*, escorted by the military and the artillery, was also there. By the morning of Saturday, the plain of Arafat, which remains almost lifeless and lonely throughout the rest of the year, was humming with life and the bustle of teeming masses.

The concourse of about 10,000 people of different colours and climes, and speaking different languages, but all dressed alike in the white wrappers (ahram) and all inspired by the same pious thoughts of prayer and penitence and yearning after Divine Truth, presented a unique sight, almost superhuman and sublime. Every heart there unconsciously felt touched by the Gracious Spirit which rules over Heaven and Earth:

A gracious spirit o'er this earth presides,
And in the heart of man; invisibly
It comes to works of unreproved delight
And tendency benign; directing those
Who care not, know not, what they do.

After the khutba delivered by the *Khatib* on the *Jabal-e Rahmat* in the afternoon, all departed peacefully to Mina after halting at a place called Mudalfa for the night. At Mina, which is about three miles from Mecca, all the hajjis have to stop for three days for sacrifice and for performing other ceremonies. On the third day, all left Mina for Mecca, and performed the final ceremony there. This completed the hajj. Barring the complaint of bad water at Mina, the hajjis passed a happy time during their hajj tour from Mecca to Arafat and back.

The sanitary arrangements at Mina were most unsatisfactory. Filth and dirt had accumulated everywhere and people drank water stored in dirty and un-cleaned subterranean tanks. It was, however, fortunate that their health was not affected and an epidemic did not break out. The reason for this was that their numbers this year were not large and that the weather was good.

The Sherif and his Address

On the next day of Id, the Sherif gave an address at Mina to the assemblage of Meccans and the hajjis. He explained to the audience his position and duties with regard to the Holy Places and the Islamic world, and expressed his solicitude and care for the protection and welfare of the pilgrims coming to Mecca.

Return at Jiddah

As under the present circumstances, it was not safe to go to Medina, which is in the hands of the Turks, the hajjis made up their minds to return home as soon as possible. The first pilgrim ship, 'Hijaz', arrived in Jiddah on 20 October 1916, by which date about 1,000 pilgrims had already arrived in the town. On the next day, the steamer left for Camaran with 952 pilgrims on board. Camaran was reached on the morning of 24 October. All the pilgrims were taken to the disinfection camp and were disinfected with promptness and care under the supervision of a qualified doctor. The pilgrims returned to the ship in the afternoon and sailed for Bombay the next morning.

Condition and Arrangements of the Pilgrims' Ship

The *S.S. Hijaz* is really a cargo ship but it has been temporarily fitted up for carrying pilgrims. It is not a very convenient or comfortable ship for passengers. The pilgrims were packed on its decks like sardines. Some parts of its decks were open and exposed to the rigours of the heat and cold. Poor hajjis complained about lack of water and fuel. Water was doled out at the rate of one gallon per head and fuel was given in the shape of big unhewn logs of wood, which were difficult to split up. The water supplied was about 20 days old in the tank, because a quantity of water was brought from Bombay. The Parsi Karani or purser of the ship was a terror to the hajjis, who were openly bullied, insulted and even thrashed by him. There were many complaints, on this score.

The dogs of the Captain and other officers of the ship were a source of nuisance to the pilgrims. The dispensary arrangements were rather defective. The doctor complained about the lack of necessary splints and bandages to treat cases of fracture and dislocation of bones, and of some medicines required for serious cases.

The pilgrims also complained of loss of their bags of corn and other articles from the ship, while they landed at Camaran for quarantine on their first voyage to Jiddah from Bombay. It was reported that some bags of stolen rice were subsequently traced and returned to them, when they lodged a complaint at Jiddah.

General Remarks

Most of the pilgrims are generally illiterate and unacquainted with Arabic and the conditions of Arabia. They thus fall easy victims to the tricks and intrigues of the wily muallims at Jiddah and the mutawwifs at Mecca. They also suffer much from the ruthless Bedouin camel-drivers and others. To remove their grievances and to protect their interests, it is considered very desirable by Mohammedans that a Protector of Pilgrims be appointed by the Government, for both Jiddah and Mecca. This officer must be a Mohammedan, knowing Arabic and some Indian languages, and he should be under the control and orders of the British Consul or Vice-Consul at Jiddah.

It is also the desire of hajjis that in every pilgrim ship, the doctor should be a Mohammedan, specially deputed by the Government, and that one Mohammedan police officer of the Government should be on board the ship to look after the person and property of the pilgrims.

Some of the other suggestions which will be welcomed by Mohammedans are that dogs should be excluded from pilgrim ships, that sufficient provision for water and fuel is made, that hospital arrangements should be adequate and satisfactory, and that a Mohammedan should be employed to dole out water to the pilgrims on the ship.

The need for establishing a free, charitable dispensary at both Jiddah and Mecca for the benefit of the pilgrims is one, which may with advantage be brought to the notice of generous and philanthropic Mohammedan millionaires of the Bombay Presidency.

Table showing the names of pilgrim ships, the names of shipping companies, with their advertised and actual sailing dates, the number of pilgrims who actually embarked and the passage rates of the deck charged by the company during the outward season of 1929

S. No.	Name of ships	Name of shipping company	Advertised date of sailing	Actual date of sailing	Carrying capacity	Men	Women	Boys	Girls	Infants	Total	No. of deaths during voyage	Single	Return	Single	Return	Date of arrival at Jeddah	Remarks
1	S.S. Jehangir	Messrs. Turner Morrison & Co.	—	4th January 1929	..	4	—	—	—	—	4	—	—	—	—	—	—	Sailed as passenger ship.
2	Khosrou	Do.	24th January 1929	17th January 1929	1,503	360	134	14	15	25	548	Nil.	125	195	125	195	30th January 1929	
3	Alawi	Do.	—	24th January 1929	..	52	—	—	—	—	52	—	—	—	—	—	—	Do.
4	Rehmani	Do.	14th February 1929	14th February 1929	1,773	1,168	220	22	9	12	1,437	1	125	195	125	195	1st March 1929	
5	Jehangir	Do.	28th February 1929	26th February 1929	1,158	138	57	5	6	9	215	1	125	195	125	195	12th March 1929	

No. of pilgrims actually embarked columns: Men, Women, Boys, Girls, Infants. Passage rate for deck columns: Single, Return, Single, Return.

Contd ...

Contd...

S. No.	Name of ships	Name of shipping company	Advertised date of sailing	Actual date of sailing	Carrying capacity	No. of pilgrims actually embarked					Total	No. of deaths during voyage	Passage rate for deck				Date of arrival at Jeddah	Remarks
						Men	Women	Boys	Girls	Infants			Single	Return	Single	Return		
6	Arabestan	Mr. M.K. Khaleeli	21st March 1929	23rd March 1929	1,199	514	167	5	3	3	692	Nil.	125	195	25 to 125	195	5th April 1929	
7	Sultania	Messrs. H.S. Shushtary & Co.	27th March 1929	27th March 1929	1,520	624	137	4	3	5	773	Do.	125	195	125	195	11th April 1929	
8	Akbar	Messrs. Turner Morrison & Co.	3rd April 1929	28th March 1929	1,503	1,288	308	4	1	6	1,507	Do.	125	195	125	195	8th April 1929	
9	Rehmani	Do.	9th April 1929	4th April 1929	1,773	1,477	290	2	3	4	1,776	3	125	195	125	195	14th April 1929	
10	Zayani	Messrs. H.S. Shushtary & Co.	15th April 1929	6th April 1929	981	817	124	5	1	5	952	4	125	195	125	195	18th April 1929	

Contd...

Contd...

S. No.	Name of ships	Name of shipping company	Advertised date of sailing	Actual date of sailing	Carrying capacity	No. of pilgrims actually embarked					Total	No. of deaths during voyage	Passage rate for deck				Date of arrival at Jeddah	Remarks
						Men	Women	Boys	Girls	Infants			Single	Return	Single	Return		
11	Alawi	Messrs. Turner Morrison & Co.	11th April 1929	9th April 1929	1,156	969	160	17	9	16	1,171	2	125	195	125	195	19th April 1929	
12	Arabestan	Mr. M.K. Khaleeli	22nd April 1929	22nd April 1929	1,199	567	209	11	12	11	810	Nil.	125	195	25 to 125	25 to 195	6th May 1929	
13	Sultania	Messrs. H.S. Shushtary & Co.	25th April 1929	25th April 1929	1,520	552	202	4	3	15	776	2	125	195	125	195	10th May 1929	
14	Khosrou	Messrs. Turner Morrison & Co.	29th April 1929	29th April 1929	1,508	177	68	4	3	3	255	Nil.	125	195	125	195	15th May 1929	
15	Englistan	Mr. M.K. Khaleeli	30th April 1929	30th April 1929	1,038	298	99	5	3	6	411	Do.	125	195	25 to 125	25 to 195	14th May 1929	
				Total		9,005	2,081	102	71	120	11,370	13	—	—	—	—	—	

Table showing names of ships with their arrival dates, the total number of pilgrims who embarked from Jiddah deck and other ports, deaths and births during the voyage, the total number of pilgrims who disembarked and the passage rates charged by \the Companies during the return season of 1929

S. No.	Name of the steamers	Name of the owners or the agents of the ship	Date of arrival	No. of pilgrims who embarked at							Total	No. of pilgrims who disembarked at							Number of deaths	Number of births	Grand total	Rate of single ticket issued at Jeddah
				Jeddah	Mussawah	Port Sudan	Kamaran	Makalla	Aden	Karachi		Kamaran	Hodeida	Bijouti	Makalla	Aden	Karachi	Bombay				
1.	S.S. Rehmani	Messrs. Turner Morrison & Co.	6th June 1929	1,776	—	—	—	—	—	—	1,776	—	—	—	—	—	—	1,765	11	—	1,765	
2.	Khosrou	Do.	9th June 1929	1,509	—	—	—	—	—	—	1,509	—	—	—	—	—	—	1,501	8	—	3,266	
3.	Shuja	Do.	12th June 1929	1,436	—	—	—	—	—	—	1,436	—	—	—	—	—	—	1,427	9	—	4,693	
4.	Sarvistan	Mr. K.K. Khaleeli	13th June 1929	1,574	—	—	—	—	—	—	1,574	—	—	—	—	—	1,184	383	7	—	5,076	
5.	Zayani	Messrs. H.S. Shushtary & Co.	14th June 1929	983	—	—	—	—	—	—	983	—	—	—	—	—	876	93	14	—	5,169	

Contd ...

S. No.	Name of steamers	Name of the owners or the agents of the ship	Date of arrival	No. of pilgrims who embarked at							Total	No. of pilgrims who disembarked at							Number of deaths	Number of births	Grand total	Rate of single ticket issued at Jeddah
				Jeddah	Mussawah	Port Sudan	Kamaran	Makalla	Aden	Karachi		Kamaran	Hodeida	Bjibouti	Makalla	Aden	Karachi	Bombay				
6.	Sultania	Do.	17th June 1929	1,495	—	—	—	1	—	—	1,496	—	—	—	148	—	1,111	218	19	—	5,387	
7.	Englistan	Mr. K.K. Khaleeli	18th June 1929	928	—	—	—	—	—	—	928	—	360	98	—	107	259	96	8	—	5,488	
8.	Dara	Messrs. Turner Morrison & Co.	20th June 1929	1,448	—	—	—	—	—	—	1,448	—	—	—	—	—	1,129	298	21	—	5,781	
9.	Alawi	Do.	15th July 1929	1,182	—	—	—	—	—	—	1,182	—	—	—	—	—	969	208	6	1	5,989	
10.	Akbar	Do.	16th July 1929	473	—	—	—	1	7	—	481	—	—	—	192	81	—	207	1	—	6,196	
11.	Arabestan	Mr. K.K. Khaleeli	18th July 1929	1,264	—	—	—	—	4	1	1,269	—	196	—	—	4	740	323	7	1	6,519	

Contd...

S. No.	Name of steamers	Name of the owners or the agents of the ship	Date of arrival	No. of pilgrims who embarked at							Total	No. of pilgrims who disembarked at							Number of deaths	Number of births	Grand total	Rate of single ticket issued at Jeddah
				Jeddah	Mussawah	Port Sudan	Kamaran	Makalla	Aden	Karachi		Kamaran	Hodeida	Bjibouti	Makalla	Aden	Karachi	Bombay				
12.	Sultania	Messrs. H.S. Shushtary & Co.	27th July 1929	1,395	—	—	—	2	2	—	1,399	—	—	—	126	19	905	338	11+	—	6,857	
13.	Jehangir	Messrs. Turner Morrison & Co.	31st July 1929	466	—	—	—	—	—	—	466	99	—	—	—	—	199	167	1	—	7,024	
14.	Alawi	Do.	29th August 1929	369	—	—	—	7	—	—	376	—	—	—	128	—	—	246	2	—	7,270	
15.	Jehangir	Do.	7th September 1929	163	1	—	—	—	—	—	164	—	—	—	—	—	—	165	—	1	7,435	
16.	Alawi	Do.	11th October 1929	220	—	12	—	—	60	—	202	—	—	—	—	25	—	267	—	—	7,702	
17.	Jehangir	Do.	5th November 1929	100	—	—	1	—	28	—	129	—	—	—	—	18	—	111	—	—	7,813	

Contd...

Contd ...

S. No.	Name of steamers	Name of the owners or the agents of the ship	Date of arrival	No. of pilgrims who embarked at							Total	No. of pilgrims who disembarked at							Number of deaths	Number of births	Grand total	Rate of single ticket issued at Jeddah
				Jeddah	Mussawah	Port Sudan	Kamaran	Makalla	Aden	Karachi		Kamaran	Hodeida	Bjibouti	Makalla	Aden	Karachi	Bombay				
18.	Alawi	Do.	28th November 1929	58	—	—	—	—	49	—	107	—	—	—	—	5	—	102	—	—	7,915	
19.	Jehangir	Do.	24th December 1929	25	—	—	—	—	—	—	25	—	—	—	—	—	—	25	—	—	7,940	
				16,864	1	12	1	11	150	1	17,040	99	556	98	594	259	7,372	7,940	125	3		

١٣٩٩

Labbaik Allahumma Labbaik

SAFAR-I SA'ADAT

Propitious Journey

Masjid-e Nabawi: The Prophet's Mosque at Medina, AD 1907 (AH 1325)

1

The Religious Awakening

19 Sha'baan, AH 1347 (31 January 1929)

I left home on Thursday at 8 o'clock in the morning. Scores of relatives crowded the ladies' quarter. Every person, related or unrelated to me, appeared sad. My mother had urged the people not to cry. Hence, the stoic composure of silence. I felt dismal but controlled myself. I tried to talk about this and that but no one would look me in the eye or talk to me. My condition can best be expressed in that verse by Mir Anis[1] wherein he describes the condition of Hazrat Fatima Sughra[2] in her own words:

حیرت میں ہوں باعث مجھے کھلتا نہیں اس کا

وہ آنکھ چرا لیتا ہے منہ تکتی ہوں جس کا

Hairat me hoon baais mujhe khulta nahin iska,
woh aankh chura leta hai mooh takti hoon jiska.

I am amazed by this situation which I cannot fathom
Why is it that whoever I look at turns his gaze away?

---

1 Mir Babar Ali Anis (1802–74/75) was born in Faizabad in northern India. Poetry came to him as an ancestral heritage, for his great grandfather Mir Hasan authored the immortal work, *Masnavi, Sehr-ul-Bayaan*. Anis's fame rests on his elegies on the tragedy of Karbala.

2 Fatima (605–32) was the youngest daughter of the Prophet Mohammad and his first wife Khadija. Muslims regard her as an exemplar for women. She remained at her father's side through the difficulties suffered by him at the hands of the Quraysh of Mecca. She married Ali ibn Abi Talib, Mohammad's cousin.

To end this poignant (*hasratnaak*) scene I got up from my place, performed my ablution, and offered two *rakat*[1] prayers. Then I took my leave, first from my mother, followed by the relatives. My middle daughter stood at the door. She clung to me and wept. Her tears signalled others to do the same. Everyone joined in. I consoled her as best as I could, controlled my own tears, and stepped out into the *mardana* (men's quarter). Here, too, friends, relatives, and neighbours had gathered. I left everyone to Allah's safekeeping and approached the car. My younger son Nawab, who is physically challenged and therefore dearer to me than the others, and who has spent ten years with me, stood beside the car. He saw me and stepped away. I beckoned him to come close. He did so without looking at me. I won't forget that gesture. Like him, I remained composed and got into the car. Some of my relatives drove with me to Lucknow. My middle son Bashir Ahmad works in Aurangabad.[2] He would accompany me until Manmarh.[3]

Invoking the name of Allah, we left Kakori and, in about half-an-hour, reached Lucknow's Char Bagh station.[4]

The Dak Train was to leave at 10.55 p.m. It was only 9 o'clock. We had booked a berth on the train from Lucknow to Bombay. My brothers had already purchased the ticket. With my luggage weighed and the excess baggage paid for, we stood at the railway platform beside the bogie where the rail company had already pasted my name on the door. After some time, my son Bashir Ahmad arrived with some of my relatives from Lucknow. Two of my dear friends from Kakori had got on to the local train.

Quite a crowd had assembled to see me off. An hour passed amidst this anxious, well-meaning company. I took my leave and got on board. Just then, I saw my old servant, Hafiz Abdul Karim. He had come with me from Kakori. While he wiped his tears, I moved away lest I too started crying. The train blew its whistle and I bid adieu to Lucknow.

1 Rakat implies an individual unit or section of the prescribed prayer.

2 Named after Aurangzeb, the city was founded in 1610 by Malik Ambar. It is surrounded by many historical monuments including the Ajanta and Ellora caves, which are UNESCO World Heritage Sites.

3 A town in present-day Maharashtra, it is situated 100 kilometres from a sacred Jain site, Shri Mangi Tungiji Digambar Jain Siddha Kshetra.

4 The north was served by the Awadh and Rohilkhand Railway, with a station near Kakori, and close to this ran the road from Lucknow to Malihabad and Hardoi, from which a metalled road took off at the railway station and gave access to the town of Kakori. See H.R. Nevill (1904), *Lucknow: A District Gazetteer*, Allahabad, p. 194.

ہم نے جب وادیِ غربت میں قدم رکھا تھا

دور تک یادِ وطن آئی تھی سمجھانے کو

Hum ne jab waadi-i-ghurbat men qadam rakkha tha
door tak yaadi-watan aai thee samjhane ko.

When we had set foot in the valley of nostalgia
For long, memories of home had come to comfort us.

The train journey was uneventful. The night was cold. I had enough (woollens) to keep me warm, yet, I kept awake all night. The next morning my son got off at Manmarh, leaving me alone. Sometime in the afternoon, the train entered a series of tunnels and, at about 3.30 p.m., pulled into Bombay's Victoria Terminus.

My benefactor was Syed[1] Samiuddin Sahib[2] Fatehpuri, a retired Inspector of Police. His two sons are employed in the railway office. They received me at the railway station. With them taking charge of my luggage, I didn't experience any inconvenience.

A police constable posted at the railway station took one look at my face and asked, 'Are you going for hajj?' Just then, I recalled what a well-travelled friend had told me. According to him, Bombaywallahs could tell a hajji from his face.

Accompanied by my hosts, I took the car to Mahim,[3] a qasba[4] located at a distance of about eight miles from Bombay. Or, you can say, a far-flung mohalla in the city. The young men had rented a modest flat.[5] They would take the electric train to the city, work in office, and return home in the evening. Saeed Qureshi and his brother also lived

---

1 Syed or Sayyid is an honorific title given to males accepted as descendants of the Prophet through his grandsons, Hasan ibn Ali and Husain ibn Ali. They were the sons of his daughter Fatima and son-in-law 'Ali.

2 A title added to the name of the position somebody holds, commonly used with Muslim names to show respect. Sahib literally means 'friend, companion', and is also used to show respect, meaning 'sir, master, or lord'.

3 A neighbourhood in Mumbai. The old Mahim mosque was built in the fourteenth century. The dargah of Makhdum Ali Pir was constructed in 1431.

4 For a man belonging to Kakori, the author uses the word qasba quite consciously. It gives some idea of his mental horizon.

5 We have used the words 'flat' and 'quarter' simply because the family could not have afforded *ghar* or house, the word used in the Urdu text.

in the same quarter. I also became their guest. *Alhamdulillah!*[1] Their hospitality made me feel at home.

Saturday, 2 February

Today, I drove with Saeed Qureshi to the Allahabad Bank to obtain a letter of credit for the Netherland Trading Company in Jiddah for Rs 400.[2] I had already completed the paperwork through its Aminabad branch in Lucknow. Afterwards, we went to the booking office of the Turner Morrison Company. It is located near Sabu Siddiq's Guest House in Crawford Market.[3] I booked a first class passage for Rs 550.[4]

I have been informed by an official that I would receive the passport the day after, that is, Monday, from the police station. He issued a letter for the purser of *The Rehmani S.S.* so that I could choose my own cabin on the ship. The ship was to sail on 14 February, but the official informed us that it could also leave a week before.[5] Saeed Qureshi, an employee in the office of the Traffic Manager, BBCIR, was going to let me know the exact date.

I was still in the booking office when Hasan Sikandar, my muallim, showed up. He had bid me adieu in Kakori. He wanted to treat me to a cup of tea. I chose to accompany him because Saeed Qureshi was required to get back to his office. My host Syed Samiuddin Ahmad Sahib and some of his friends urged me to meet the Assistant Traffic Superintendent and enquire about my baggage that had been stolen en route from Neemuch four months ago. I had already claimed compensation from Kakori, but I had no hope of receiving any recompense. But, upon the young men's insistence, I met the Superintendent with the necessary

1 Meaning, 'Praise be to Allah': a statement of thanks, appreciation and gratitude from the creature to his Creator.

2 The Dutch trading company, founded in 1621 mainly to carry on economic warfare against Spain and Portugal by striking at their colonies in the West Indies, in South America, and on the west coast of Africa. The Dutch West India Company was much less successful than the Dutch East India Company, its counterpart in Southeast Asia.

3 Officially, Mahatma Jyotirao Phule Market. Completed in 1869, it was named after Arthur Crawford, Bombay's first municipal commissioner. It is situated opposite the Mumbai Police headquarters, just north of Victoria Terminus railway station, and west of the J.J. flyover.

4 The first class ticket cost Rs 450; the second class cost Rs 195.

5 This was not unusual. Abdul Majid Daryabadi had to stay in Bombay for twelve days. See *Safar-i Hijaz*, p. 40.

details. He found my correspondence in his office and offered me Rs 124. Delighted by this unexpected gift from Allah, I accepted the offer.

I reached the station and boarded the train to Mahim.

Sunday, 3 February

My hosts took me to the dockyard. After a great deal of search, I found the *Rehmani S.S.*, a brand new ship of a very high quality. Owing to its proximity to the toilets, I chose cabin no. 10. Then, I went to Sabu Siddiq's Guest House where a group of hajjis, led by Mir Raham Ali Sahib, had come from Neech. The manager was absent. Therefore, I took time locating Mir Sahib. Hasan Sikandar, also staying there, took me to his room. Therein, I tasted my first sip of Arabian tea.[1] After a hectic day, which involved a great deal of running around, the tea without milk tasted wonderfully refreshing.

Soon, on hearing that Mir Rahim Ali was on the third floor, we trooped into his room to meet him. A water-carrier from Neech had accompanied him. He used to collect money at the Jama Masjid on Fridays for meeting the mosque's expenses. Obviously, Allah has rewarded his devotion. Now, he was on his way to being blessed by the ziyarat of Mecca and Medina. I was glad to see him and to be joined by two of God-sent friends.

The rules required that I be inoculated. Hasan Sikandar proposed that I pay a rupee or two and obtain a false certificate. Instead, I chose to abide by the rule.

After some time, we returned to Mahim, sipped tea, and then set off for the famous Chowpatty beach.[2] A broad boulevard runs beside the sea. A carnival-like atmosphere prevails here every evening. However, having gone there with a great deal of expectation, I found the place lacklustre. If one is not at peace with oneself, no amusement park can be interesting.

هجر میں عاشق ہنسے کیا رو سکے
جی ٹھکانے ہو تو سب کچھ ہو سکے

Hijr mein aashiq hanse kya ro sake
Ji ithikaane ho to sab kucch ho sake.

1 Using the prepared leaves of a shrub, or small tree, Arabian tea has the effect of a euphoric stimulant.

2 Apart from Juhu, Chowpatty is Mumbai's most famous beach.

In separation, the lover can neither laugh nor cry
If one is at peace, then everything is possible.

Meanwhile, it was time for the *Maghrib* (fourth of the five daily prayers performed after the sunset prayer). My companions were not keen on namaz. I could see no suitable place for offering my namaz. After fretting over the matter for some time, my fellow-travellers directed me to a nearby mosque. Even though it did not look like a mosque from the outside, a *jama'at* (lining up for namaz) stood in place. I joined them.

After namaz, I enjoyed the fresh sea breeze for a long, long time. By about 8.00 p.m., I boarded the train to Mahim.

Monday, 4 February

I have been nursing a cold all morning. Yet, I went to the Turner Morrison Company. Accompanied by Saeed Qureshi, we obtained the chit, and went to the Biswari Car Passport Company. There, I was inoculated and, after answering a few brief questions, completed the departure formalities. I was told that the passport would be sent to the shipping company the next day. After completing this necessary paperwork, I returned to Mahim.

Tuesday, 5 February

The cold worsened today. I stayed home. In the afternoon, I heard of the outbreak of riots in Bombay. I also hear that a few Afghans had been arrested on the suspicion of allegedly kidnapping children.

Wednesday, 6 February

Hafiz Nasr Ahmad, my third son, came from Aurangabad. He reached Mahim after facing a lot of problems. In the afternoon, I took the electric train to Bombay with him. At the Turner Morisson Company, I discovered that the passport had yet to come, and that the ship's departure date had not yet been fixed.

From there we went to the Guest House. Hasan Sikandar offered us tea. We met Mir Reham Ali and chatted for a long time. We also met the water-carrier from Neemuch. He had only Rs 400 with him, of which he spent approximately half the amount on purchasing the ticket. Now, he was left with less than Rs 200. He told us that he intended to walk from Mecca to Medina. By around 2 o'clock, we took the train back to Mahim.

Thursday, 7 February

Rioting continues. I didn't go anywhere today. Hafiz Nasr Ahmad went with Saeed Qureshi to purchase some cloth, etc., from the city. He bought a box with a lock, *chadars*[1] for ihram,[2] an urn, some besan[3] and few other essential items.

Friday, 8 February

I went to the city with my son Nasr and received the compensation cash card from the railway office. We offered our Friday namaz at the mosque in the Fort area. Although this mosque too does not look like a mosque from outside, it is fitted with electric fans and lights. I enjoyed listening to the recitation of the Quran by the mosque's Imam,[4] who has a sonorous voice.

After namaz, we went to the office of Turner Morrison. I finally obtained my ticket and passport. The officer told us that the ship was ready to sail but its departure had been delayed due to the riots. Everything had come to a standstill. It seemed unlikely that the ship would sail before the 13th or 14th of this month. A curfew had been clamped. I hired a car to Grant Road,[5] to encash the cash card. The amount of Rs 124 was god send. Nasr returned to Aurangabad because he had been summoned through a telegram.

Saturday, 9 February

The riots continue unabated. It is said that thousands have been wounded and killed. I did not step out all day. In the evening, I went for a stroll up till Colaba and returned safely.

---

1 A chadar is a full-length semi-circular outer garment or open cloak worn by women when they venture out into public. It is thrown over the head and held shut in front. It is also the Islamic *hijāb* dress. But here it is just a sheet.

2 Two pieces of unstitched cloth, donned by the person performing hajj or umrah.

3 Flour made from pulses. Indian besan is a staple ingredient in Indian cuisine, and, when used in the form of a paste with water or yoghurt, a popular facial appliance.

4 Imam is the one who leads a congregational prayer. Imam or *Amir* is also an honorific title for a religious leader, who leads his community in political affairs.

5 Named after Sir Robert Grant, Governor of Bombay between 1835 and 1839. Grant Road railway station is a centrally located arterial station in South Mumbai.

Sunday, 10 February

With Saeed Qureshi in tow, I bought biscuits for the sea journey from Andheri.[1] In the evening, I walked along the beach at Mahim. The sea breeze seemed cooler than at Chowpatty. I heard that the famous Bombay businessman, Seth Chotani,[2] had been wounded in the riots. I was worried. A little later, we heard that this was a rumour and an entirely baseless one at that. The moon has not been sighted.

Monday, 11 February

I did not step out of the house all day today. Peace has still not returned to the city. Saeed Qureshi telephoned to find out that the ship would sail on 14 February at 5.00 p.m. The luggage could be loaded a day before, but for this I will be required to go to the office. Letters came from Kakori telling me that all is well. The new moon was sighted in the evening. Tomorrow, *Inshaallah*,[3] I shall observe the first of the Ramazan fasts.[4]

Tuesday, 12 February

I went to the shipping company's office for the last time. Owing to the riots and disturbances, the company did not allow the baggage to be loaded a day earlier. The babu issued a slip which stated that the heavy bags would be loaded at 7.00 a.m. on 14 February. The ship would be fumigated at 9.00 a.m. The passengers would board the ship an hour later, and it would set sail by mid-day. I was concerned. How will I, at 7.00 a.m., even before sunrise, transport the bags from Mahim to the port, 10 miles away? But Allah is the one who gets things done. He will doubtless find a way out.[5]

---

1 A suburb of Mumbai city; also a railway station on the Mumbai Suburban Railway, Western line. In the early 1900s, as urbanization spread from Bombay northwards, Marathi, Gujarati, and other settlers began to colonize the area.

2 1883–1932; timber merchant from Bombay; disciple of Maulana Abdul Bari of Firangi Mahal; president, Central Khilafat Committee, 1919–23; his last days were spent in Medina.

3 God-willing.

4 Ramazan is the ninth month of the Islamic calendar. Fasting in the month of Ramazan is one of the five pillars of Islam. The month is spent fasting during the daylight hours from dawn to dusk.

5 Literally, Allah is the one who gets things done.

I returned home by 11.30 a.m. Owing to the fast, I began suffering from constipation. My head was also aching. By afternoon, I felt quite listless. Allah says, 'And whosoever of you is sick or on a journey, let him fast the same number of days [later].'[1]

I am feeling weak. My health appears to be failing. I have been travelling for the past 12 days; a longer journey is ahead of me. I must, therefore, avail of the exemptions provided by the Shariat.[2] It looks as if I will not be able to observe fast tomorrow. However, I felt better after *iftar*,[3] though the headache stayed for a while.

Wednesday, 13 February

Alas, I cannot fast. All day long I fretted over my luggage being taken to the docks. My hosts, Syed Mohiuddin Ahmad and Saeed Qureshi, promised to rent a car. In the evening they bought me some paan, but failed, despite their best efforts, to organize transport. Finally, they hired a car and took me to the Bandra station in the morning. My sea journey begins tomorrow. Fear weighs upon my heart.

Thursday, 14 February

I woke up at 3.00 a.m. I was done with my prayers by 5.30 a.m. Tea followed. Syed Mohiuddin Ahmad and Saeed Qureshi's brother were kind enough to arrange a car from Bandra. I left their home at 6.00 a.m. On reaching Bombay, I saw a lot of pilgrims heading towards the docks in order to get their luggage stowed. The sight was overwhelming. Pride in the unity of Islam surged within me. A great many pilgrims had reached well before sunrise. The docks were crowded.

I discovered my mistake in rolling and tying up my bedding instead of packing it in a trunk or box. The porter at the dock told me that the bedroll would be put through the fumigator. I was worried how my bedding would make it to the ship because I had heard that coolies were unwilling to carry the luggage to the ship after fumigation. Here, at the dock, I could see no way of either hiding from sight or packing my bedroll.

1 Quran, Al-Baqara: 185.

2 Islamic Law: considered to be divine.

3 Iftar refers to the breaking of the daily fast immediately after Maghrib (sunset) during the month of Ramazan. Iftar is often done as a community, with Muslims gathering in groups to break their fasts.

A policeman told me that the bedding of first class passengers is not put through fumigation. Others present, however, did not accept this. Another said that if the bedding was new, it would not require fumigation. I was not satisfied. In fact, till all my bags were stowed away I was not at peace. The loading started at 8.30 a.m. My cabin had already been reserved. So I was in no hurry to board. But the third class passengers were jostling to get on board. It is said that once aboard the ship, the hajjis can spread their bedding on any spot and that spot becomes theirs for the duration of the journey. And that is why everyone is in such a rush to grab the best place. An English sergeant stood beside the ship's plankway; he was stopping everyone from getting on board. The Englishman was rude; he beat several hajjis with his cane and kicked others. I was at some distance. I was shocked and dismayed by this brutish behaviour; I found it revolting. Most of the hajjis bearing the brunt of this brutishness were Bengalis. Had they been Punjabis or Afghan, this ill-tempered Englishman would have got his just desserts. There were approximately 1,200 Mussalmans were on the dock. Had a riot broken out, it could not have been controlled without a machine gun. Every lash of that tyrant's cane bled my heart and roused my anger. But the Bengali Mussalmans were either entirely insensitive to the humiliation or so overwhelmed by the excitement of the pilgrimage that they seemed impervious to the pain and humiliation.

2

On the Coastline
Bombay to Karachi[1]

Thursday, 14 February

At long last, we received permission to get on board. When the crowd thinned somewhat, I found my way to my allotted Cabin No. 10. It had two berths. My co-passenger is Mohammad Yusuf, resident of Sadiabad in Zilla Allahabad.[2] A zamindar, he receives a pension for his services in the army.[3] He seems hospitable and friendly. I hope, Inshaallah, to enjoy his company.

The cabin is comfortable with electric lights, an electric fan, and a basin with sweet tap water. With two Turkish towels, the beds and pillows are soft and comfortable. The bathroom and toilets are clean. With Allah's grace, there is comfort all around.

A purser handed me a key to the cabin. I locked my luggage and got off the ship. The vexed issue of fumigation remained unresolved.

Fumigation is designed to harass the hajjis. It takes place in a tin-shed where they are held hostage for an hour or two. The tin-shed has electric fans. Intermittently, a blast of hot air jets out. First and second

---

1 Karachi was the original capital of Pakistan until the construction of Islamabad, and is the location of one of the region's largest and busiest ports. It was conquered by Charles Napier in 1843 and was made the capital of Sind in the 1840s. Its population was about 1,05,000 by the end of the nineteenth century, with a mix of Muslims, Hindus, Europeans, Jews, Parsis, Iranians, and Goans.

2 An administrative district.

3 They were employed by the Mughals to collect taxes from peasants. The practice was continued under British rule in India. They constituted an important force in rural society, and the bulwark of the Raj.

class passengers are made to sit on the benches, while a doctor checks their pulse and places a stamp on their passports and tickets. Thereafter, the doctor issues a slip of paper to certify the passenger's fitness.

People travelling in the third class are seated in rows like animals. They hold their passports in one hand, while they hold up their shirts with the other hand to reveal their stomach. The doctor touches their bellies cursorily and gives them a clean medical chit.

O Qadir-e Zuljalal [Exalted and Powerful], have pity on the state of the Muslims! Steeped in their passion to see your Exalted House, they are willing to undergo every manner of humiliation and not a word of protest escapes from their lips. They are treated no better than goats and sheep in a slaughterhouse; yet they do not pollute their tongue with grievance or complaint:

در ره منزل لیلیٰ که خطرهاست بسے
شرط اول قدم آنست که مجنوں باشی

Dar rahe manzil-e-Laila ke khatarhast basey
Shart awwal-e-qadam aanast ke Majnun bashi

In the way to the house of Laila, there are a lot of perils
The first condition to step into is that you should be a Majnun.

For the first time, we saw the members of the Hajj Committee[1] and the *muhafiz*. The pilgrims vociferously condemned the beastly behaviour of the British Sergeant at the ship's plankway. We found that the same person had repeated the atrocities even at the entry of the fumigation house. The pilgrims were constrained to complain to the muhafiz. As a result, someone approached me to seek confirmation. I narrated the pitiful scene at the ship's plankway. I was asked to pen my account in English. I did so briefly and handed it to him. My new friend, Mohammad Yusuf Allahabadi, co-signed. We don't know if our account will serve any purpose, and whether or not the gentleman who asked for it will have the courage to report to the newspapers.

The time fixed for fumigation was 9 o'clock. We have been locked up inside this cattle house since 9.30 a.m. Orders to free us were issued at

1 The Hajj Committee in India was formed for making arrangements for the pilgrimage of Muslims of India. A special hajj passport was issued to aspiring pilgrims for this purpose. The first formal meeting of the Hajj Committee was held in 1927 in Bombay.

11.30, and, we were, finally, granted permission to get on board the ship. Having escaped from the fumigation shed, we were taken to yet another shed before the platform on the dockyard. Like prisoners, we were made to squat in rows on the floor. After about ten minutes, a white-skinned officer allowed us to leave this second round of imprisonment. We reached the ship around noon. The ship blew its whistle at 1.30 p.m. Two small steamers had emerged to tug it out of the quay. Ropes pulled us out into the open seas beyond the Bombay harbour.

> In the name of Allah who is (this ship's) mover and its docker.
> Indeed my lord is most merciful.

I stood on the deck, watching. The ship's movement caused no discomfort. Those who had come to see us off stood on the dock, watching and waving; I saw a man wiping his tears. Obviously, he had come to bid farewell to someone very dear.

The *Rehmani*, a new ship, is equipped to cruise along smoothly and comfortably. If one doesn't look at the water, it is hard to tell whether it was sailing or had dropped anchor. For an hour or two I could sight the buildings of Bombay. I paced up and down the deck and looked longingly towards land. By four, we had sailed far beyond the shore. Now, except for the blue water and sky, there was nothing around us. Suddenly, a passenger recited a verse from the Quran:

> How many a portent is there in the heavens and the wrath which they pass by with face averted. (Quran: 105 Yusuf)

His solemn and sonorous recitation moved me.

There is a Muslim Hotel on the ship, but its arrangements are unsatisfactory. The hajjis found nothing to eat at iftar. The dinner, served by 8.00 p.m., was inadequate. Some passengers went to bed hungry. I was finally served my dinner at 9.00 p.m.; fortunately, the food wasn't too bad. I had performed my *Isha* prayers (prayers prescribed to be performed once the night settles until dawn). After dinner, I went to bed. This being my first night on the sea, I felt nervous.

Friday, 15 February

I performed my morning chores, had tea which came from the English Hotel, and took a walk on the deck by 7.30 a.m. In the distance, I saw the shore of Kathiawar.[1] I spent the better part of the day walking on

---

1 It is part of Gujarat state, bounding the great wetland of the Rann of Kutch, on the

the deck and talking to fellow-passengers. At 11.00 a.m., I wired a telegram to the contractor of the Muslim Hotel on board about his poor management. An Arab helped me with the drafting of the telegram; the 19 or 20 words cost me Rs 11 and 14 annas[1]. By the evening, I received an answer. The Hotel's manager was brought to book and given a warning. He was pardoned on the grounds that a few hiccups on the first day of a journey were expected. The hotel's staff, having been warned and admonished, produced a delicious dinner.

Till 4.00 in the evening, the Kathiawar shore glimmered in the distance. After that, we saw nothing but the sea. All the Muslims offered the *Juma* prayer on deck. The Imam was a *ghair-muqallid* (one who does not follow the historic law schools but consults the Quran and hadith). His Urdu-language *khutba*,[2] took up a great deal of time due to his verbose lecture-*baazi* (long-winded speech). I too participated in the namaz. My health, thank Allah, is good, though the constipation is beginning to aggravate me.

Saturday, 16 February

The hills of Karachi have become visible since the morning. Several steamers have cruised past us. An aeroplane also flew overhead. At 11.30 a.m., we dropped anchor off the port of Karachi at a distance of about a mile. By 4.00 p.m., we were towed closer to the shore but

---

northwest, by the Gulf of Kutch, on the west and southeast, and by the Gulf of Cambay, on the east.

1 Anna is an Indian coin equal to 1/16th of a rupee.

2 An Islamic sermon delivered before Friday prayers and after Id prayers. There is also a khutba delivered during hajj in the plains of Arafat, just outside Mecca. The following description of Arafat is useful: 'And as I stand on the hillcrest and gaze down toward the invisible Plain of Arafat, the moonlit blueness of the landscape before me, so dead a moment ago, suddenly comes to life with the currents of all the human lives that have passed through it and is filled with the eerie voices of the millions of men and women [who] have walked or ridden between Mecca and Arafat in over thirteen hundred pilgrimages for over thirteen hundred years. Their voices and their steps and the voices and the steps of their animals re-awaken and resound anew; I see them walking and riding and assembling—all those myriads of white-garbed pilgrims of thirteen hundred years; I hear the sounds of their passed-away days; the wings of the faith which has drawn them together to this land of rocks and sand and seeming deadness beat again with the warmth of life over the arc of centuries, and the mighty wing beat draws me into its orbit and draws my own passed-away days into the present, and once again I am riding over the plain—.' Muhammad Asad, *Road to Mecca*, p. 373.

not allowed to berth. A few officers from the port climbed aboard. We heard that 30,000 bags of wheat would be loaded, and that we would be required to stay for three days. By evening, a small bazaar had come up all around our ship. Merchants selling dry fruits, cigarettes and fish rode on small boats and clamoured all about us as they began to hawk their wares. I didn't need anything; in fact, I didn't buy anything because I had enough provisions. The Karachi harbour is pretty. On one side of it is the Army garrison, where canons are positioned and barracks lined in a row. Scores of small boats and motley steamers crowd the waters. The lights of the sprawling city can be seen only a short distance away.

Unfortunately, only the upper class passengers can enjoy this view for, today the third class passengers are in distress. Thirty thousand gunny sacks full of wheat will be loaded on the ship in order to be transported to Africa. The planks have been taken out and the hold opened up. The sacks that were brought up in several small boats were picked by a crane and dropped into the ship's storage compartment. This cumbersome exercise began in the evening, and lasted all night long; it is still continuing. In order to position the crane, even first class passengers were removed from the deck. Of the 1,400 pilgrims aboard, at least a 1,000 were inconvenienced through the night. May Allah have mercy on them!

Had Muslims been owners of ships, they would never have put innocent hajjis to such hardship, and for the sake of a few extra rupees they would never have troubled hapless pilgrims in this manner. The *Rehmani*, on which I am travelling, belongs to the Mogul Line; ships belonging to this line are considered superior. But since the British own them, the revenue earned through profit from transporting goods is given greater premium than the comfort of pilgrims. In comparison, the ships of the Nemazi Company and the Shustri Company sail to Jiddah without making the poor hajjis take a needless detour through Karachi. Moreover, their ships are not docked there for two or three days in the hope of earning extra money by carrying cargo.

O Lord, have mercy on the people belonging to Mohammad. May peace and blessings of Allah be upon him!

Sunday, 17 February

Since this morning, the third class passengers have been complaining of a water shortage. Such is their plight that even the saltwater taps have been turned off. Several have had to miss their *Fajr* namaz.[1] Still, the tormentors have not provided them with water. A poor thirsty soul wandered into my room and took some sweet drinking water from my tap. He could offer his prayers thereafter.

It is ten in the morning. Thousands of sacks of grain are still to be loaded. The ship has to pick up 15,000–16,000 *maunds* of coal. A huge boat carrying coal has pulled up close to our ship. Scores of coolies, men and women, are engaged in loading the coal. The grain is being stowed in four storage compartments in the ship's hold. It seems as though this loading operation will continue till tomorrow afternoon.

Interestingly enough, on 14 February, the day of embarkation, 70–80 per cent of the hajjis observed *roza*, by the second day, this number was down to 20–25 per cent. Today, a bare 5 per cent of the men appear to be fasting. I can't say much about the few women on board.

Bengalis constitute the great majority of hajjis. Some are from Java and Burma, too. One family hails from Cape Town; their women wear Western clothes and go about unveiled. A man has come all the way from Shiraz with his wife.[2] Indians constitute not even 10 per cent of my fellow-passengers.

The water shortage was taken care of by 8.00 a.m. The pilgrims, thereafter, got busy with their chores. A crowd of vendors' boats swarms around the ship and the passengers are buying their assorted wares. Everything is sold at exorbitant prices, and why not. Some pilgrims wanted to go offshore, but the ship's officers did not let them do so. By sunset, the coal had been loaded. The vendors too sailed away. But the stacking of the sacks of grain went on till 1.30 in the night, and the constant, painful creaking of the crane bothered the pilgrims.

جام ٹوٹا بت بد مست کہ مینا ٹوٹا

دل حاجی بھی کوئی چیز تھا ٹوٹا ٹوٹا

Jaam toota but-e bad mast ke meena toota
Dil-e haaji bhi koi cheez tha toota toota

The cup of wine has been broken but the drinker thinks the wine glass is broken. The heart of the hajji is of no account—whether it breaks or not.

1 The first of the five daily prayers recited from the beginning of dawn to sunrise.

2 Located in the southwest of Iran, Shiraz remained the provincial capital throughout the Safavid empire (1501–1722). It was a leading centre for poetry and literature. Sadi and Hafiz, the two outstanding Persian poets, belonged to Shiraz.

Monday, 18 February

At 8.00 in the morning, the tiresome sound resumed. Sacks of grain are being pulled from the boats and dropped into the ship's hold. May Allah give us speedy relief from this calamity [*azaab*]!

Tuesday, 19 February

All day yesterday, the sacks were loaded. It finally got over at 6.00 in the morning. A few sacks were loaded five hours later. After 12.00 noon, the ship pulled anchor and, an hour later, we entered a berth in Karachi's harbour. We were still not allowed to get off the ship. People stood on the quay, in the hot sun, waiting for the ship to berth. A plankway was set up for the coolies to load the luggage of those hajjis who were embarking at Karachi.[1]

Here, on the Karachi docks, I could not see a British officer in charge of the pilgrims. A few police constables and some members of the Hajj Committee were around. As far as I could see, the baggage was loaded without a glitch in a fairly smooth manner.

Two British officers appeared at the time that the pilgrims boarded the ship. They stood quietly. The hajjis in Bombay would have been spared of the needless anguish if things had been managed so smoothly and in so pleasant a manner there too.

Sindh has a predominantly Muslim population. With our government being sensitive to the opinion of the majority, they value the Muslims. Moreover, members of the Hajj Committee do not behave as nominal

---

1 After passing through the quarantine station at Kamaran, the pilgrim would reach the harbour at Jiddah. The reports of the British Consul showed that the procedure of landing Indian pilgrims at Jiddah compared very unfavourably with that adopted in the case of Javanese and Malay pilgrims. The captains of the ships conveying pilgrims of the latter class did not allow the coolies from Jiddah to board their ships, but unloaded the luggage of the pilgrims into the *sambuks* waiting alongside by means of their own crews and the ships' cranes, whereas, at least until recently, on Indian ships, coolies from onshore went on board and seized the pilgrims' luggage indiscriminately and carried it away to the sambuks, with the result that portions of it were frequently lost by the time the pilgrims had disembarked and passed the quarantine station on shore. Attempts were made by the shipping companies to improve the arrangements, but these were not successful. The British Consul suggested that the shipping companies engaged in the Indian pilgrimage traffic should be requested to afford the same facilities for the unloading of baggage as were afforded by the Blue Funnel Line, namely, that the ship's derricks should be employed, and only coolies and boatmen provided by the company allowed on board.

office-bearers, but serve everyone earnestly in order to fulfil what they regard as their primary duty. Consequently, they take care of the pilgrims' amenities and comfort.

Rail tracks were laid out on the dockyard. A woman with a baby in her arms stumbled on the track and fell. Fortunately, her baby was not hurt and both climbed safely on board. Members of the Hajj Committee collected the tickets from the pilgrims and showed them, individually, to the officers of the shipping company. They, in turn, guided them about the necessary formalities and escorted them right up till the ship. May Allah grant the same zeal to the Muslims of Bombay to enable them to work like this!

Four to five hundred pilgrims boarded at Karachi. Most of them were Punjabis and women. There are also some Arabs from Basra,[1] some covered in black *burqas*. I spotted three unveiled women walking around on the dock. Their awful appearance saddened me. Later, I found out that they were prostitutes. Perhaps, they had come to bid goodbye to a relative.

Fifty-odd Kabulis from the Frontier Province came on board—by hook or crook I don't know. The shipping company had reserved a lower deck for the Karachi passengers. The Punjabis and Arabs went to their allocated places but the Afghans seized control of the deck. A young British officer tried in vain to check them, but they spread out their rugs and blankets and spread themselves out on both sides of the deck. This prevented first class passengers and officers from walking about the deck. The ship's Hindustani and British officers, who had been roaring like lions and bullying the passengers all this while, became quiet as mice and slunk away. The Afghans established their *swarajya*[2] on the best part of the deck.

When it comes to arranging water, the ship's employees trouble the poor passengers who travel third class. In fact, a clerk from Goa even hit a couple of passengers from Chittagong when they asked for water. But these fifty-odd Afghans have caused havoc among the ship's management. 'Each Pharoah begets a Moses (To teach him a lesson or subdue).'

---

1 Iraq's fourth largest city after Baghdad, Mosul, and Arbil, Basra is also the country's main port. It has played an important role in Islamic history.

2 'Self-rule' through individuals and community building. The word usually refers to Mahatma Gandhi's concept for Indian independence from foreign domination.

The first whistle blew at 6.00. A small steamer appeared to tow the ship out to sea. By 6.30, our ship had left Karachi.

There was no place to walk. So I went and sat in the upper berth occupied by Mohammad Yusuf Sahib in my room. From the porthole, I enjoyed seeing the sea. With our ship taking the north-westerly direction, our journey [of faith] has, in actual fact, started. The further we travel from India, the closer we get to our cherished goal. *Alhamdulillah ala zalik.* Praise be to Allah for it!

The Afghans have commandeered the lavatory door! A bearer has locked one of the special toilets meant for first class passengers and handed us the key so that the Kabulis don't seize control of that too. We ate dinner after Maghrib and went to sleep after the Isha prayers.

Wednesday, 20 February

Tea was served late this morning. The reason: I discovered that my watch was still showing 'railway' time whereas here it is 'sea' time. I performed namaz at six according to my watch but the sunrise occurred at 7.45. My friend Yusuf carried two watches. I told him to set one according to the 'sea' time, and the other according to 'railway' time so that we can tell the difference between the two.

The decks are washed each morning. Today, the sweepers were up to mischief. They released the water with such force that the Afghans scurried to collect their belongings from getting wet. For some time, the passage was cleared. But the Afghans re-occupied their territory when the deck dried out. I took advantage of this respite and paced up and down the deck. I walked for a long time, enjoying the fresh sea breeze. Water all around! Water below and the sky above! There isn't a bird in sight.

Who has supreme authority today? Allah, the Almighty, has it.

In the afternoon, I spotted the flying fish. They swoop to a height of the span of a hand or two above the water's surface, fly for a little while, and then disappear underwater. Mohammad Yusuf Sahib spotted some birds as well. This meant that we were not too far from land. In order to keep myself occupied, I visited Mir Rahman Ali, and, for a long time, sat with Mohammad Akram Sahib[1] from Bengal. The latter, a leader

1 1868–1968; a journalist-editor of great fame. He edited *Mohammadi* and *Al-Eslam*, followed by *Azad*. He was a nationalist, having supported the Swadeshi movement and the Khilafat and Non-cooperation movements in Bengal. He organized mass meetings

from Calcutta, had spent some time in jail during the Non-cooperation movement. He told me that a certain young British officer had kicked some pilgrims at the time of distribution of water.[1]

Water is in chronic short supply. For nearly 1,900 pilgrims, there is provision for only three sweet water taps; hence, water gets distributed only once a day. Over 600 pilgrims swarm around a single tap. Each one of them tries to be the first to get it. On such occasions, the company's employees trouble the poor hajjis to their hearts' content, and the young British officers do not even hesitate to kick them. For one, the black man from Hindustan is, in any case, an animal and deserves to be kicked around. On top of that, he wants to go on hajj, which is nothing but an illustration of his stupidity and misguided enthusiasm. I have heard a company employee say, 'These hajjis are silly fools.'

I learnt from Akram Sahib that the company's employees had smuggled in some passengers from the third to the second class. He said that he would investigate the matter and inform me of his findings. I learnt from the Assistant Manager of the Muslim Hotel about a particular place that has been labelled the 'Inter Class'. The company's employees charge a certain fee, entirely illegally of course, and create a space by screening it off with curtains and begin to call it 'Inter Class'. Such activities simply add to the woes of the poorer passengers. Some of them don't even have enough space to sleep. The water-carrier from Neemuch complained to me that he could not sleep all night on several occasions. In desperation, he spent the night in one corner of the deck. All this is because Muslims do not own shipping companies. If a Muslim company had known that a ship from some other line was heading towards Jiddah, it would not have treated its passengers so shabbily.

There is very little space on this ship. Scores of fires are lit for cooking meals on makeshift stoves. In the afternoon, the smoke reaches our cabin's door. It is due to Allah's grace that we have not died of suffocation. The shipping company, clearly, could not care less.

---

and collected funds for the Khilafat in Turkey. In 1921, he published his biography of the Prophet entitled *Mostapha Charit*. For a while, he was involved in peasant politics. Later, he joined the Muslim League. He opted for Pakistan and lived in Dhaka.

1 Characteristically, here as elsewhere, he mentions the two persons travelling in the first and second class, respectively.

The sun set at 7.25 p.m. by our time, that is, the railway time; the ship's clock showed 5.55 p.m., a difference of an hour and a half between our time and the ship's time.

3
Journey of Faith

Thursday, 21 February

I woke up at six in the morning. It was 4.30 a.m. according to the ship's time. The Afghan passengers were eating *sehri*.[1] I prayed, performed my early morning chores, and, as always, sent for tea from the English Hotel. The sun rose at 8.00. After tea, I turned my attention towards my treasured hoard of paan. I had packed 400–500 of them before leaving Bombay; I have been dipping into my stock ever since. The leaves are beginning to rot and need extra care. More than half are still green. Hopefully, they will see me through till Jiddah. Tea came from the Muslim Hotel at 8.30. By 10.00 o'clock, my muallim, Hasan Sikandar's deputy, who has come with us from Bombay, offered me some Arab tea. I helped myself to two cups.

There are only four of us in the first class on this ship—one is an Arab merchant, the others are Indians. Besides me, there are Mohammad Yusuf Sahib of Allahabad and Dr Abdur Rehman from Zilla Munger.[2] Dr Rehman is a doctor from Great Britain. The Nizam of Hyderabad financed his travel.[3] Dr Rehman presents himself at the Haram

1 Refers to the meal before dawn taken by the person who intends to fast during the month of Ramazan. The meal is eaten before the Fajr or dawn prayer.

2 One of the thirty-seven districts of Bihar state in eastern India.

3 Nizam, a shortened version of Nizam-ul-Mulk, meaning Administrator of the Realm, was the title of the native sovereigns of Hyderabad state, India, since 1719, belonging to the Asaf Jah dynasty. Seven Nizams ruled Hyderabad for two turbulent centuries until India's independence in 1947. The Nizams were among the wealthiest rulers in the world. Mir Osman Ali Khan Asaf Jah VII ruled Hyderabad between 1911 and 1948. He was the richest man in the 1940s, having a fortune estimated at $2 billion.

Sharif[1] to treat the poor and to distribute medicines among the hajjis every year. May he live forever! Dr Rehman does not receive a salary; he undertakes this annual pilgrimage to serve the pilgrims and the residents of Haramain. He intends to proceed directly to Medina from Jiddah and be at Mecca at the time of hajj. According to him, the residents of Medina need far more medical attention because a great many of them are poor. May Allah grant him entry into paradise for this great service!

Last year, he published a short pamphlet describing his services. He has given me a copy. Inshaallah, I shall read it soon.

Friday, 22 February

Today, according to my watch, sunrise was at 8.30: the difference between my watch and the ship's watch is 1.45 hours. In the morning, I spotted two sea birds, which looked like eagles. By afternoon, some dark hills appeared on the south-western horizon. At first, I thought this was just the mingling of the sea and sky or an illusion. But after an hour or two, I could clearly make out the hills. The sight gladdened my heart. This must be the shore of Mukkala [East of Dhufar in Oman] or Socotro. We are getting closer to the land of Arabia. I learnt that the hills belong to an island called Khuriya Muriya;[2] the shores of Arabia were afar yet. By *Asr*, these hills were drawing closer. Till Maghrib, we kept looking longingly towards land.

قدر هر نعمت است بعد زوال

Qadr-e-har neamat ast baad-e-zawal

One values a blessing only after it's lost.

Saturday, 23 February

The difference between our time and the ship's time is exactly two hours. The sun rose at 8.45 a.m. according to my watch. All around me, there is nothing except water. By afternoon, we spotted some more hills.

---

1 Haram means an Islamic holy site of sanctity. The two sites whose Islamic sanctity is the highest of all are Mecca and Medina in Arabia. In addition, the term 'haram' is commonly used to refer to certain other holy sites, such as the Haram-al Sharif in Jerusalem.

2 Situated 25 miles off Oman's southeastern coast. The five islands have a total land area of 28 square miles. In 1854, the Sultan ceded them to the British, who included them in their colony of Aden in 1937.

Gradually, we were getting closer to them. The chain of hills continued with us on the left seaboard till sunset. At some point in the night, we left this chain behind, for till there was daylight left we had seen the hills hulking beside us. We saw a strip of land beside the hills. The land was, no doubt, inhabited because we saw a few boats with sails. They probably belonged to fishermen or passengers who had been ferried from one island to another. Several small birds were also flying around, but the most interesting experience was the shoal of fishes attacking our ship. A vast shoal, measuring approximately three or four yards in length and a half or three-quarters of a yard, rushed towards us from the land. Like trotting deer, they came towards us at full throttle, rising as much as a yard above the water surface. Just as they came close to the ship, they would disappear under the water! The spectacle was repeated several times and we spent almost two hours in rapt enjoyment. Onlookers crowded the deck as I watched from the porthole of my cabin's upper deck.

All morning I felt a little run down. I drank some fruit salt. By *Zuhr*, despite a dose of quinine, I was feeling unwell. By late afternoon, I had a mild headache. So I chose to forego dinner. At Munshi[1] Mohammad Yusuf Sahib's suggestion, I bought a tin of condensed milk from the Muslim Hotel. Adding milk to water, I took a tablet for constipation and retired for the night. Although I could not sleep well, the headache finally left me by midnight.

Sunday, 24 February

Feeling buoyant, I took a hot water bath. I felt good. To be on the safe side, I took two pills of quinine. There is a difference of two-and-a-half hours between my watch and that of the ship. Our qibla[2] now faces north. Tonight, we expect to pass the port of Aden;[3] but without a halt.

---

1 A degree in South Asia awarded after passing a certain course of basic reading, writing, and mathematics. The advanced degree was Munshi Fazil. In British India, Munshis were hired as clerks, accountants and secretaries.

2 The direction that Muslims face when they offer their prayer. It is in the direction of the Kaaba in Mecca. Kaaba is the spiritual and ritual centre of the Islamic world.

3 The Gulf of Aden is located in the Arabian Sea between Yemen on the south coast of the Arabian Peninsula and Somalia in Africa. In the northwest, it connects with the Red Sea. Captured by the British in 1839, Aden was chosen as the most suitable location and in 1937, Aden became a British crown colony. To Indubhushan Majumdar, a traveller in 1902, 'Aden constituted by her black mountains shorn of vegetation stood before me stern and naked. Coming as I did from the infinitely green and divinely

While there is nothing but water all around, we could see a chain of hills on the right-hand side. This probably belongs to the Arabian Peninsula.[1] Alhamdulillah!

Our ship will approach the Sea of Socotra[2] today. It is very hot now. The lower decks are, in particular, unbearably so. I went to visit Munshi Mohammad Akram and sat with him in the second class for a long time. There was an elderly gentleman from Rampur sharing the room with him. His family has been living at Haramain Sharifain. A devotee of the Naqshbandi order,[3] he is related to Mohammad Masoom of Naqshband. During the First World War, his family lived in Medina. He narrated the calamitous events of those years with anguish. I was saddened to hear

---

fertile land of India I felt strange in this harsh and infertile environs'. See Simonti Sen (2005), *Travels to Europe: Self and Other in Bengali Travel Narratives 1870–1910*, Delhi, p. 67.

1 The Arabian Peninsula is a peninsula in Southwest Asia situated at the junction of Africa and Asia, consisting mainly of desert. The area is an important part of the Middle East and plays a critically important geopolitical role because of its vast reserves of oil and natural gas. Politically, however, the peninsula is separated from the rest of Asia by the northern borders of Kuwait and Saudi Arabia.

2 Yemen's coastline has 182 islands, the most important of which is the Island of Socotra. Lutfullah described it as follows in his *Autobiography* published in 1857: 'On 2nd April, we came in sight of the island of Socotra, as predicted the day previous by a number of birds, called bostons, flying in that direction in the afternoon. This bird seems to be gifted with a wonderful power of flight over the seas. The island of Socotra was not less than two hundred miles distant from the spot where we saw them the day before. Hence it might be concluded that the bird, leaving the island in the morning and returning to it in the evening for its rest, must travel about five hundred miles a day. Praise to the power of the Omnipotent Being! In one stroke of whose mysterious pen, innumerable dexterities and arts can be seen, if one has an attentive eye and comprehensive mind. I witnessed another wonder in this part of the sea—the flying fish. From one of these flocks that happened to fly across our streamer, three flying-fish having fallen upon the deck, I seized upon one; and a close view of the animal showed that it was a pretty little creature, and that nature had furnished it with two pairs of wings, one to be used in the water and the other in the air. Besides, when it was fried, I found it to be a very delicious food.' See Lutfullah (2007), *Seamless Boundaries: Lutfullah's Narrative beyond East and West*, edited, annotated, and with an Introduction by Mushirul Hasan, Delhi, pp. 198–9.

3 One of the major Sufi orders (*tariqa*). Formed in 1380, the Naqshbandi order is considered by some to be a 'sober' order known for its silent *dhikr* (remembrance of Allah) rather than the vocalized forms common in other orders. The Naqshbandi order is also notable as it is the only Sufi order to trace its spiritual lineage (*silsilah*) to Prophet Mohammad through Abu Bakr, the first Khalifa. In contrast, most other *turuq* trace their lineage to Ali.

of the atrocities perpetrated by Sharif Hussein. I had come here looking for distraction, but the events described by the elderly gentlemen left my heart heavy with sorrow:

سمجھے تھے مرزا سے ہوگا غم غلط
ایسی باتیں کیں کہ دل گھبرا گیا

Samjhe the Mirza se hoga gham ghalat
aisi baatein keen keh dil ghabra gaya.

We had thought the Mirza would comfort us
But he spoke of things that worried us even more.

The sea is turbulent. Walking on the deck makes one stumble. I still felt dispirited; so I decided to turn in early without having my dinner.

نیند آتی ہے کب لاکھ جو پٹکے وہ سر اپنا
یاد آتا ہے منزل پہ مسافر کو گھر اپنا

Neend aati hai kab laakh jo patke wo sir apna
yaad aata hai manzil pe musaafir ko ghar apna.

One can't sleep even though he tries a lot.
The traveller remembers his house at a destination.

Monday, 25 February

We spotted the lighthouse of Aden before sunrise.[1] Its beam of light is strange—never still, it strikes again and again like lightning and disappears just as quickly. With more daylight, we could see the shore of Aden. Military barracks and the Lasilki[2] station could be seen. Some canons were also visible. We also saw lots of boats with sails. Thank Allah for having blessed us with the land of Arabia. The fragrance of

---

1 This is what Lutfullah wrote: 'On the morning of the 4th, we came in sight of Aden, and let down our anchor in its harbour at 1.30 p.m. The distance reckoned from Ceylon is 2215 English miles. So far, our voyage was, on the whole, a very pleasant and very comfortable one. We had smooth and calm water almost all the way from Ceylon. After our arrival, the ship's company got permission to go to the land if they liked; so we landed at once and placed ourselves on the lap of Mother Earth after eight days' separation. There is no much thing as a wheel-carriage known in Arabia; we had, therefore, no alternative left but to hire some asses for our short travel to the town of Aden, six miles from the harbour.' See Lutfullah (2007), *Seamless Boundaries*, p. 199.

2 Wireless station.

faith blows in from Yemen. By the grace of the Merciful Allah, may this fragrance bring comfort to my heart!

The distance from Karachi to Aden is 1,450 miles; we have covered it in 132 hours. Therefore, our ship has travelled, on an average, at a speed of 11.5 miles an hour, which is not bad for a freight ship [baarbardaari]. It is 675 miles from here to Jiddah. Accordingly, it would now take two-and-a-half days to reach Jiddah. But we shall waste a lot of time in quarantine. So it looks like we shall not reach the port before Friday.

The sun set at 9.00. Now there is a difference of almost 2.45 hours between my watch and that of the ship. The Piram Island is six hours away.[1] By late afternoon, we expect to enter the Strait of Ahmar.[2] We didn't berth at Aden; in fact, we didn't even venture close to the coast.

The ship's speed has slackened for some reason. That is why the Piram Island appeared before us at 4 o'clock (according to the ship's time). Its lighthouses (minar i-raushni) were visible from a distance. There are several of them across the length of this island. The Lasalki station can be seen with its barracks, mounted canons, and a military ship anchored close to the coast, and petrol and kerosene depots. The buildings are beautifully built in the English style. We see smaller dwellings for coolies. Our government has turned this tiny island into a fortified stronghold.

---

1 Piram Island is approachable by a machine boat in about an hour's sailing by ML *Piram* of the Lighthouse Department from Ghoga Port. The lighthouse is about 1.5 km from the landing point. Researchers claim to have found evidences of the Jurassic age there.

Piram Island before Independence was part of Bhavnagar State, whose rulers had built a bastion on the southwest corner of the island to keep a watch on the maritime activities in the region. The British realized the importance of the location and built the 24 m high circular masonry lighthouse tower on the bastion in 1864–5. A wick lamp with catadioptric arrangement in the lantern house was installed which started functioning in November 1865. The Custom Supervisor of Ghoga regularly visited the station. The equipment was replaced by a 4th order dioptric system in 1895. The lighthouse expert D. Alan Stevenson visited the station in February 1927 and appreciated the maintenance but pointed out certain defects in optic and lantern. According to the old inspection book available at the station, John Oswald, Chief Inspector of Lighthouses, visited the station on 18 February 1931, 10 March 1935, and 14 February 1938.

2 Bahr al-Ahmar in Arabic. The Red Sea branches off the Indian Ocean between Egypt and the Arabian Peninsula, and thus forms the boundary between the two continents of Asia and Africa. At its northern end, it is divided by the Sinai Peninsula into two long inlets—to the west, the Gulf of Suez, which is linked with the Mediterranean by the Suez Canal, and to the east, the Gulf of Aqaba. At its southern end is the Bab al-Mandeb (Gate of Lamentation).

The Suez at one end of the Red Sea and the Piram Island at the other end of the Persian Gulf are the custodians of Hindustan. No European power can attack us from this sea route. There is no one to equal the British Empire—either in its navy or its military might.[1]

(As for 'Aad, they were arrogant in the land without right, and) they said, who is mightier than us in power?

It is 8.00 p.m. by my watch (by the ship's watch it is 5.15 p.m.). There are still 40–5 minutes left for the sun to set. The ship sails north. We have entered the Strait of Ahmar. On our left is the dark continent of Africa, on the right the coast of Tihama[2] and Yemen. The qibla moves from the north to the east. By the time we reach Jiddah, it shall point directly towards the east. God-willing, we'll reach the Kamaran (Qumran) Island tomorrow (an island west of Yemen).

Tuesday, 26 February

From early morning, there was much hustle and bustle on the ship. Everyone was busy collecting their belongings and setting things apart for the quarantine to take place. There was a slight cover of clouds on the sky and a brisk wind. The sea was turbulent. We were worried. It seemed dangerous to get off the ship's ladder to get into the boats that would row us ashore. But Allah's benevolence intervened. The clouds dispersed as we reached Kamaran and a rainbow appeared on the northern sky slowly arching down to the sea. With the turbulence dying down, the strong winds weakened. By 9.00 in the morning, we safely reached Kamaran. The island's governor came on board with a doctor. A small steamer pulled two big boats from the coast. The pilgrims started boarding them. I stayed on board, having decided to take the last boat. The other passengers were ferried to the shore.

Each boat carried approximately 250 hajjis. The last one left at 4.00 p.m. My friend Munshi Mohammad Yusuf and I, along with the remaining passengers, boarded it. Given the pleasant weather, we hit the shore leisurely and comfortably. First, we entered the fumigation shed, removed our clothes, and tied lungis[3] around our legs.

---

1 In India, Mirza Abu Talib first expressed this idea.

2 Tihamah or Tihama is a narrow coastal region of Arabia on the Red Sea. It refers to the entire coastline from the Gulf of Aqaba to the Bab al-Mandeb Strait, but it usually refers only to the section adjacent to southern Hijaz (south of Jiddah), Asr and Yemen.

3 A garment consisting of a piece of cloth, in which a variety of designs and colours are used. It is worn wrapped around the hips and extends up to the ankles.

I had already kept my cash and papers in a cigar box. I held on to it firmly so that the papers would not get wet during fumigation. Clothes and shoes were placed in the fumigator. We had carried our beddings with us, which Munshi Mohammad Yusuf Sahib had packed in a bag. Fortunately, his glass and *lota*,[1] along with some fruits and sweets, escaped the fumigator.

Having left our belongings, we entered a chamber where the people stood in row upon row like prisoners. A doctor came, checked our pulse without saying anything, and went away. Thereafter, we entered the bathroom. Jets of water gushed from the ceilings like fountains. Everyone was forced to have a shower under it. Afterwards, we went back to the first room with no clothes on, except for the lungis around our waists. Here we expected to get back our clothes after fumigation, but that did not happen for a while. For almost an hour, we stayed locked in the room without any clothes on. Eventually, they came in bundles. As luck would have it, ours were in the last lot. We put them on and came out of the prison. There was hardly much time left for the Asr namaz (the afternoon four *rakat* prayer; the third of the five daily prayers). We offered two rakat namaz quickly and hurried towards our camp.

The island's weather is pleasant. The camps for the hajjis are constructed in an orderly fashion. They are spacious, with electricity and sufficient provisions for ablutions. The mosque is good. But the toilets are not. For 1,800 hajjis there are only 20 latrines, of which eight are for women and a dozen for men.

I feel immeasurably good. Maybe, it is owing to the island's climate or perhaps the result of having set foot on land after a week and a half. Everyone seemed happy. With a new teahouse, the camp wore a festive mood all night long. Groceries, bread, and boiled eggs were being sold. Chicken, too, was inexpensive. First, I had tea, biscuits and eggs at the tea stall. Then, I dined with Dr Abdur Rehman Sahib, whom I have mentioned earlier. A little later, upon the insistence of Akbar Umar, the muallim of Mohammad Yusuf and his friend Khalid Bisauni, I tasted a few morsels of biryani. It had been cooked in the Bedouin style,[2] after the slaughter of a lamb. I didn't approve of it.

---

1 A small brass pot used for carrying water. It is also used for purposes of ablution prior to the namaz.

2 Member of a community of Arabic-speaking desert nomads. Bedouins have

Wednesday, 27 February

We had been preparing for our departure all morning. The sea was rough again. The wind had whipped up and the boats were bobbing so violently that it filled my heart with dread to even look at them. For the first time, I experienced sea sickness. By Allah's grace, we reached the ship safely but I was so mentally disturbed that I could not find the way to my cabin. I reached my room after taking several wrong turnings. It was an especially hard day for women. With the difficulty faced in aligning the boats with the ship's stern, everybody apprehended that an untoward incident might take place. But that did not happen. Allah kept everyone safe and the hajjis managed to reach the ship safely. The ship pulled anchor after 1.00 p.m. The wretched matter of quarantine is finally behind us. Now we await Yalamlam,[1] approximately 22 hours away from Kamaran.

At this point, it would be appropriate to record an incident that should instil the fear of Allah in everyone. A Muslim who was employed on the ship told me that every year he received almost Rs 300–400 as bribes from the hajjis, but this year he had received nothing. He was sad that the company had made better provisions for water and, as a result, he had lost his earnings. He was aggrieved that water taps had been installed in the first class; till last year, he used to earn a handsome sum from the first class passengers. I had taken exception to the hardships endured by the passengers in securing enough water this year, but now I gather that it was much worse during the previous years. Sadly,

---

traditionally made their living through animal husbandry, and rearing of camels, sheep, goat, and cattle. The tribe is a community of equals headed by a sheikh.

1 Nearly five or six miles from Mecca on different sides there are stages called 'Miqat'. These are Zul Hulaifa on the vicinity of Madina-Hujfah on the Syrian road, Qarn on the Najd road, Zate Iraq on the Iraq road, and Yalamlam on the Yalamlam road. When a hajji reaches any one of these stages he wears his 'ihram' or white wrappers after which he is not allowed to wear any garment such as shirt, trousers, cap, and so on. He should cover his head and face and should not cut his hair and beard. He should abstain from hunting and quarrelling with any one. He must put a stop to sexual intercourse also. Thus, consecrated entirely to God he should proceed towards the sacred territory till he arrives at an elevated place or descends a valley or enters the city of Mecca, when he should mutter continuously 'Labbaika' meaning 'Here I am O God'. On reaching the enclosure of the city he should go to the 'Masjidul Haram' first and standing before Kaaba recite Allah-o-Akbar. He then should kiss *Hajr-e-Aswad* or the Black Stone. Afterwards he should fulfil the ritual of Tawaf or circuit around Kaaba seven times.

even Muslim employees were a party to inflicting torment upon their brothers and extracted illegal bribes from them!

هر کس از دست غیر ناله کند

سعدی از دست خویشتن فریاد !!

Har kas az dast-e-gheir naleh kunad
Saadi az dast-e-kheeshtan faryaad.

Everyone blames others, but Sadi blames himself.

A man from Kashgar,[1] accompanied by his wife and daughter, is also a fellow-traveller. He had reached Kashmir from Kashgar (Chinese Turkestan) after travelling on horseback for 40 days. He boarded the ship from Karachi. I marvelled at his courage. Truly, the hajj belongs to such men of piety. May the Merciful and Beneficent Allah accept our hajj too because of him! Their daughter, who is eight or nine years old, is extremely pretty. She looks like a Chinese doll. She too travelled with her parents on horseback for 40 days and reached here after a long and arduous journey.

Now there is a three-hour difference between my time and that of the ship. By our time, the sun set at 9.00 p.m. but it was 6.00 p.m. according to the ship's watch.

Thursday, 28 February

Just before daybreak, I saw my dear departed father in my dream. I embraced him and cried. It is all because of his blessings that a sinner like me has been granted the privilege of hajj. The moment for which I have waited for months has finally arrived. In a few hours, the ship shall reach Yalamlam. I took a bath, wore the ihram, offered two rakat namaz, and prayed to the Almighty Allah:

O Lord! Cause not our hearts to stray after you have guided us, and bestow upon us mercy from Thy Presence. Indeed only you are the bestower. (Quran: Al-Imran 8)

I made the *niyat* (literally, intention) for umrah and began saying,

---

1 Now an autonomous region of China. It has been a political and commercial centre from very early times. It is almost directly north of Tashkurgan through which traffic passed from the ancient Buddhist kingdom of Gandhara, in what is now Pakistan, and Jalalabad in eastern Afghanistan.

O Lord, I respond to your call, I respond to you who has no partner, I respond to you, indeed you deserve all praise and you bestow all blessings, you have all the might, there is no one who shares your power, your authority. I respond to you, O Lord.

It is owing to Allah's infinite mercy that a sinner like me has been allowed to see this blessed day and brought this close to His door. Overwhelmed by emotion, I wept tears of joy. It is 12.15 a.m. I write this diary wearing the ihram. The ship has not sounded the siren for reaching Yalamlam. This was done, upon the Captain's orders, after 4.00. We could not see Yalamlam, but the Captain could, through his binoculars. He would have also calculated the distance and estimated our approaching Yalamlam. Most hajjis had worn the ihram before noon, because they wanted to err on the side of caution and not wait for the Captain's signal. We had heard that Yalamlam can be reached after 22 hours from Kamaran but today it took 27, almost 28 hours. It is being said that our ship will reach Jiddah by eight or nine. Let us see when it does so, and what occurs there.

By now, all passengers are virtually in the same uniform. They wear nothing but a *tehmad*[1] and a chadar.

It is worth noting that I had left my homeland on a Thursday and I have tied the ihram on a Thursday.

O Lord bless my people on their arrival on Thursday.

---

1 Often sewn into a cylindrical shape, it is worn around the waist, running to the feet.

4
In Jiddah

Friday, 1 March

The ship docked near Jiddah at 9.00 a.m. A couple of officials from Hijaz came aboard to talk to the Captain and inspect the sanitary conditions. Thereafter, they let the passengers disembark. Sailboats surrounded our ship from all sides. Arab sailors clambered aboard and began to fling the pilgrims' luggage on their boats. Our ship was anchored three to four miles from the coast. Fearing that the sailboats would take long to ferry us ashore, my fellow traveller Munshi Mohammad Yusuf tried through his muallim, Akbar Umar, to arrange for a steam launch. The muallim, a resourceful man, arranged for a place for us through the good offices of a head clerk in the Mogul Line. We handed our luggage to him, got into the steamer, and headed towards the shore. As we approached Jiddah, we came across cliffs under the water. That is why boats take a circuitous route to reach the shore. The colour of the waters, too, is green in some places and turquoise at other places. It is possible that these rocks are mines (*maadan*) for precious stones. One day, this patch of sea may turn fertile.

There are two stations beside the dock: one for passengers and another one close by for the unloading luggage. We reached 15–20 minutes before the other passengers. After walking about the dock for some time, the port officers allowed us to enter the station door. Every passenger was charged 15 annas per head for the boats. We had not come on the hired boats but on the steamer of the Mogul Company. We had boarded it with the permission of the Company's head clerk, Munshi Azizuddin Sahib, who had come with us from the ship till the shore. We got a chance to know him on the ride; we learnt that he belonged to Zilla Barabanki.[1] But when we were asked to pay the boat's fee, it seemed unnecessary to give all the above-mentioned details; we quietly paid the 15 anna fee. We entered another room to find several gentlemen sitting on chairs. I was asked who my muallim was.

I said: 'Abdul Qadir Sikandar.'

Immediately, someone seized my arm, handed me over to his servant or slave, and impounded my passport and return ticket. Mohammad Yusuf Sahib and I had planned to stay together in Jiddah and Mecca, but we were already being separated.

The gentlemen in chairs were the lawyers for the muallimin of Mecca. Abdul Qadir Sikandar's lawyer caught hold of me, and Akbar Umar's lawyer did the same to him. Swaleh Bisyoni was my lawyer; Yusuf Sahib's lawyer was called either Abdur Razzaq or Abdul Karim. Abdur Razzaq was a reasonable man. He came to know that Mohammad Yusuf Sahib and I wanted to be together, so he told my lawyer to either take away the two of us or hand me over to Abdur Razzaq. Clearly, Swaleh and Razzaq were on good terms. Swaleh agreed to let his victim stay as ransom with another bounty-hunter. Mohammad Yusuf Sahib and I were thus united after a few minutes of separation. An employee of the lawyer's was appointed to look after us. He took us to the dock where the luggage was being unloaded. After about two hours, our bags were taken off the boat. My new trunk was broken in the process, and Mohammad Yusuf's canister, half-filled with ghee (clarified butter, an important ingredient in Indian cuisine) got washed away. These were the only losses we suffered.

I had heard that passengers who come by sea were subjected to a severe search of their belongings; now the roughness of the Indian port authorities seemed nothing when compared to the Immigration Department of Jiddah. Every suitcase was opened up. Every article of clothing was closely inspected. Pillows were stripped of their cases and torn open to see if they hid valuable bolts of cloth. Books were impounded. My cigar box was taken away. Mohammad Yusuf Sahab and I had two or three electric lamps and a couple of spare batteries, which we had kept, fearing that these might be difficult to find in Arabia. The

1 One of the districts of Uttar Pradesh in India. Being in close proximity to Lucknow, the district assumed some degree of importance under the British. Located within the district were a number of qasbas. Barabanki was also the home of some prominent Sufis, notably Haji Waris Ali Shah and Shah Abdur Razzaq of Bansa Sharif. The ulama of Firangi Mahal belonged to the Barabanki district.

lamps were returned to us after due inspection but the government servants carefully pocketed our batteries. We had a couple of bottles of English candy. Some of those too found their way into their pockets.[1]

We stood still and silent, patient and praise-giving, supine in following God's will. Had they stuffed all our belongings into their pockets, what right did we have to complain? Each box and bedding was stamped after inspection and after much mishandling we were finally allowed to take away our damaged and diminished belongings. I was told that my cigar box would be handed over to me after I had paid the toll tax. About the books, I was told that nothing could be said at this point; there was no knowing whether they would be allowed to go beyond the port or not. Grateful to have our lives intact and believing that what we had lost was a small recompense, we came out of the station and loaded our luggage on a cart. The servants of the lawyer, Abdur Razzaq, took us to his house.

Approximately 1,900 hajjis had stepped off the *Rehmani*. Almost all would have faced the same trauma. So, one can speculate that not all hajjis would have been freed on the same day. The checking of luggage, having gone on till late, is likely to continue over the next few days. I have decided to leave my cigar box and books behind and proceed to Mecca. If the government decides to return my belongings, my lawyer can accept them on my behalf, and it is not worth fretting over them too much.

By 2 o'clock, we reached the lawyer's house. After the Zuhr prayers, lunch was laid out on the *dastarkhwan* and we sat down to eat. The food was delicious. Tonight, we'll sleep here. Our passports are with the lawyers. They are, in turn, busy getting the bags of the other passengers inspected in the Immigration Department. Tomorrow, Inshaallah, we shall head towards Mecca.

Saturday, 2 March

The day dawned at the house of the lawyer, Abdur Razzaq. He is a hospitable and sincere man. An employee of (another) lawyer named Abdul Karim, he has been asked to put us up at his home. We shared

---

1 Nawab Sikander Begum described how her goods were lost or stolen. See Nawab Sikandar Begum (2007), *A Princess's Pilgrimage*, Edited, introduced and with an Afterword by Siobhan Lambert-Hurley, Delhi, pp. 7–26.

our room with a Munshi Muniruddin from Hyderabad.[1] The three of us, that is, Mohammad Yusuf, Munshi Muniruddin, and I are guests of Abdur Razzaq. My passport is with Swaleh Bisyoni. I don't know where he lives. Mohammad Yusuf Sahib's passport is with Abdur Razzaq. We do not know his whereabouts either.

A new rule has come into effect this year: that the hajjis have to deposit their return tickets at the office of the British Consul. The tickets were to be returned after hajj. The hajjis are angry at this stringent regulation, because, besides making rounds of offices, they are expected to pander to the whims of the clerks. But why should a ruler be concerned with the plight of the pilgrims? Their real design is that the number of pilgrims should go down and all the wealth of the world should not reach the Jaziratul Arab [the Island of the Arabs][2] to be expended. But this secret can never be revealed in clear words; instead, expediency is resorted to and attempts are made to inflict inconveniences so that, frustrated, the hajjis might drop out of the journey to Hijaz. Forcing the poor pilgrims to deposit their tickets at the British Consul's office and, on this pretext, making them come several times to bow subserviently before the embassy staff is obviously a ploy meant to benefit the locals.

I tried in vain not to deposit my ticket at the embassy, but the lawyers admonished me and warned that those failing to deposit their tickets would face official retribution. Hence, they too were helpless. The Afghans were told, despite their defiance, that they would not be allowed to leave Jiddah till they had deposited their tickets and presented themselves at the embassy. How could the Afghans know that the embassy is also the Kaaba[3] and its circumambulation is more sacred than going around the Baitullah!

To cut a long story short, my return ticket was forcibly taken away and deposited at the British Consul. It is a good thing that I did not have to go to the embassy personally; otherwise, I would have spoken to the officials and refused to hand over my ticket. As one who holds a first class ticket, I was not required to be there in person. Instead, the ticket was deposited through my lawyer and I was given a receipt.

---

1 A Quranic scholar and former *khatib* of Mecca Masjid, Hyderabad, India.

2 The name given by the Arabs to the Arabian Peninsula.

3 The Prophet stated, 'Turn then thy face in the direction of the Sacred Mosque: wherever ye are, turn your faces in that direction.'

We set out to explore the city in the afternoon. We found the markets closed because of Ramazan. All through this holy month, business is conducted during the night and people spend the better part of the day sleeping. Later in the afternoon, we saw a compound that once had a grave, which is said to be that of Eve. Peace be upon her! It has been razed by the order of Ibn Saud, the ruler of Hijaz.[1] There is no trace of the grave but those who know point it out and believing Indians turn in its general direction and offer fateha. We returned from the compound and once again saw the bazaar. By now, the shops had opened and there was much hustle and bustle. All sorts of essential commodities are available here. The sun was about to set. I looked for the office of the Netherland Trading Company in whose name I had brought a letter of credit (hundi). But we couldn't find it. Time was short and I had no immediate need of money so I didn't try very hard.

As we headed back home, we met Akbar Umar. We had to join him for iftar. We were not fasting but since we had not bought anything to eat from the market during the day, we had virtually been on a fast. We ate well. Then came the delightful news that a car would pick us up in an hour's time and we would be on our way to Mecca. This good news washed away the day's troubles. Why just the day's troubles—in fact, all the inconveniences of the journey. After Maghrib, we waited for the car at home.

After the Isha prayers at 8.00, we left Jiddah. The small car was a four-seater. It had three other people besides me: Mohammad Yusuf, Muniruddin Hyderabadi, and a certain hajji from Etah. We paid Rs 8 per head for the ride. The car could not carry much luggage; so, we had to hire a camel to transport the rest of our baggage. We gave Re 1 to the lawyer Abdur Razzaq so that he could send our luggage on to Mecca the next day. Muniruddin Sahib too had to pay only half the fare for hiring the camel. The government had fixed 8 annas for the lawyer's fee. We paid this, but I had to pay double the amount because Abdur Razzaq had served me and I should, rightfully, pay him. But I couldn't deprive my appointed lawyer, Swaleh Bisyoni. We were so overjoyed at the prospect of going to Mecca that we did not mind paying the lawyers

1 Abdul Aziz Al-Saud, King of Saudi Arabia (? 1876–9 November 1953) was the first monarch of Saudi Arabia. He is also known as Ibn Saud. He was born in Riyadh in the House of Saud, which had historically maintained dominion over the interior highlands of Arabia known as the Nejd.

extra money. In fact, the three of us ended up paying far more than the prescribed fee to Abdur Razzaq. Apart from this, we also offered 4 annas to Swaleh Bisyoni.

It used to be a two-day journey from Jiddah to Mecca. It meant traversing waterless deserts and mountains. There was the fear of dacoits and Beduoins. But now, thanks to the motor cars, the journey can be made in two hours. Along the way, there are four or five halts where tea is ready and waiting to be served. Policemen are stationed who keep a watchful eye on the motors to make sure that they don't carry more than the prescribed number of passengers. One can walk alone on this road at midnight no robber can dare waylay you. These days, because of Ramazan, most passengers prefer travelling during the night but there are no incidents of looting. My motor broke down near the mountains at 10.00 in the night and we had to get off. For nearly half an hour, we stood by the road while the driver tried to change the wheel. But there was no cause for fear. We saw several pilgrims walking alone. They looked fearless. Whenever we approached a halting station, a small fair would spring up.

At Behra, we did the *tajdeed* (literally, renewal) for *wuzoo* and drank tea. As we left, our fellow traveller, Muniruddin Hyderabadi, forgot his pouch with all his papers and money on a stool. The pouch carried his passport and the receipt for his return ticket. We had to plead with the driver to take us back. The driver belonged to a place called Sumatra. We had offered him tea. So he was kind enough to take us back. As we approached Behra, the owner handed us the pouch with all its contents intact. Till a few years ago, it would not have been possible to return to the halting station, nor would we have hoped to find our belongings. The present government has brought about such peace in this island there can be no other place like this after Quroon-e-Ula.[1]

Around midnight, we saw the lights of Mecca. First the driver, then the rest of us, shouted 'Labbaika' loudly! Our hearts jumped with joy. Like moths to a flame, we raced towards that light with abandon. The tongue and the pen cannot describe the state of our mind at that instant.

Alhamdulillah ...

The car station is at a distance of about a mile from the Haram Sharif. The muallim gather here to welcome the hajjis. Yusuf, Sikandar's

1 The people of ancient times.

employee, who had come to the ship to welcome us, was there. Akbar Umar's brother came to receive Mohammad Yusuf. Muniruddin's muallim was in Hyderabad. Therefore, there was no one to receive him. We tried to stay together here, as we had in Jiddah. The muallims told us that we must perform the first tawaf[1] separately, each with our own muallim, and later we could decide where to stay. Therefore, I left with Yusuf, and Mohammad Yusuf Sahib, along with Muniruddin Hyderabadi, left with Jafar Umar. We encountered a problem at the station itself: Muniruddin Sahib's baggage, which also had his clothes, was missing from the car. There was no way of knowing if it had got left behind in Jiddah itself or whether it had been lost somewhere on the way. For a few minutes, we enquired at the station itself but learnt nothing. Eventually, we gave up and walked towards the Haram Mohtaram. The muallim, Yusuf, took me to an Arab who was Abdul Qadir Sikandar's lawyer and, in Sikandar's absence, led the hajjis for tawaf. The Arab knew no English. I don't know what he was trying to ask me in his language. After some time, a man who knew some broken Hindustani, offered to translate and I discovered that he was merely enquiring about my health. After a few minutes, I was asked what I would pay as fee for my first tawaf. Already, I was getting impatient with the Arab's attitude; now, his question saddened me. I answered that my friend Mohammad Yusuf Sahib had gone for the tawaf with Akbar Yusuf Sahib. Whatever amount he would offer his muallim, I would do the same. This suggestion was turned down and I was instructed to first decide an amount myself, and if I didn't have the money with me (because due to the ahram I had no pocket), I could take a loan from someone and offer it to the Arab. But this was not acceptable to me. The Arab was greatly offended by my impertinence and Allah knows what he said in his language to me. He told Yusuf to remove my belongings from his home. Yusuf pleaded with the Arab to allow my bags to stay there for another ten or fifteen minutes, at least till my tawaf and saii.[2] Later, my bags would be transferred somewhere else. Having received the go-ahead, Yusuf took me to the Masjidul Haram[3] and did the tawaf

1 Literally means 'circumambulation'. In Islam, it refers to the act of walking around the Kaaba. People usually do this during umrah or hajj.

2 The act of walking between the two hills—Safa and Marwa—during the hajj.

3 Masjidul Haram, 'The Sacred Mosque', is located in the city of Mecca. It surrounds the Kaaba, the place which Muslims turn towards while offering daily prayer. The mosque is also commonly known as the Haram or Haram Sharif.

with me. The needless unpleasantness with the Arab had cast a shadow over me. Also, there was the sorrow that here I was doing my first tawaf with a person who was not learned or versed in the correct way of doing the tawaf. Maybe, if I had held my head and postponed the decision of choosing the muallim till we had reached Jiddah, this entire unfortunate episode could have been avoided.

چرا کارے کند عاقل کہ باز آید پشیمانی

Chara kari kunad aaqil ke baaz aayed pashemani.

Why do wise men do things which cause embarrassment?

When I return to India, I shall surely tell friends and acquaintances to beware of falling into the deceiving traps of the muallims who come to India to ensnare unwary pilgrims, and that they should not sell their freedom to any muallim till they have reached Jiddah. My muallim, Abdul Qadir Sikandar, is having a good time in Lucknow. His son hunts for prey among the hajjis at Bombay. Yusuf, his employee who received me at the ship, is ignorant about the correct way of performing the tawaf and saii. Such muallims have no right to charge a fee of Rs 25–30 from their clients. *Barguzishta salwat ainda ra ehteyat* (He first salutes then neglects). Having completed the tawaf, I was made to stand beside the Maqam-e-Ibrahim,[1] where I offered two rakat namaz. Meanwhile, my friend Mohammad Yusuf Sahib along with Muniruddin Hyderabadi showed up at this holy spot. They were accompanied by their lawyer Akbar Umar's brother, Jafar Umar, who came after having finished the *tawaful bait*. Yusuf handed me over to Jafar Umar for going to Safa-Marwa.[2]

He himself went off towards the Arab's home to transfer my belongings. Jafar Umar looks like a nice young man. He instructed us how to do the saii and read the *Dua-e Masura*. I am grateful to Allah that we were able to perform the umrah. Having received this great privilege, we went to Jafar Umar's house. We met his father, the Khalifa of Hajji Imdadullah Muhajir (a person who migrates) Makki and a pious old gentleman. Yusuf had already brought my belongings and deposited

1 Maqam-e-Ibrahim, said to be a stone from Paradise, is 30 metres away from the Kaaba door where Prophet Abraham used to stand when he was building the Kaaba.

2 Al-Safa and Al-Marwa are two small hills, now located in the Masjidul Haram in Mecca, Saudi Arabia, between which Muslims travel back and forth seven times during the ritual pilgrimages of hajj and umrah.

them before our arrival. After some time, tea was served and with it we had some food for sehri. I drank tea and made the niyat for roza. Then I went to the Haram Sharif with Umar Sahib, and offered my Fajr namaz with the congregation. Later, we returned home and went to sleep before sunrise.

Sunday, 3 March

We woke at about 9.00. A barber was sent for. This was the first time that I had my head shaven. I took off the ihram and wore stitched clothes. Then we set off in search of our lodgings. A man from Munshi Mohammad Yusuf's part of the country, Mohammad Hanif Zardoz, had been living in Mecca for a long time. He is in India these days due to some reason but his two wives are here. Both belong to Allahabad. Mohammad Hanif has gone to India on the *Rehmani*. He had met Mohammad Yusuf Sahib in Jiddah and it was decided that Mohammad Yusuf Sahib and I would stay at his house. Our breakfast and dinner too would be taken care of by him. A lump sum of Rs 150 would be given to cover our board and lodging; of this, half would be paid immediately and the rest later.

We left Umar Sahib's house and came to Mohammad Hanif's. The Haram Sharif is a five-minute walk away. The house is not too good but the food is. We agreed to live here hoping to have Indian meals. We informed Mohammad Hanif's elder wife that our bags would reach by the evening. Later, we went to the Haram Sharif and offered the Zuhr namaz. We returned to Umar Sahib's house and went to sleep.

By Asr, we had our bags sent to Mohammad Hanif's house and offered our prayers at the Haram-e Mohtaram. Until iftar, we read various *wazifa*.[1] We opened our fast with the zumzum water and dates. After Maghrib, we went to Umar's house as he had invited Mohammad Yusuf Sahib and me for dinner. We ate dinner, drank tea, and returned home. We ate a couple of paans and once again left for the Haram Sharif, and were blessed to be able to offer our Isha prayers and once again perform the tawaf. We returned home after 9.00. Exhausted by the journey, we decided to call it a day. This city is infested with mosquitoes

---

1 A wazifa normally consists of prayer formulas, invocations and verses from the Quran, which is read by devout Muslims. Also, the Sufi practice of reciting and meditating the qualities of Allah either aloud or in silent thought.

and ticks. There isn't much of a breeze either. The mosquitoes troubled us so much that we could not sleep for even half an hour.

Monday, 4 March

The Maghrib prayer is offered at 12.00; the beginning of the day too is said to be mid-day. There is a difference of not more than three hours from the Indian time, but since it has been assumed here that both morning and evening are at 12.00, in this holy city—albeit in all of Arabia—clocks are set according to this calculation. We have to live here for several months and so we decided to set our watches according to the local time. A canon is sounded at 7.30 a.m. to mark the time for the *tahajjud*[1] namaz and sehri. Two canons are shot at 10.15 a.m. to mark the end of sehri. There are still ten minutes left for sehri. The morning *azaan*[2] is sounded at 11.00 a.m. and normally one has performed the namaz by 11.30 a.m. The sun rises by about 12.30. By 6.00 p.m., the azaan is sounded for the Zuhr namaz and the congregation assembles by 6.15 p.m. The Asr azaan is at 9.30 p.m. and the namaz is 15 minutes later. The time for iftar is 12 sharp. That is when the canon is sounded yet again. The Isha azaan takes place at 2.00 a.m.; the namaz is offered 15 minutes later.

In order to adhere to the schedule, we woke the ladies who were our hosts at 8.30 in the morning. Sehri was sent to us at 9.00. By 10.00, Mohammad Yusuf Sahib and I reached the Haram Sharif and offered Namaz-e-Tahajjud and performed the tawaf. By 11.30, we had completed our Namaz-e-Fajr and returned home. We hadn't slept the previous night. Now it was pleasantly cool and the mosquitoes too had taken pity on our plight. We slept for three or four hours, and then came out and went to Akbar Umar Sahib's house. Here we found everyone to be fast asleep. It is the practice here for most people to stay awake all night and then to sleep till the Zuhr namaz. As in Jiddah, here too the bazaars open at night. Lights and festivities go on all night long in the streets and bazaars.

1 An optional prayer that is supposed to be performed in the middle of the night. It is not one of the five obligatory prayers required of all Muslims, yet Prophet Mohammad is recorded as performing it many times and encouraging his companions to offer it for its many rewards and benefits.

2 The call for the daily prayers five times a day. The azaan is composed of specific words and phrases to be recited loudly in the Arabic language so that the neighbours can recognize the time schedule for the prayers.

While returning from Akbar Umar's house, we met Nawab Ali Katbi, a resident of Rampur. This gentleman has lived here for the past ten or fifteen years. He has got married here, and has children. He has a bookshop near Baab-e Salaam, which is the source of his income and livelihood. My younger brother, Shafiq Ahmad Alawi is employed in the princely state (*riyasat*) of Rampur, and they are known to each other. And so I had decided to meet him before setting out from Hindustan. And I had instructed all my friends and relatives to send my letters in his care. I was pleased to meet him thus by chance. I enquired about my post and was told that a letter was waiting for me at the shop. Mohammad Yusuf Sahib and I reached the Baab-e Salaam before Zuhr. We met Nawab Ali, took the letter that was, incidentally, from my younger brother Shafiq. The letter also contained a missive for Nawab Ali, sent by some relative of his. Nawab Ali Sahib had met us with every sign of delight; after receiving this letter, he began to be even more kindly disposed towards us.

The mosquitoes troubled us all night. So we enquired about mosquito nets. Nawab Ali told us that they were commonly used and could be found in the shops. He then instructed his munshi to purchase two of them so that we could get them by Asr and not be troubled in the night. We also learnt that the post from Hindustan reaches here on the 6th, 16th, or 26th of every month according to the English calendar, and is sent out on the 9th, 19th, and 29th. Except for Shafiq Ahmad's letter, Mohammad Yusuf Sahib and I have not received any other letter. We began waiting for the 6th of March to come, offered the Zuhr namaz, and returned home. Having rested for an hour or two, we went to Baab-e Salaam.

At Asr, we found the mosquito nets waiting. The big net cost 2 riyals and the smaller one 1.15 riyals. Mohammad Yusuf Sahib and I bought both and thanked Allah for freeing us from the mosquito menace. The riyal is the bigger currency here. It is bigger than the Indian rupee and is equivalent to 24 qarsh. Half a riyal and a quarter of a riyal are also in vogue; and they are equivalent to 11 qarsh and five and a half qarsh, respectively. The qarsh is made of nickel and is equal to an Indian anna. A half qarsh is equal to half an anna and a quarter qarsh is equal to one paisa.[1] No copper coins are accepted here. A silver Indian coin is accepted but with a deduction.

---

1 A coin, equivalent to 1/100th of a rupee, is used in several countries including India, Nepal and Pakistan.

I opened my fast with Umar Sahib in the Haram Sharif with dates and zumzum. After namaz, Umar Sahib took us to Bataif-ul-Heel and offered us dinner. We had barely finished eating when the camels carrying our luggage from Jiddah arrived. I found Mohammad Yusuf Sahib's bags and mine loaded atop the camels. The bags would be unloaded at the lawyer's house tonight and reach our house some time tomorrow. We finished dinner and came home, drank tea, ate a few paans, and presented ourselves at the Haram Sharif for the Isha prayers. We were blessed by the tawaf, returned home, put up our mosquito nets, and went to sleep. Today our friend, that is, the paans from Hindustan, finished and we began to use dry paan leaves.

Tuesday, 5 March

I offer all the five namaz in the Haram Sharif. I also offer the tahajjud and partake of iftar in the Haram. Therefore, there is no need to mention these daily occurrences. I shall only record the changes, if any, in my daily programme.

Our bags, which had come from Jiddah, reached our house by Zuhr. The customs have freed the books, though they have not reached me yet. Perhaps, they are with the lawyer. The cigar box has still not arrived. It won't be much of a loss in case it doesn't come, because from the moment I have entered Mecca, I stopped smoking cheroots. May Allah be praised, so far I have felt no discomfort.

Nawab Ali Sahib hosted a dinner for Mohammad Yusuf Sahib and me. His shop is inside the boundary of the Haram Sharif. He served us a delicious meal. But the savour of opening the fast with dates and zumzum in the Haram Sharif was missing in these delicious and lip-smacking dishes.

Eight or nine of my garments have vinegar stains and they need to be washed. There are laundry shops where you can get clothes washed. I asked a launderer the charge for washing one garment. At first he said three qarsh; then he said that he'd first ask his master and let me know. We were pleased, thinking that the master would reduce the amount but, unfortunately, the master took one look at our faces and said he would charge four qarsh per garment and return the clothes after two days. We could scarcely afford to pay this much. Mohammad Hanif's wife told us that she would get our clothes washed by a woman at a much less fee. So we abandoned the idea of giving our clothes to the laundry.

Wednesday, 6 March

There is no letter from Hindustan. Nor is there any hope of getting any news before the 16th of March. In the evening, we spotted the ihram-clad Dr Abdur Rehman Sahib who had come to distribute medicines on behalf of the state of Hyderabad. He was supposed to have travelled straight from Jiddah to Medina. We found out that he was not able to get a car to take him straight to Medina. Since he didn't want to waste time hanging around Jiddah, he chose to come here instead so that he could enjoy the benefit of doing the umrah during Ramazan.

Thursday, 7 March

After the Isha prayer at the Masjid-e Taneem,[1] Mohammad Yusuf Sahib, Muniruddin Hyderabadi and I performed the umra. We finished the tawaf and saii after midnight. Alhamdulillah ala zalik.

Friday, 8 March

I am blessed by being able to offer namaz for the last Friday of Ramazan in the Masjidul Haram. A lakh or a lakh and a half people have assembled from almost every part of the world. The largest numbers are from Java. Its inhabitants come for the hajj with the utmost sense of devotion and piety in their hearts and minds. It is said that they don't get married till they have performed this sacred duty. They bring much reward to the shopkeepers of Mecca, because the Javanese consider it essential to buy one entire outfit—from a cap to the shoes—from Mecca. They are courageous. Everyday, they do the niyat for umra from the Masjid-e Taneem and spend the entire day reading the Quran. Their most singular quality is that they do not indulge in begging. I have never seen anyone begging in the Haram Sharif. Those from Arabia or Sudan ask for alms with impunity and a big chunk of pilgrims from our heavenly Hindustan possibly undertake this journey to Saudi Arabia, on the way to Mecca so that they can adopt the profession of seeking alms in the Baitul Haram. *Inna lil-laahe wa inna ilaihi rajioon.*[2]

---

1 This place is near Mecca and acts as a miqat for people living in Mecca. The ihram for umrah is worn at this place. It is also known as Masjid-e Aisha.

2 When struck with a calamity, he/she submits to Allah and says this expression, which means: 'We belong to Allah and to Him we shall be returned.'

A small contingent of pilgrims has come from Anatolia. I am struck with amazement when I see their faces. Once upon a time they were the rulers over this land and now no one bothers about them. The bigger part of the present building of the Masjidul Haram is a memorial to Sultan Selim[1] and Suleiman the Great.[2] Every nook and corner of Mecca is buried under the weight of the benevolence and determination of the Turkish Sultans. In fact, the Islamic world can never disregard the great service rendered by the Turks to the Haramain Sharifain. On the one hand, they have protected the Islamic sultanate with their blood and, on the other, enriched Mecca with their gold and jewels and their fabulous wealth. It is heart-rending to watch the poverty of the small Turkish contingent as it goes about performing the tawaf. May Allah bless them for their piety and may He restore them to their former glory so that they can once more serve Islam! *Een dua az man wa az jumla jahan Ameen baad.* Blessing of mine and from all people of Aminabad![3]

Today being the 27th day of Ramazan, Id[4] will probably be celebrated on Monday or Tuesday. In Hindustan, it is still the 25th day of Ramazan.

Saturday, 9 March

Everything went according to the schedule. There is nothing unusual to record.

---

1 Sultan, an Islamic title meaning 'authority' or 'power'. Later, it came to be used as the title of certain Muslim rulers, who claimed almost full sovereignty in practical terms (that is, the lack of dependence on any higher ruler), without claiming the overall Khilafat, or it was used to refer to a powerful governor of a province within the Khilafat. Selim III (24 December 1761– 28/29 July 1808) was the Sultan of the Ottoman Empire from 1789 to 1807. He was a son of Mustafa III (1757–74) and succeeded his uncle Abdülhamid I (1774–89). He had associated a lot with foreigners, and was thoroughly persuaded of the necessity of reforming his state.

2 The tenth and longest-reigning Ottoman ruler (1494–1566). He is known in the West as Suleiman the Magnificent.

3 Lucknow's busy and congested market. The market was started under the nawabs of Awadh. They were successors to the Mughal emperors.

4 Literally means 'feast' or 'festival'. Id is a Muslim holiday that marks the end of Ramazan, the month of fasting. It is a time of giving and sharing, and many Muslims dress in holiday attire on this day. Id al-Adha, also called Baqrid, is celebrated on the 10th of Zul Hijja as a commemoration of Prophet Ibrahim's (Abraham's) willingness to sacrifice his son Ismael for Allah. On this day, animals such as the goat and sheep are sacrificed in the name of Allah.

Sunday, 10 March

Today, I went with Dr Abdur Rehman, Muniruddin and Mohammad Yusuf Sahib to watch the bazaar where slaves are bought and sold. Five black women were seated on chairs in a house. The minimum price for each slave girl was 65 guineas. Of the five, one was slightly less dark; she was, therefore, priced at over a 100 pounds. But she also had two children with her, who were free.

Owing to Ramazan, the trade in slave girls is slow and the *maal* (wares) is not being shown freely. After Id, business will be brisk, and one will see every kind of slave—male and female. But the rates too will soar. Our guide knew Dr Abdur Rehman. He promised to bring us to this market again after Id and show us the shops dealing in slave trade.

Today, we went around the markets of Mecca and found shops stocked with all sorts of commodities. You find everything from all parts of the world. *Mashaallah la quwwata Illa billah!*[1]

I carried my essentials all the way from Hindustan and took the trouble of carrying them from place to place. What a pity! I had thought that those essentials, which have entered our lives courtesy the British, might not be available in Arabia. And so I had packed every possible essential commodity. However, after my arrival here, I realized that everything was available here. Moreover, one is helping the Meccans by buying from them.

Shops are all around the Haram Sharif. On entering the market you will find a treasure trove of every possible item. Nowadays, because of Ramazan, there is much hustle and bustle in the markets all night long. Gas lamps keep the city illuminated like a cupola of light. Such is the people's enjoyment that they are reluctant to leave the alleys of the shops. It is about this place that Hazrat Ibrahim[2] had said:

---

1 Meaning: 'Allah has willed it, there is no power and no strength save in Allah.' This expression is read by a Muslim when he is struck by a calamity, or is taken over by a situation beyond his control.

2 Prophet Ibrahim was born in a leading family of priests at Urwa (now in Iraq). Image-carving was the occupation of his ancestors, who were also the keepers of the biggest temple in the town, the Hebrew patriarchs, and a figure revered by the three great monotheistic religions: Judaism, Christianity and Islam. He was the father of the Prophet Ismael (Ishmael), his firstborn son. Ibrahim is commonly termed as 'Khalil-Allah', or 'Friend of Allah'.

Our Lord! I have settled some of my posterity in an uncultivable valley near Thy Holy House. (Quran: Abraham 37)

Monday, 11 March

According to the Hindu astrologers, tonight is *Somwari amawas* or the moonless night. Therefore, the moon will not be sighted. Here it is the 30th of Ramazan AH 1347, and Id must be tomorrow. After iftar, 21 canon shots were fired announcing the end of the most blessed month.

Tuesday, 12 March

I woke up four hours before sunrise. Owing to the kindness of our hosts, I had hot water for my bath. I changed, drank tea, and presented myself in the Haram Sharif. After offering the Namaz-e Tahajjud, I stood beneath the Mizab-e Rehmat. Touching the cover of the Kaaba with my eyes, I prayed for my own well-being, that of my near and dear ones, and of all Muslims. I had barely done one tawaf when the proclamation of Id was announced from the royal palace. In the sweet light of the early morning, the floating, lyrical voice of the muezzin, the heartbreakingly sweet music of the azaan, mingled with the sound of the canon shots, combined to create a strange ambience—one that cannot be described.

After the Fajr namaz, as I sat beside the prayer rugs, Abdul Qadir's employee, whom I have earlier referred to as Yusuf, showed up, and took me and Munshi Mohammad Yusuf to the top storey. This was where the *mukabbirin* (those calling people to come to mosques for prayers) meet. Yusuf is the brother-in-law of Hasan bin Abdul Qadir Sikandar; his father is employed by the Mukabbirin-e Hanafi. That is why we were allowed access to their section. After sunrise, the entire city was in the Masjidul Haram. According to my estimate, there were at least 2 to 3 lakh people. But some people tell me that there were less than 2 lakh people. Anyhow, one could see heads in every direction and there wasn't any place to keep the proverbial lintseed in the Masjidul Haram. The rich brocade gowns of the Arabs, the plain white clothes of the hajjis, the colourful burqas of the women—it looked as though there was a garden of people and the courtyard of the masjid looked like a bouquet of colourful flowers.

The mukabbirin resumed their sermon. They would loudly chant *Allah-o-Akbar* (Allah is the Greatest) *Allah-o-Akbar, La ilaha illal-*

laah,[1] *Wa Allah-o-Akbar, Allah-o-Akbar, Wa lillahil-Hamd.* The hajjis would join in. At every few intervals, they would say *Allah-o-Akbar Kabiran, Alhamdulillahi Kasiran, Subhan-Allah Bukratan wa asila* (Praise be to Allah every morning and every evening), *wa sallallaho Ala Syedna Mohammad wa Aalihi wa As-haabihi wa sallam-kasiran kasiran* in a most heartrending manner. At such times, it would seem as though a river of brightness flowed from the skies to the earth and the Mercy of Allah had gathered the entire masjid under its cloak. There was more bustle around the Kaaba than I had ever seen before. It seemed as though my heart moved from its place when the mukabbirin chanted *Sallal laaho Ala Syedna Mohammad*[2] and a vivid picture of the glory of Islam shimmered before my eyes. I was reminded that this is the name of that pious man who was once forbidden from entering the Kaaba, and all of Mecca had become his sworn enemy.

Our Lord, do help Islam and Muslims.

Today, however, every child recites the name of the same person after the name of Allah.

---

1 Meaning: 'There is no Lord worthy of worship except Allah.' This expression is the most important in Islam. It is part of the first pillar of Islam.

2 'May Allah's blessings be on our master Mohammad, his family and his companions'—the most profuse of all blessings.

5
Celebrating Id in Mecca

According to local time, the Id namaz began at 12.45, half an hour after sunrise. There were 12 *takbirs*;[1] according to our Hanafi tradition, there are six. There were half-a-dozen in the first rakat after *sana* and before the fateha, and another half-a-dozen in the second rakat before fateha. I was not too far from the khatib.[2] One could hear his voice well but not his words. When the khatib reached 'O Lord, do help Islam and Muslims' (*Allahummun-suril Islama wa Muslimeen*) after the second khutba, small flags were waved and canons were shot from the royal palace. The roar of the canons made my heart race and I sensed the might and glory of Islam all around me. Not a fraction of the gaiety and festivity with which Id was celebrated by the Ottomans remains, say members of the older generation. But this show of pomp and splendour was good enough for me.

از دوزخیان پرس که اَعرافِ بهشت است

Az doza khyan purs ke aeraf behesht ast

Ask the hellites – they say airaf is paradise.

After namaz, I went with Mohammad Yusuf to his house and partook of the Id banquet. On my return, I saw Arab boys and girls prancing around and playing English musical instruments on the streets. Happiness and gaiety prevailed all around. The faces of everyone—the

---

1 A proclamation of the greatness of Allah, such as 'Allah-o-Akbar' meaning, 'Allah is the Greatest'.

2 An Arabic term used to describe a person who delivers the sermon (khutba), during the Friday prayer or Id prayers. The khatib is usually the Imam (prayer leader), but sometimes the two roles can be played by different people.

noble as well as the plebian—gave clear evidence of happiness. I use
the word plebian by mistake. No inhabitant of Mecca is plebian. Our
forefathers have said, 'Allah disdains save that He shall perfect His light,
however much the disbelievers are averse.' Even the illiterate and half-
witted here are better than the ulama of other places. When a child
turns 40 days old, he is wrapped in a cloth and placed in front of the gate
of the Kaaba and when he dies, his corpse is placed for a few minutes
again in front of the gate before being taken to the graveyard through
the Baab-e Salaam.

The Namaz-e Janaza is offered in front of the Kaaba gate; the fortunate ones have it after the Fajr namaz when thousands of Muslims pray
for the deliverance of the deceased Muslim. Allah knows better about
the activities of the Meccans. He is the One who draws a curtain over
man's misdeeds and knows both the hidden and the revealed deeds of
every soul. But a peculiar quality of the Meccans—apparent to all—is
their great faith in Allah and their supreme trust in His ability to provide
for them. Sheikh Saadi[1] had said:

" آن قدر تعلق کہ انسان را با روزی است۔ اگر

با روزی دہ بودے در مقام از ملائکہ در گز شتتے "

*Aan qadr taaluq ke insan ra ba rozi ast, agar barozi deh boode dar maqam az malaeka
dar guzashte.*

If people be as incumbent upon the Provider of daily bread (God) as they are
attached to their sustenance, they would have surpassed the Angels in their status.

But when I came here I saw that the Meccans have complete trust in
Allah's ability to provide them with a livelihood. Whatever they earn,
they spend and consider it futile to save for another day. They believe
that He who has given today shall also provide tomorrow, Inshaallah.

There are no leftovers to feed the dog, as it were! Those who had
been spotted begging a few days before Id could be seen walking around
dressed in resplendent clothes. Tomorrow, they might sell their bright
new plumes for a few cowries and pawn the expensive robes to earn
their daily bread. Today, however, they are out in their full glory. This

---

1 Saadi (1184–1283/1291?) is one of the major Persian poets of the medieval
period. He is recognized not only for the quality of his writing, but also for the depth
of his social thought. His best known works are *Bostan* (The Orchard) in 1257 and
Gulistan (The Rose Garden) in 1258.

confidence illustrates their complete conviction just as every Believer is a likely candidate for gaining *maghfarat* and entering heaven. Therefore, the saying of the elders, 'The fools of Mecca are better than the wise of other places', should not be disclaimed.

That is the bounty of Allah, He gives to whosoever He wishes and He is full of bounties.

I am a native of India, weak of faith, timorous of belief, and oblivious of the intricacies of dogma. A man like me, though dazzled by the splendid celebrations in this citadel of Islam, is also distressed by a few things. You have heard my paeans of praise; listen now to my tale of woe.

Thank Allah, the better part of Hijaz is semi-independent. Yet Great Britain rules over much of the Arab lands. Its markets are flooded with British goods. You can buy toys worth thousands of rupees—all produced in Europe. Rubber balls, rubber blow toys, tin engines, toy trains, organs and musical implements are sold here in hundreds of thousands. I didn't see a single child without a few toys clutched in his hand. Yet, the poor Hijazi's earnings are of no use to the Meccans. This is unfortunate. What they earn finds its way to England just as surely as it does from our benighted country. It is a matter of great surprise that car accessories imported from Great Britain are worth 81,000 pounds. They are sourced from other European markets as well, but those are not included here. Why just talk of one car; every single commodity is imported from Great Britain. And all the wealth of the world of Islam finds its way to Europe through Mecca.

It is a pity that the women here are enamoured by Western fashions. The burqa, once meant to cover a woman's beauty, is now a means to draw attention. Burqas made of vividly coloured silks and brocades draw everyone's eyes like magnets. Young girls roam about unveiled, dressed in Western clothes from head to toe, and wearing the same silken robes and high-heeled boots.

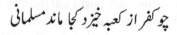

Chun kufr az Kaba khizad kuja manad Musalmani

If infidelity rises from Kaaba itself, then where would faith be.

English sweets and biscuits are found in all the shops. Tea and cigarettes are a way of life. Bullets and ammunition come from abroad.

Postal stamps are printed abroad (*wilayat*). Riyal and qarsh are minted in London. Cloth comes from English mills. And this valley has always been inhospitable for the cultivation of wheat. The only native produce is watermelon and the water of the sacred spring of zumzum. Camels were once a source of livelihood. According to Sharif Hussein, the former ruler of Hijaz, a camel would support 140 families. The coming of the automobile put an end to this.

A matter of great shame, something that causes pain even to write about, is to see women embracing pilgrims to seek alms. To say any more is to go against the norms of propriety.

'We sent Allah's protection from the evils of our heart'.

This was the state of the economy; now let us look at politics. Although Sultan Ibn Saud rules over Jiddah, the real power is wielded by the British. Ibn Saud's slaves run away and take refuge in the British embassy where the Consul General puts them on ships and transports them to safe havens abroad. And the King can do nothing. No caravan can cross from Jiddah to Medina or Nejd without the Consul's permission. The King has no say. The embassy has warned the Afghans that they must submit their return tickets to the Vice-Consul[1] or else they will not be allowed to travel to Mecca. And the self-proclaimed sovereign Arab King dare not say a word.

Mecca and Medina are in Allah's protection but the British Consul can, in a matter of minutes, occupy it if he so wishes. The Nejd soldiers who are stationed here are not even properly armed. When I saw them on Jumatul-Wada (the last Friday of the month of Ramazan) and earlier today in a procession, some wore boots, some slippers, others walked barefoot with guns on their shoulders. Belts of cartridges are looped about their waist; no one knows if they are full or empty. But, as everyone can see, the guns are broken and rusted. In India, the troops of Hyderabad, Gwalior, and Indore are far better organized and equipped than this 'royal' force. One machine gun is enough to make mincemeat out of this entire force. These soldiers cannot face an organized army for more than five minutes. And, on top of that, the Meccans are weary of the Sultan. I have been here for ten days and I have yet to meet a person who is not critical of the Nejdis or condemns Ibn Saud. The inhabitants are (on the other hand) beholden to the Turks. Sharif Hussein betrayed

---

1 A public officer commissioned for overseeing the commercial affairs of its citizens in an overseas country. He or she also issues visas and renews passports.

the people and unleashed barbaric cruelties upon the Turkish soldiers because the elite of Mecca had begun to hate him and had begun to furtively fawn upon the Nejdis merely to humiliate him.

After defeating Sharif, the Nejdis unleashed mass mayhem and slaughter in Taif.[1] When the population went out of sight, they made a declaration of peace. Many innocents were beguiled by this and appeared in public. Then, they reneged on their promise of mercy and people were ruthlessly put under the sword. Thousands of innocents were killed. This aggression and brutality shook the Meccans. The rich and poor alike silently paid allegiance to the ruler of Nejd. Today every Meccan—May God be with him—is an inveterate enemy of the Nejdi and is biding the time when he can shake off the yoke of tyranny. The tragedy is that the Nejdi have managed to defeat the Bedouin. Thousands of Bedouins—innocent and blameless— were slaughtered. Peace was restored after this terrible bloodbath. The roads became safe once again. Today, if one were to throw gold all the way from the shores of Jiddah to Amman there would be not the slightest of looting. But consider the price that has been paid for this peace. The soldiers who were stationed to defend Haramain Sharif too were killed. Now the field is clear for an enemy to attack. May Allah save all from evil times!

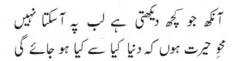

Aankh jo kucch dekhti hai lab pe aa sakta nahin
meh ve hairat hoon keh duniya kya se kya ho jaai gi

I cannot put into words what my eyes see
I marvel at how the world has gone awry.

The Turks had served the rich and poor alike, awarded handsome scholarships to the Syeds and other respectable men, and fixed stipends for widows and orphans. And they did not impose any tax on the hajjis. Nowadays, the Nejdis extract almost 10 pounds through the muallims. A sum of 6 guineas is fixed for those travelling to Medina by car. The camel-owners from Arafat and Jiddah are charged a few riyals per hajji. I had heard these details but don't remember them exactly.

1 For a brief description, see Husain Ahmad Madani (n.d.), *Safarnama Asir-e Malta: Hayat-e Mahmud wa Sawanah Shaikhul Hind*, Delhi, p. 36.

Briefly, the Sultan receives 10 pounds per hajji. One can, thus, calculate how much the royal treasury earns from the hajjis in a year. Earlier, this money was used in the welfare of the people of Mecca; now it is used to buy goods according to the latest English fashion in Nejd and Mecca. The people of Mecca are in dire straits. Poverty makes them commit such acts of omission that are the necessary consequences of being penniless. But the Nejdis can't care less. They know and are well aware that their rule over Mecca is temporary and it shall not last for more than a few years. Therefore, they want to amass as much wealth as they can from here. The son of Sultan Ibn Saud, who is the Crown Prince of Hijaz, lives in Mecca. Every Friday, he comes to the Haram Sharif but no one looks at him with affection. Whether he will gain permanent rule over this land or the Nejdis will retain control over Mecca is known only to God. One can only pray that the Malik-ul Mulk keeps this holy land free from the rule of the infidels and except for this anything else is tolerable.

نہ بود نصیب دشمن کہ شود ہلاک تیغت

سرِ دوستاں سلامت کہ تو خنجر آزمائی

Na buwad nasib-e-dushman ke shawad halak-e-teighat
Sar-e-doostan salamat-ke tau khanjar aazmaii.

The enemy does not deserve death by your dagger
To test your sword, friends have heads to offer

This tale has become too long. So I bring it to a close. I shall write about it again some other time. After Zuhr, Mohammad Yusuf Sahib and I went to greet Akbar Umar Sahib for Id. And from his house we recovered our books that had been confiscated at Jiddah's custom house. These books, having been in the muallim's safe custody, were released after several days. My confiscated cigar box shall be auctioned after two years and the money earned will go to the government's coffers.

From Asr to Isha, we stayed in the Masjidul Haram, performed tawaf, and read *wazaif*. After every namaz, we heard canon shots from the royal palace. A 20-gun salute was sounded. We didn't eat dinner and went to bed.

Wednesday, 13 March

The canon shots were sounded after each of the five namaz. The shops remained closed. People were busy meeting each other and celebrating.

Mohammad Yusuf Sahib and I were invited to Akbar muallim's house in the morning and offered the choicest Arab dishes. I did not have much of an appetite but because of the hosts' urging, we ate and ate well. I spoke at length to Akbar Umar's father, who narrated several interesting incidents about the Haramain Sharifain. These left a lasting impression on me. Some of his impressions are worth remembering, but for fear of making this narration tediously long, I cannot record them in this diary.

From the muallim's house we went to the home of Mohammad Salim Sahib, the trustee of the Madrasa Saulatiya. Here too, we exchanged notes with each other for quite a while. We went to the Masjidul Haram and stayed there from Asr till Isha.

I sat on the Musalla-e Hanafi (place of prayers for the followers of the Hanafi school) watching those doing the tawaf and at the same time relishing the sight of the Kaaba. Turkish, Chinese, Bukhari, Shafai,[1] Afghani, Javanese, Hindi hajjis were going round and round the Kaaba with great gusto—like moths around a flame. And watching them engaged in prayer was a sort of worship too.

Sultan ibn Saud has introduced several innovative changes in the Haram Sharif, the most remarkable one being the organization of only one jama'at. Shia,[2] Hanafi, Shafai, Maliki,[3] Hanbali[4] and Ahl-e-

1 Abu Abdullah Mohammad ibn Idris al-Shafi'i, an Islamic jurist (AH 150/AD 767 –AH 204/AD 820), was born in Gaza and moved to Mecca when he was about ten years old. His teaching led to the Shafi school of *fiqh* (or *madhab*) named after him. Hence, he is often called Imam al-Shafi'i. He is reported to have studied with the School of Mecca and then he moved to Medina.

2 Shia refers to the largest minority denomination based on Islamic faith after Sunni Islam. Shias claim to adhere to the teachings of Prophet Mohammad and the religious guidance of his family (who are referred to as the Ahl-i Bait) or his descendants known as Shia Imams, whom they consider to be infallible. Thanks to the Shia Nawabs of Awadh and their patronage, a large number of Shias lived in or were drawn to the qasbas of Awadh. Kakori, too, had a substantial Shia population. The ruler of Rampur, a princely state in Rohilkhand, was a Shia.

3 The Maliki *madhab* is one of the four schools of fiqh or religious law within Sunni Islam. It is the third-largest of the four schools, followed by approximately 15 per cent of Muslims, mostly in North Africa and West Africa. The other three schools of thought are Shafi, Hanafi, and Hanbali.

4 Hanbali is one of the four schools (madhabs) of Fiqh or religious law within Sunni Islam (the other three being Hanafi, Maliki and Shafi). The school was started by the students of Imam Ahmad bin Hanbal (780–855 CE, AH 164–241), a prominent scholar and theologian of Persian background. His full name was Ahmad bin Mohammad

Hadith[1]—all stand in unison and offer namaz behind the Imam. The Malikis are usually from Habsh [Ethiopia] and Sudan. They offer namaz with open hands. The Javanese follow Imam Shafai; they constitute the largest number among the hajjis. They do the *raf'i yadain* (with both hands raised behind the ears). Their saying 'Ameen'[2] in chorus makes the masjid resound with their sound. Muslims of different denominations and from different countries come together to praise the One Allah in whose Oneness no one can share. At such moments, the picture of Islamic brotherhood flashes before the eyes. One has not seen such a scene for a very long time.

May Allah give the Saudis the good sense to make one more necessary correction that would benefit the entire world of Islam, that is, fix a time for women to do their tawaf! The Nejdis are criticized from all sides and thousands of true and false allegations are levelled against them. If this change is added to the list of changes that they have brought about, they can atone for many of their past deeds. In the past too, women did the tawaf with the men. But then the wave of freedom that is currently coursing through the world did not exist. Earlier, women hid their modesty, *zeenat*. They would try to keep their bodies away from the bodies of men and somehow, with the utmost decorum and modesty, manage the tawaf. But this is the age of freedom. Women do the tawaf alongside men, shoulder to shoulder. And those from Egypt and Java don't mind their bodies jostling against the men. Sadly, this isn't the state of affairs only at the Hajr-e-Aswad but all over the circumambulatory path for the tawaf. Some women wear burqas with *zardozi* and gold lace. Where is the need to wear such burqas? Some wear veils of such gossamer fabric that their entire face is visible. Why wear the veil at all?

---

bin Hanbal Abu 'Abd Allah al-Shaybani and he was born at Merv in Khurasan. He is considered to be the founder of the Hanbali school of Fiqh (Islamic jurisprudence). The Hanbali school is followed by less than 3 per cent of the world's Muslim population. Hanbali jurisprudence is predominant among Muslims in the Arabian Peninsula.

1 They differ from orthodox traditionalist Sunnis in rejecting the concept of *taqlid*, which is dubbed as blind adherence.

2 This is the standard ending to *dua* (supplication) meaning: 'Verily', 'Truly', 'So be it', and 'Let it be'. Muslims use the word 'Ameen' not only after reciting the first sura (Al-Fatiha) of the Quran, but also when concluding a prayer or dua, with the same meaning as in Christianity.

Na uzu billahi min shuroori anfusina wa min sayye aate aamaalina

We seek Allah's protection from the evils of our hearts and from our evil deeds.

Thursday, 14 March

The canons were sounded at Fajr, Zuhr, and Asr. When they were not heard after Maghrib, it sounded oddly empty. However, I cannot imagine why the Saudis have permitted this bid'at (heresy).

Today, we had planned to go to the cave at Hira,[1] but were told that the Nejdis had placed guards so that no one could get close to this sacred site. It is a pity that we were denied the chance to pay our respects at that holy cave where the Emperor of the Two Worlds had prayed for such a long time and where the Revelation had descended. *Inna lillahi wa inna ilaihi rajioon.*

Friday, 15 March

Today I was blessed by being able to offer the Friday prayer at the Masjidul Haram for the second time. The size of the crowd was no less than what it had been on the previous Friday.

After the prayer, Mohammad Yusuf, Muniruddin, and I went to the shop of Abdul Jabbar Dehalvi. I had got a hundi worth Rs 500 in his name from Lucknow. Out of it, I took Rs 200 in order to pay [the fare] for the car to Medina. Mohammad Yusuf Sahib had a hundi from Ali Jaan's shop. He too received Rs 200 and got a hundi for Rs 300 written for Medina Munawwara.

Although we are consumed with the desire to see Medina, we have yet to arrange a car. All businesses have been virtually closed [after Id] and there is no chance of getting a vehicle. So far we have been patient, but now we are beginning to get restless. May Allah arrange our travel [to Medina] at the earliest!

Dr Abdur Rehman had bought a one-way ticket worth 5 guineas from the Kaukabush-Sharq car company at Jiddah, but he has still not hired a car to take him. The rest of us wanted to buy a return ticket so that we wouldn't face any problems while coming back. We are willing to pay more than 10 guineas but still nothing is working out. We did

---

1 Hira, also known as Jabl Nur, is a small mountain near Mecca, Saudi Arabia. Prophet Mohammad used to visit a small cave in Mount Hira's secluded place. It was in the same cave that he received the first *Wahi* (Message of Allah).

not find Nawab Ali Kutbi at his shop or we would have tried through his good offices. We are trying to make some arrangement through Dr Rehman; the result is in Allah's hands.

Our hostesses served us moong dal *khichdi* (cooked dish of rice, dal, vegetables), along with green chillies fried with spices and turnip pickle. This easy-to-digest meal was more pleasurable than the tastiest morsel we had eaten since stepping on Arab soil. Alhamdulillah! As always, we prayed at the Masjidul Haram and performed tawaf.

Saturday, 16 March

With Mohammad Yusuf, Muniruddin, and Dr Abdur Rehman, I called upon Shebi Sahib, the caretaker of the keys to the Kaaba. He extended his courtesy to us because Rehman had treated his son last year. He offered us tea and English biscuits. He had a box of English soap called Peerless Erasmic. He showed it to us, expecting us to praise it.

Before departing for Hindustan, an elderly gentleman had requested me to bring back a piece of the Kaaba cover. He had even specified the measurements. The cover, once taken off, becomes the property of Shebi Sahib. He, in turn, sells its pieces. He quoted a price of 3 guineas for a cloth of one hand width. According to this rate, I would have had to pay almost Rs 300. Given my budget, I couldn't be extravagant. And so I did not buy the cloth.

We kissed Shebi Sahib's holy hands and left. We roamed around the bazaars of Safa and Marwa looking for an English medicine for Yusuf Sahib. Unfortunately, we could not find it though almost everything else of daily use is available. In fact, the stuff we had brought with such care all the way from Hindustan is stocked in Mecca's shops. By lugging all the stuff [from home] we have denied ourselves the opportunity of helping those living in the vicinity of the Kaaba. Except for fresh paan, ginger, and little-known English medicines, everything is plentifully available in the bazaars. Even though there is no land suitable for agriculture nor water for irrigation, green coriander, green parsley, parsenum and spinach—so fresh as though they have just been brought from the fields—are available in abundance. Allah alone knows how these fresh fruits and vegetables are available in the local markets. It's a miracle wrought by the prayer of Rehman.

And gave its people sustenance from its bounties.

The mail came from Hindustan today. Thank Allah I received a letter from home that brought news of my family's well-being.

Efforts are still underway to organize a car, but there is as yet no sign of success. It is said that the authorities have not yet granted permission for the caravans of hajjis to travel.

Sunday, 17 March

We went to Akbar Umar Sahib's house in the morning and spoke to him about finding a car for us. We were told that we would have to pay 15 guineas per head for it. We are ready for this, but we were required to find four passengers. Mohammad Yusuf Sahib and I are willing to pay this dear price but Muniruddin Hyderabadi is not. Dr Rehman has already bought a one-way ticket for 5 guineas, so we don't know whether we will have his company on this holy journey or not. Although obsessed with finding a car, we've made no headway so far. May Allah help us!

From Umar Sahib's house we went to meet Mohammad Salim, the trustee of the Madrasa Saulatiya. He lives in Kairana[1] and is the grandson of the famous Hindustani gentleman, Maulvi Rehmatullah Muhajir.[2] He was extremely hospitable and served us Hindustani tea.

I found out that Umar Sahib's father is not the Khalifa of Hajji Imdadullah Muhajir; he is only one of the disciples and is close to the Hajji Sahib because he lives in Mecca.

After Zuhr, we went to meet Nawab Ali Rampuri near the Baab-e Salaam. I found another letter from home waiting for me. It too had come in yesterday's post but the postman delivered it late. This letter came from my employee Hafiz Abdul Karim and had been put in the mail on 19 February. I came to know, in detail, the well-being of my sons and other dear ones. Thank Allah everyone is well at home!

Today, for the first time after reaching Mecca, I committed a dietary indiscretion. I bought kababs[3] from the bazaar. Of course, they didn't taste like the ones in Hindustan, but they weren't too bad either. They tasted all right because I was hungry. I didn't eat dinner.

---

1 A city in Muzaffarnagar district in the Indian state of Uttar Pradesh.

2 An Islamic religious title often, but not exclusively, given to Muslim religious scholars or ulama preceding their names. 'Maulvi' generally means any religious cleric or teacher.

3 Refers to a variety of grilled/broiled meat dishes in West Asian and South Asian cuisines. Kababs usually consist of lamb and beef, though particular styles of kababs have chicken or fish.

After Asr, Akbar Umar told us that we should not expect transport for the next 3–4 days. The government had yet not permitted cars to leave, whereas pilgrims wanting to travel on foot could do so. Similarly, the camel caravans were expected to leave tomorrow.

The government had received [its share of] 6 guineas from each passenger travelling to Mecca by car. Soon, it wanted to charge more. That is why everything hangs in the balance. Moreover, the authorities have formed a union of sorts for the car vehicles, that is, cars belonging to different companies were to leave one by one. Each one of the 18 companies owns at least 30 cars. A dozen or so companies have already run their cars by the end of Ramazan. The rest will take their vehicles once they receive the travel permission. And when all these cars have run their course, the general cars will be allowed to move. The worst thing about this 'union' is that one is not allowed to stay in Medina Munawwara for more than 72 hours. It is unacceptable to travel such a long distance for just 72 hours. So, naturally, there is little hope for us to travel till this union disappears.

We became constant with what Allah had pre-ordained for us.

Monday, 18 March

After the Fajr namaz, I went to Dr Abdur Rehman's house and ate the famous Arabian dish called *harisa*. Its special ingredients are meat, wheat, dates and ghee. Besides its nourishment value, the meal tastes good and isn't too expensive either. A bowl, which is enough for one man's breakfast, costs two qarsh. After tea, we called on the famous *mujahid*[1] of Tripoli, Hazrat Sheikh[2] Sanosi. The Sheikh lives on Jabal Bu Qabees. With a huge khanqah and an attached mosque and houses, he has owned this property for a very long time. The place is pleasant by Meccan standards. Its climate is favourable.

The sheikh welcomed us graciously, because Dr Rehman is his physician. He served us green tea. He is an elderly man with an extremely youthful face that can easily pass for a man of less than 40 years. With a florid, fair complexion, stout arms, and strong hands, he has a charismatic face. But he was extremely modest while conversing

1 Mujahid means a 'struggler'. It is the singular form of *mujahidin*.
2 Sheikh, also rendered as Shaykh or Shaikh, means elder of a tribe, lord, revered wise man, or Islamic scholar. The term literally means a man of old age, especially in the Arabian Peninsula, where Sheikh became a traditional title of a Bedouin tribal leader.

with us. An interpreter had accompanied us; we struck a conversation with his help.

The sheikh had come here for ziyarat and tawaf but has been placed under house arrest. He cannot cross the seas and go home for fear of the Europeans. Indeed neither he nor the Kings of Hijaz[1] and Egypt have the power to ensure his safe passage to Tripoli. May the Lord of the Universe make the seas safe and secure with His infinite mercy or else Muslims will have no hope of progress!

After Asr, Maulvi Akram Khan Sahib Bengali came to see us and we spoke for a long time. As luck would have it, our tea came; it had milk in it. Akram Khan Sahib told us that the Arabs object to mixing milk with tea and are critical of the Hindis because they 'eat food with spices and kill tea with milk'. Just then we heard of arrangements being made for Dr Abdur Rehman's travel to Mecca. A travel company had agreed to offer him a place in a car lorry. He could, therefore, leave tomorrow. May Allah bless him and bless us too with a similar opportunity!

Just a little before Maghrib, I was sitting woebegone in the Haram Sharif, fretting over what I could do to make the journey to Medina. I didn't have the courage to travel on camelback. Moreover, even if I were to make the effort, the caravan would not halt there for more than eight days. If I motor the journey it would cost 12.5 guineas per head and I would not be able to stay for more than 72 hours. If I go on a lorry the travel cost would be less, that is, 10.5 guineas per head. But even then, I can't stay for more than three days. I had come with the intention of staying at Medina for much longer, but the Saudi's interference has made it increasingly difficult to extend the duration of my stay. May Allah have mercy!

A hajji from Delhi came up to me after the Maghrib namaz. He told me that we should buy a one-way ticket to Medina for 5.5 guineas. In the absence of a return ticket, we shall have the right to stay there. We shall return, somehow or the other, close to the time of hajj. He had made such an arrangement for himself and suggested that we do the same. I immediately reported this conversation to Mohammad Yusuf

---

1 The Hijaz was part of the province of Arabia. Under the control of regional powers, Egypt or the Ottoman empire through most of its history, the Hijaz had a brief period of political independence in the early twentieth century. In 1916, its independence was proclaimed by Sharif Hussein ibn Ali, the Sherif of Mecca. In 1924, however, ibn Ali's authority was usurped by Ibn Saud of the neighbouring region of Nejd and became known as the Kingdom of Hijaz and Nejd, and later the Kingdom of Saudi Arabia.

Allahabadi. Sad and dejected, he agreed. We set off for Akbar Umar's house. He promised to arrange one-way tickets for us and later, closer to hajj, organize our return through the 'Nejah' or some other car company. I thanked him. My problem is that my own muallim is absent. Without him, no hajji can leave Mecca. Akbar Umar promised that he would meet the muallim's lawyer and obtain the necessary permission, and that he would also arrange for Muniruddin Hyderabadi to travel with us because his lawyer too is not around.

I have made the most terrible mistake. Upon the urging of a relative, I made Abdul Qadir Sikandar my muallim. At every step, my foolish mistake has caused immense trouble. People from Hindustan will do well to be wary of the false traps of such predators! And they will do well not to appoint some smooth-talking deceiver as their muallim until they reach Jiddah. Unfortunately, the muallim who has once been appointed for you cannot be changed once you reach here [Mecca], and you can do nothing without the permission of your muallim. Forget Medina, you can't even go to Arafat without his approval! This great respect is not accorded to the muallims because of their high birth, but simply because the government extracts its fee through them. And so it was found to be necessary to stretch the rights of the muallim.

بہ ہر زمین کہ رسیدیم آسماں پیداست

Behar zamin ke rasideem aasman paidast

Whichever land we inhabit gets a sky over it.

Thanks to Umar Sahib's friendly conversation and heartwarming promises, the burden on my heart is lifted. We happily returned to the Haram Sharif and offered the Isha namaz.

Tuesday, 19 March

After the morning prayers, Muniruddin Hyderabadi invited Mohammad Yusuf Sahib and me to a meal. He gave us an Arab dish called *matbakh* and tea. Matbakh is a sort of bread with eggs and a little mince, and large helpings of a special kind of green vegetable called *kurraath* whose leaves are a bit like onion springs and mixed generously into the bread. It is a tasty and wholesome dish. We ate well and gave thanks to Allah. The desire to go to Medina Sharif is all-consuming. Akbar Umar Sahib has promised to come by at 3.30. Let's see what he has to report.

6

Medina, the Home of Plenty

We packed a few essentials for the journey to Medina. Having bathed and dressed in clean clothes, we waited for Akbar Umar. Maulvi Akram Khan Sahib showed up. Seeing our preparations, he was also inspired to go to Medina. In fact, he resolved to leave at the earliest. We were discussing political matters when Dr Abdur Rehman arrived to bid us farewell. He was setting out for Medina right away. I requested him to present my salaams in the Holy House and intercede on my behalf to hasten our departure. I could wait no longer.

Umar Sahib came a short while after Rehman. He collected our car fare in order to obtain the government's permission and purchase our tickets. Umar Sahib went to meet the lawyer for my muallim and had some argument, the details of which I do not know as yet. Yusuf, the lawyer's employee, told me that the lawyer wanted to see me. Having had an unpleasant altercation with him on the very first day, I hesitated to meet him again. But I had no choice but to do so, because I required his permission to go to Medina. Consumed with the desire to visit the holy shrine, I turned up at his home. As he was out somewhere, I waited a long time for him to return.

As on the first day, anger and resentment rose inside me. Yusuf, the lawyer's employee, was ingratiating and supportive. At his insistence, I did the wuzoo because by now, the azaan for the Zuhr namaz had sounded. The Haram Sharif was close by. I went there to offer namaz before returning to the lawyer's house. By now, the lawyer had returned and got busy with his namaz. After he had finished, he began talking to me through an interpreter. He was aware of my anger and sorrow at the way things had turned out between us. And so he began to speak gently. Every now and then, he would pat me on the back and seek forgiveness for the unpleasantness of the first day. Seeing him like this, I too sought forgiveness for my behaviour. I sat before him respectfully, with folded hands. He said that he had signed my permission letter and that I could go to Medina. He also said that the muallim usually charges his fee from the hajjis beforehand, but because I was now a 'dear one', he would not demand his fee now. I could give it to Sikandar upon my return from Medina. I agreed. It was not the occasion to ask for the amount of the fee. What, after all, had Hasan or his lawyer done to earn it? I did not deem it fit to carry this fight any further. This unpleasant episode was coming to an end with the help of Allah and so I kept up a respectful conversation and did nothing that could be seen as disrespectful or indiscreet. Although I harboured reservations deep inside my heart, and I still have them, may Allah cleanse my heart of ill will! I don't know why I lose my head the moment I step into a lawyer's abode and become angry.

Forgive me O' my Lord and have mercy, you are the best forgiver.

The muallim also informed me that the fee for my ticket had been deposited, and that 1.5 guineas had been returned from the 6 guineas given to Akbar Umar. He asked me to recover this amount from Akbar, and to inform him if he (Akbar) refused to give it. He wanted me to meet him before leaving so that he could take me for the *tawaaful-wada*.[1] Agreeing to all his suggestions, I took my leave.

At night, I discovered that the muallim had got angry with Umar for arranging a one-way ticket for me. Moreover, the muallim fumed, even if Akbar had misguidedly done so, why did he quote a rate of 5.5 guineas? And why did he not take the entire 6 guineas? Normally, the muallims make half a guinea from each hajji travelling by car. If Akbar Umar had realized the entire 6 guineas from me, he—that is, the muallim—would have received one entire guinea from me. *Maale muft dil beraham!* (The stoney heart spurns not the free goods!)

The muallim was also angry because Akbar Umar had not arranged transport for me. If he had not interceded, I would have been forced to pay obeisance in the lawyer's court. May Allah grant him better sense, and may my countrymen have the foresight to stay clear of those muallims who are not present in Mecca during the time of the hajj and leave their clients to fend for themselves! As far as I know, the

---

1 The final tawaf.

tawaaf alvida is performed after hajj and just before one is leaving for one's country. There is no need to do a tawaaf alvida, especially if one is leaving Mecca for a short while. Tomorrow morning I shall do the tawaaf, as I always do, and not flatter the lawyer. If I happen to meet him in the Haram Sharif, I shall greet him by paying cash. He is a *mujawir*, a caretaker, in the House of Allah, and I have come to serve and obey and not to engage in fights and arguments.

Briefly, I waited until Asr for Umar to return but he didn't show up. Lorries leave Medina regularly. Their rumblings cause an excitement to well up in my heart. I was leaving for the Haram Sharif to offer my prayer when I came across a contingent from Java that was on its way to Medina Munawwara. Contraptions made of wood and leather called shaqdaf were fastened atop the camels and every camel carried two passengers. It was a very moving sight. The long line of camels, the colourful shaqdaf, and the pilgrims waiting eagerly to catch their first sight of the house of their beloved Messenger of Allah caused a strange welling up of emotions inside me. Tears came into my eyes. I was reminded of my parents and other relatives who had travelled like this on camelback long ago to visit the holy sites in Medina. It was because of the benevolent sight of these zealous pilgrims that, after namaz when performing the tawaf, a strange sense of heedlessness came upon me. I tried to stem my tears but a few drops would still fall uncontrollably. After tawaf, my restless heart found some comfort. I became engrossed in wazaif. I met Muniruddin Hyderabadi who told me that Akbar Umar had found a car for him and that he too would leave for Medina after Zuhr.

بریں مژدہ گر جان فشانم رواست

Barin muzdah gar jan feshanam rawast

It is quite permissible if I sacrifice my life on this very good news.

Today, I noticed patches were being stitched on the cover of the Kaaba today. The cloth was an ordinary black one. Traditionally, the cover, made of the finest silk, came from Egypt. But after the fight between the Nejdis and the Egyptian caravans, the cover was produced last year in Hindustan and brought to this place with much fanfare. The weavers of Hindustan are workers.

نہ ہر کہ موبّرا (مبّرا) شد قلندری داند

Na harke mubarrah shud qalandari danad

Those taken as absolved and pure need not know *qalandari* for sure.

Once upon a time, the Egyptian girls used to stitch the cover. The Hindustani cover has been in place for less than a year and is already torn. There are tears and gashes everywhere; one can see the wall of the Kaaba in places. Moreover, the cloth's black colour has faded in the rain and sun. It is now reduced to a pale almond colour that is no match for the earlier Egyptian colour. The Hindustani artisans could neither give a permanent black colour nor a strong enough fabric. Although this year weavers from Benares are staying here and are engaged in preparing a cover, they are not likely to match the Egyptians.

In order to check out the exact state of affairs, Mohammad Yusuf Sahib and I went to Umar Sahib's house after the Maghrib namaz. He told us that tickets had been bought from the Harmain Company, and that we would leave tomorrow before Zuhr. Alhamdulillah! We took our leave and returned to the Haram Sharif, offered the Isha prayer, and went home to sleep.

Wednesday, 20 March

All morning we have been looking forward to our journey [to Medina]. We have packed our luggage and are waiting for the car to arrive. Umar Sahib sent word that it would reach us at 3.30 pm.

Maulvi Akram Khan Sahib and Khalilul Nabi arrived. We discussed political affairs for a long time. Akram Sahib wished to meet Ibn Saud and place before him the grievances of the hajjis. During the conversation, Akram Sahib criticized the government employees who, at the time of the namaz, forcefully drive people out of markets and into the mosques without even giving them time to perform the wuzoo. These employees—*Amr bil Maroof* (those who order people to goodness)—are entrusted with the task of pulling anyone they spot outside at the time of the namaz into the masjid—be they shopkeepers or buyers, Meccans or outsiders—and, if they refuse, to arrest them and put them behind bars. Owing to such strictness, thousands enter the mosque at the time of prayer without the wuzoo. These people have decided that when the imam says Allah-o-Akbar they do the niyat ('I am performing the Saudi namaz without ablution or wuzoo and without intention to pray') and go into rukoo[1] and sajda[2] with the Imam.

We spoke about such matters for almost an hour before Akram Khan Sahib took leave. His host had promised to arrange his travel to Medina on Friday.

In the afternoon, Muniruddin Sahib brought roti[3] and kabab from the bazaar for our late brunch. Hoping to leave at 3.30 p.m., we had asked our hostesses not to cook lunch. After Zuhr, Umar Sahib and his employee Yahya arrived. They told us that the car was parked besides the road. They carried our luggage and gave us a good seat next to the driver. They placed some of our bags under the seats and some on top of the roof. In a car lorry, the seats close to the driver are considered good because one experiences fewer bumps here. The back seats near the door and those furthest from the driver are uncomfortable. Umar Sahib told the car driver that he would be suitably rewarded if he took care of us. The driver, an Arab, knows Hindi. His name is Sadiq and he seems to be a good sort.

This lorry has 14 people including the driver. Besides me, there is Mohammad Yusuf and our new friend Munir Hyderabadi. There are four Dilliwalas, one gentleman from Hyderabad accompanied by two women and children, and two Javanese, the only two foreigners in this group.

There are three or four police posts on the way from Mecca to Jiddah. At each point, they count the passengers. We left Mecca at 4.00 p.m. according to the Indian time. We offered the Asr and Maghrib namaz on the way. A little before Isha, we reached Jiddah. Umar Sahib had very kindly informed his lawyer, Abdur Razzaq, about our arrival telegraphically. He welcomed us at the gate of Jiddah. We felt good to meet him. He drove the car close to his home and had our luggage taken in. We offered the Isha prayer. Muniruddin and Yusuf bought food from the bazaar, but I had no appetite. I simply drank some tea and went to sleep.

---

1 It means to bend down in the prayer in the prescribed way. During prayers, a Muslim bows forward at the waist, and stands with the hands on the knees and the back parallel to the ground to glorify Allah.

2 To fall prostrate on the ground in prayer in the prescribed way.

3 Bread of certain types, usually cooked over a griddle. Roti refers to many different kinds of Indian bread, such as chapatti and phulka in India, in contrast to the naans or breads originating primarily in the north-west of South Asia and Central Asia.

Thursday, 21 March

The morning dawned at the home of Abdur Razzaq, the lawyer. We finished the wazaif and our ablutions and toilette, and went to the bazaar with the nephew of Abdur Razaq, Abdul Karim. He is the son of an Indian Memon,[1] who lost his father and came here with his mother and younger sister to live with his maternal uncle. Sitting in a hotel we ate harisa and drank tea before returning home. Abdur Razzaq offered us tea once more. Then, we proceeded to meet Ahsanullah Sahib, the Vice-Consul, along with Abdur Razzaq. He was courteous, offered us tea, and talked for nearly an hour about national and cultural affairs. We learnt that at the time of the recognition of Jiddah, the British Empire and Ibn Saud had engaged in a dialogue through him. Therefore, he was still quite influential in the present government. Unfortunately, this otherwise deeply courteous man is bitterly opposed to the Turks and considers the present educated Turks to be outside the circle of Islam. He tried converting us to his way of thinking but Alhamdullilah he did not succeed.

The Vice-Consul is deeply disillusioned with Shah Amanullah Khan. He does not consider Shah Ghazi and his Queen Suraiya Begum to be worthy of the throne of the Afghan kingdom a second time round. In the past, all the Afghan hajjis he had met narrated innumerable stories about Queen Suraiya's freedom and free thinking. And her photographs printed in the foreign newspapers too were meant to instigate the Afghans. The Vice-Consul Sahib also said that he had told the Afghans that they were pimps and procurers because they were slavishly obedient to such an emperor. He was pleased that the Afghans had proved themselves not to be pimps and had risen in revolt and banished Amanullah Khan from Kabul. Now, no damage will be done even if Afghanistan were to break up into tiny fragments. There was nothing to worry about if the entire life's work of the late 80-year-old Amir Abdur Rehman Khan went to nought, but an emperor whose wife was a free-thinking liberal had no right to rule over Afghanistan.

In the course of the conversation, I asked the Vice-Consul why our return tickets were forcibly deposited in the Consulate. But he gave us no satisfactory answer.

---

1 A minority business people and entrepreneurs, who trace their roots largely to Sindh, Kutch, and Kathiawar in Gujarat.

We took leave of Ahsanullah Khan and went to meet the Head Clerk of the Mogul Company, Munshi Azizuddin Sahib, whom we had first met upon our arrival in Jiddah. Meeting us with great warmth, he offered us tea and paan. A Hindustani, even though he has been working here for 25 years, he pleaded with Abdur Razzaq on our behalf saying that we should not be inconvenienced. Azizuddin Sahib is a pious man and his heart beats for Islam. Meeting him was pleasurable. I felt I was back home and talking to an old friend.

Abdur Razzaq telephoned the Haramain Company and was told that the car would leave after an hour. We took leave from Azizuddin with the intention of packing our belongings and making some provisions for food. Razzaq took me to the Netherland Trading Company in whose name I carried a hundi from Hindustan. As I did not need any more money right now, I merely showed the European person the hundi and came away. He was courteous to me.

At this point, I was struck by the following text written on most of the houses in Jiddah: 'O the one entering this house, say Allah's blessings on the Chosen Apostle'. In the morning, I had seen the same text on the hotel wall. I was pleased to see this auspicious sentence on the bank door.

Upon our return, I bought roti and a dozen eggs from the bazaar and handed them to Abdur Razzaq so that he might get *khakeena* made for us (a spicy dish of scrambled eggs), because we were unlikely to find food suited to our taste on the way. I reached the house and packed. Mohammad Yusuf Sahib and Muniruddin had very kindly put my things in order and saved me from the trouble of tying up my bedroll. The car came at 10.00 a.m. and we occupied our seats as before. It then proceeded to its depot where it stopped for an hour. We left Jiddah at 11.00 a.m. The road skirts the sea from Jiddah till Rabigh.[1] It is impassable in some places but is all right for the most part. Gusts of cool

1 'At about noon of the second day the ship siren sounded: this was a sign that we had reached the latitude of Rabigh, a small port north of Jiddah, where, in accordance with an old tradition, the male pilgrims coming from the north are supposed to put away their everyday clothes and don the ihram, or pilgrim's garment. This consists of two unsewn pieces of white woolen or cotton cloth, of which one is wounded around the waist and reaches below the knees, while the other is slung loosely around one shoulder, with the head remaining uncovered. The reason for this attire, which goes back to an injunction of the Prophet, is that during the hajj there should be no feeling of strangeness between the Faithful who flock together from all the corners of the world to visit the House of God, no difference between races and nations, or between rich

breeze blow in from the sea. Our car is old but strong. The driver too is good. *Kishti subak wa hawa muafiq* [Smooth sailing of the ship and the favourable winds]. We travelled at a speed of 25 miles an hour. There are several *qahwa* shops along the way and the car stops at almost each one of them. We offered the Zuhr, Asr and Maghrib namaz. Everywhere you get water for wuzoo and prayer mats. The strong and bitter Arab tea helps remove the fatigue of the travel.

The journey passed enjoyably without any trouble. We reached Rabigh before Isha and rested under the huge huts built for the passengers. Thatched roofs are placed on top of palm tree stumps. A lot of beds are placed underneath, each with a small table close by. The huts, beds and tables are the sort that would be used by the Bedouins. Strong gusts of cold air came in from the sea. We offered the Isha namaz and helped ourselves to roti and khakeena. We savoured tea at the qahwa shop before rolling out our beddings for the night. A fee of 4 annas per bed is charged; so some prefer staying in the car that is parked in one corner of the shack. The rest of the space is a rest house for passengers. The teashop is inside the shack. There is a bazaar a few steps away for buying meat, fish, ghee, and other essentials. We travelled light because the drivers don't let you carry a lot of luggage with you. I made my bedroll as small as possible, so much so that I did not even carry my blanket. The wind was chilly here and so I thought I might be uncomfortable at night, but there can be no discomfort when Allah's mercy is with you. The wind died down and the chill went away. Spreading a rug I went to sleep covered by a Turkish towel. Soon, I was free of the world and its worries.

Friday, 22 March

Today's journey—it is almost 160 miles from Rabigh to Medina—is harsh. The camel caravans take eight days to cover this distance. But, Inshaallah, we'll cover this distance today itself.

We woke up two or two-and-a-half hours before sunrise. We finished our toilette and offered the Fajr namaz. My friends, Mohammad Yusuf and Muniruddin, very kindly tied my bedroll and put all our things together to load in the car. We bought tea from the shop, ate breakfast, and waited for the car to leave. With the driver still resting, we set off to

---

and poor or high and low, so that all know that they are brethren, equal before God and man.' Muhammad Asad, *Road to Mecca*, pp. 357–8.

inspect the bazaar. Balsa oil is produced in this region and is sold quite cheaply. Muniruddin settled the price of one *huqqa* (glassful) of oil for two guineas, and each of us bought it. Half is mine; the remaining half will be shared between Muniruddin and Mohammad Yusuf.

The motorcade left Rabigh by 1.00 p.m. The road is hilly and difficult to pass in places. But we are indifferent to the hazards of the journey owing to the prospective delight of entering the Home of the Prophet. The wind was chilly for the next two hours and we kept our ears covered with a cloth. Gradually, the chill lessened and the sun became warmer. By 4.00 p.m., we reached a post called Bir-e Ehsan. We had just finished our cup of tea when a car lorry drove up carrying a dead body. It was the body of a Javanese, who had been ailing for a long time, and was going to Medina with the dream of being buried in its sacred soil. But the Angel of Death did not give him the chance. He died after leaving Rabigh.

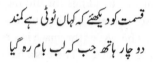

Qismat ko dekhiye ke kahan tooti hai kamand
do chaar haath jab ke labi baam reh gaya.

Look where destiny has broken the rope-ladder
When the destination is just a few hands away.

The dead body was taken out of the lorry and kept in a hut behind the qahwa shop. The Arabs gave it a funeral bath. With the shroud ready, it was wrapped around the body. We offered the Namaz-e Janaza. A pit was dug in the sand close beside the qahwa shop and the corpse was placed in the dirt. Inna lillahe wa inna ilaihi rajioon.[1]

Ten or fifteen cars were parked close to the qahwa shop; many of its passengers were Javanese. Strangely enough, except for two or three Javanese, no one from among the dead man's compatriots came

---

1 Abu Musa Al-Ash`ari (May Allah be pleased with him!) reported:

The Messenger of Allah (PBUH) said,

When a slave's child dies, Allah the Most High asks His angels, 'Have you taken out the life of the child of My slave?' They reply in the affirmative. He then asks, 'Have you taken the fruit of his heart?' They reply in the affirmative. Thereupon He asks, 'What has My slave said?' They say: 'He has praised You and said: "Inna lillahi wa inna ilaihi rajioon" (We belong to Allah and to Him we shall be returned). Allah says: 'Build a house for My slave in Jannah and name it as Bait-ul-Hamd (the House of Praise)'. (At-Tirmidhi)

close to the corpse or participated in the Namaz-e Janaza or the burial. Although our driver Sadiq did not observe the namaz strictly and we had, therefore, begun to look upon him with disfavour, he was the one who showed great alacrity in performing the last rites. He picked up the body, gave it a bath, covered it, and buried it. In fact, his involvement was such that one could have taken him to be a relative of the dead person.

Some of the passengers suggested handing over the dead body to the owners of the qahwa shop and moving on, or, at the very least, burying it without a namaz. But our driver insisted on the Namaz-e Janaza. May Allah grant him good recompense for this! There were only 10–15 people in the namaz, with the majority being from Hindustan. One Javanese, probably the dead man's relative, stood as the imam; the rest of us followed him.

We left this post after about an hour and a half. The road was uneven. The car's speed could not be increased. Every two hours, the car would halt at a qahwa shop for at least half an hour. We offered our Zuhr and Asr namaz at such shops. We had halted at the time of Asr at a police check post close to the qahwa shop. We were required to wait for almost two hours yet again because a death had occurred on the way and it had to be reported and investigated. We had been hoping to reach Medina by Maghrib, and this holy journey was supposed to have been over during the daylight hours. But we had to stay here for so long that our chances of reaching Medina even by Isha seemed dim. We left this post ten minutes before sunset. The car was stopped a short distance away at Maghrib time and we offered our namaz in a jama'at on the sand. Everyone was sad that it had already become dark. By the time we reached the last leg of our journey—Bir-e-Ali[1]—it became so pitch dark that we could not sight the high spot from where one catches the first sight of the Green Dome.[2]

1 Bir-e-Ali (Well of Ali) is not too far from Masjid Shajjarah (miqat). When returning from an expedition, the army of Imam Ali once ran out of water here. Miqat is the place where Muslims declare their intention to make hajj or umrah and begin the state of ihram. The miqat boundary is anchored by different townships and locations in different directions around the Kaaba. They are (a) Dhul-Hulaifa in the north, (b) Yalamlam in the southeast, (c) Zat Irq in the northeast, (d) Al-Johfa in the northwest, (e) Qarn al-Manazil in the east. It is also known as Zulhulaifa.

2 The Dome of the Rock is an Islamic prayer house, which Jews and Christians call Har ha-Bayit or the Temple Mount at Jerusalem. It was built between AD 687 and AD 691 by the ninth Caliph, Abd al-Malik. It is generally confused with Al-Aqsa Mosque, which was the first praying direction for Muslims before Mecca, and lies in the vicinity

We entered Medina three hours after sunset.

مقام وجد ہے اے دل کہ بزم یار میں آئے

بڑے دربار میں پہنچے بڑی سرکار میں آئے

Maqaam-e Wajd hai ai dil ke bazm-e yaar mein aaye
Bade darbar mein pahunche badi sarkar mein aaye.

I've my lover's company
It's a moment of ecstasy
I've arrived in the court of mighty
I've come before the great Majesty.

Inside the city, close to the railway station is the car depot. Here, guides and their lawyers greet the pilgrims. We had decided to stay at the Hyderabad Inn and look for a place in the morning. That is because Muniruddin carried a letter from the government permitting him to stay there [Hyderabad Inn], and the two of us, that is Mohammad Yusuf and I, could stay with him. But Sheikh Umar Effendi's lawyer insisted on taking all three of us to his house. We went along thinking that it might be difficult to go to the inn at this late hour.

Pilgrims and their guides are divided according to country, province, even district. Sheikh Umar is the guide for the Lakhnavis. Another guide is deputed for the pilgrims from Allahabad, and yet another for Hyderabad. We decided to accompany our respective guides when we go for ziyarat in order not to upset their fixed rights. But we will stay together so that we can draw comfort and solace from each other. I needed friends around me, particularly because I often feel tired while picking heavy loads. Also, I'm not used to doing my own chores. Muniruddin and Mohammad Yusuf Sahib take care of my errands when they are doing theirs and keep me out of the smallest trouble. May Allah grant them good recompense!

Sheikh Umar is an elderly man and quite deaf. He did not come to the station. His lawyer insisted on sending us to his house with an assistant, while he stayed back to greet the other pilgrims. Our luggage was loaded on a cart while the rest of us set off on foot because we considered it against etiquette to undertake this sacred journey differently.

---

of the Temple Mount. Al-Aqsa Mosque commonly refers to the southern congregational mosque that is part of the complex of religious buildings in Jerusalem known as Al-Haram al-Qudsi al-Sharif (the Noble Sanctuary) to Arabs and Muslims.

We prayed at the lawyer's house because the doors of the Haram Sharif had closed. Mohammad Sahib carried some home-made sweets with him, while Muniruddin Sahib had a box of salted biscuits. We ate this *manna*[1] from heaven. In the meanwhile, the lawyer showed up. He got some tea prepared for us. The long journey's fatigue disappeared the moment we set foot in Medina Munawwara. The tea invigorated us. We laid out our beds on the floor and, giving thanks to Allah, went off to sleep.

Saturday, 23 March

The morning dawned on the holy land of Medina. Close to the house is a Turkish bath. We took a bath, changed our clothes, applied *itr*, and proceeded to seek the Prophet's refuge. Our decades' old desire was finally fulfilled. The yearning of a lifetime welled up. The prayer beseeching the Almighty was finally answered.

دعائیں جو کی تھیں ہوئیں اب قبول

مراد ایک ہے اور ہزاروں حصول

Duaaen jo kee theen huween ab qubool
Murad ek hai aur hazaron husool.

All my prayers have been answered all through
I asked for one, but all my wishes have come true.

The guides accompanied us. We entered through the Baab-us Salam. I offered two rakat *nafil*[2] in the Jannat ki Kiyari (in the Prophet's mosque) and stood respectfully beside the Prophet's grave to say the salaam. I have no recollection of what happened to me at that point. All I remember is that a strange state was upon me. Tears coursed down my face. I don't remember what the guides asked me to recite or what I said or did.

Alhamdulillah!

آنرا کہ خبر شد خبرش باز نیامد

---

1 Manna is the name of a food mentioned in the Quran. The divine supply of manna as one of the miracles with which the Israelites were favoured.

2 Meaning 'extra'. A nafil (supererogatory) is an act of worship done because it was practised by Prophet Mohammad on at least one or two occasions. It earns a reward for the person performing it and its omission does not incur any punishment.

Aanra ke khabar shud khabrash baaz niamad

One who gets to know of Him the world does not get to know of him.

We returned from the Home of Plenty. Umar Effendi's assistant, Hamza, in whose house we had spent the night, served breakfast with tea. Afterwards, we set out in search of a house. We had heard at night that Dr Abdur Rehman was staying at the Hyderabad Inn. So, we went to meet him right away. Although he had set out from Mecca a day before, he reached only a few hours before us. He could attend the Friday prayer, whereas we entered Medina after the Isha namaz.

Doctor Sahib, who was pleased to meet us, insisted that we stay with him. A *waqf*[1] house is attached to the Hyderabad Inn. Here lives Jafar Daghistani, the trustee of the waqf properties in Mecca. The doctor occupies the top floor of the same building with two large rooms. While this place is nice and the doctor's company is desirable, it would not be proper to stay without the Trustee's permission.

We took our leave to meet Maulana[2] Abdul Baqi Sahib, the *muhajir* from Firangi Mahal. A well-to-do elderly gentleman, he has lived here for a very long time. He is married with children. I carried two letters of introduction and a couple of books. I presented the letters and books to him. He was extremely affectionate. He offered us tea and paan. As the Chief Teacher and Administrator at the Madrasa Nizamiya, he gave us permission to stay in the rooms of his madrasa and sent a servant to show us the way. Although the rooms were large and airy, they are at a distance from the Haram Sharif. So, we declined the offer to stay.

Taking our leave, we headed towards Dr Mohammad Husain Allahabadi's house. He had been posted in Jiddah for a very long time. He took his pension and went to India, but he returned to Mecca after the First World War. He belongs to the same area as my friend Mohammad Yusuf and is known to the latter's son. The doctor met us with courtesy, offered us tea, and conversed with us for a long time. He suggested that we stay at the Inn of Tonk, which is close to the Haram

---

1 A religious endowment, a property giving revenues, as regulated by Islamic law. Waqfs were vital to the religious parts of the society before the establishment of modern states in the Muslim world. Even today, institutions of waqfs finance the administration of mosques and religious schools.

2 Literally means, 'our lord' or 'our master', also used as a title, mostly in the Indian subcontinent, preceding the name of a respected Muslim religious leader, or scholars who have studied under other Islamic scholars.

Sharif and that we could live there free of charge. He wrote to Maulvi Syed Ahmad Sahib, the Trustee of the Tonk Inn, and instructed us to meet him forthwith and choose a nice room at the Inn. Accordingly, we reached Syed Ahmad's house following the doctor's instructions. It is very close to the Haram Sharif. As he was not home, we returned to Hamza's house. He wanted to rent out the top floor of his house to us. We went to look. Close to it is a cell. Herein, it is said, Syed Abdul Qadir Gilani (Peace be upon him!)[1] had prayed for a few days. Hamza expected four guineas as rent, but my friends didn't care much for this room.

We performed the wuzoo before reaching the Haram Sharif. This time we entered through the Baab-e Jibreel, offered the Zuhr namaz, and our salaam at the Prophet's grave. Then we went to Syed Ahmad's house. The maulana was back by now; he met us warmly. I showed him the letter, as also a letter sent by my relative in Lucknow. The maulana said that we could stay in any room we liked, and that he would go with us to show us around the Inn. He offered us tea and spoke at length about Hindustan and Afghanistan. Later, he took us to the Tonk Inn, a place closer to the Haram Sharif in comparison to the Madrasa Nizamiya. But the Hyderabad Inn is even closer. It is also close to the bazaar and the other populated areas. The Tonk Inn is, on the other hand, on the city outskirts in an uninhabited area.

The room shown to us was airy and faced a large courtyard but my friends did not like it. I did not want to do anything against their wishes. It was then decided that we approach the Trustee of the Hyderabad Inn, Jafar Daghistani, to seek his permission to let us stay with Dr Abdur Rehman.

Muniruddin is carrying two letters for Jafar Daghistani, one of which is a government note. Jafar is, therefore, compelled to give him a place to stay. But we don't know whether he would agree to house uninvited guests. We took our leave from Maulvi Syed Ahmad, and returned to Dr Rehman's house, and met Jafar Daghistani. He agreed, willingly and happily, to let us stay and promised that under no circumstances would he force us to change our rooms.

---

1 Shaikh 'Abd al-Qadr Gilani (1077–1166) was a noted preacher, Sufi, and the figurehead of the Qadiri Sufi order. He was born in the Persian province of Gilan (Iran), south of the Caspian Sea. Gilani belongs to the spiritual chain of Junayd Baghdadi. His contribution to thought in the Muslim world earned him the title 'al-Gauth al Azam' (the Supreme Helper).

We offered the Asr namaz in the Haram-e Mohtaram and, after the *salaam-khwani*,[1] had our baggage brought from Hamza's house. As I have written earlier, Doctor Sahib has two rooms. One serves as his clinic and bedroom. In the other room, we laid out our beds on one side, and on the other side, the doctor's compounder and servant laid out their beds. We are at ease with our lodgings. The house is comfortable. The bathroom and toilet are close by. There is enough light and air. We are also happy with Doctor Sahib's company and, above all, the proximity to the Haram Sharif.

Praise is to Allah whatever be the situation.

Sunday, 24 March

We woke up about two-and-a-half hours before sunrise. We offered the Namaz-e Tahajjud in the Haram Mohtaram. We stayed busy till Fajr, praying, reciting, and supplicating (reading durood-o-wazaif). After the Fajr namaz, we returned to our inn and sat down to write letters after breakfast. For close to two hours, I sat engrossed in performing this duty. After Asr, we went to Jannat-ul Baqi.[2] We offered salaam to the martyrs, and the truthful, noble, pious people buried here.

We had studied in the history of the Great Roman Empire that when the Vandals and Goths had attacked Rome, they had vanquished it and destroyed its ancient monuments and razed centuries-old art and architecture to the ground. The state of Jannat-ul Baqi under the Nejdis, is similar to the ruin and havoc unleashed by those barbarians.

از نقش و نگارِ در و دیوارِ شکسته

آثارِ پدیدست صنادید عجم را

Az naqsh-o-nigar-e-dar-o-deewar shikaste
Aasaar padeed ast sana deed-e-ajam ra.

Inlays and designs on broken walls suggest
These remains belong to Persian kings.

1 Paying homage at the shrine. Also known as 'birth' or 'birthday'. In this context, it refers to the birthday celebrations held for the Prophet.

2 A graveyard in Medina located across from the Masjid al-Nabawi. It contains the graves of many of Prophet Mohammad's relatives and companions. Its name means 'Tree Garden of Heaven'. It is the most sacred and blessed graveyard, followed by Jannat-ul-Mualla, which is the graveyard of Mecca.

We came out of Jannat-ul Baqi carrying the burden of longing and pity in our hearts, even though we scarcely wanted to leave such a holy and sacred site. A strange feeling came upon me, which I cannot describe, when I was saying my salaam at the grave of Hazrat Syedatun Nisa Fatima Zehra (Peace be upon her!).[1]

Monday, 25 March

Once more, I visited the Jannat-ul Baqi, after the morning namaz. Once again the same feeling overwhelmed me as I stood before the domed graves of the Ahl-i Bait (Peace be upon them!).[2] May Allah bestow his pleasure and kindness on all of them! Some of my relatives and friends from back home had given me their teeth to bury in Medina. Today, I put them in the care of this sacred soil.

We've worked out a regimen whereby everyday, we get up three hours before sunrise, offer salaam, perform wuzoo, go to the Haram Sharif, offer Namaz-e-Tahajjud, go to the Prophet's tomb (*Muwajah-e Aqdas*), and offer salaam. And then we stay there till Fajr, busy reciting different kinds of prayers and supplications. After the namaz, the guides make us offer the salaam. Then we return home, eat harisa or matbakh for breakfast, and drink tea. Then, we get busy performing various chores. Lunch is at Zuhr. We buy the bread from the market; it is extremely soft, delicious, and easy-to-digest. The Doctor Sahib's employees can cook meat. Muniruddin Sahib is in charge of organizing and cooking the meals. After the Zuhr, Asr, and Maghrib namaz, the guides instruct us to say the salaam. From Maghrib till Isha, we stay in the Blessed Mosque reciting *Durood Sharif*.[3]

We return home after Namaz-e Isha. At night, we don't eat a proper meal; instead, we make do with either milk or sweets. These are daily occurrences, which I shall forbear from recording everyday. Thank Allah I am able to join the jamaat everyday in the Masjid-e Nabawi.[4]

---

1 See also Shorish Kashmiri (1971), *Shabja-i ke Manboodam*, Lahore, pp. 164–5.

2 Meaning, people of the house or family. To Shias, Ahl-i Bait refers to Fatima Zahra, his successor, son-in-law, and cousin Ali, their two sons, Hasan and Husain, and the nine Imams from the lineage of Husain and Hasan ibn Ali's daughter.

3 Durood (also Durood Sharif) is an invocation, which Muslims make by saying specific phrases to compliment the prophet Mohammad. The Islamic view is to say durood whenever a Muslim reads, speaks, or hears the name of Mohammad.

4 The Mosque of the Prophet in Medina is the second holiest mosque in Islam. The original mosque was built by Prophet Mohammad himself. Subsequent Islamic rulers greatly expanded and decorated it. The most important feature of the site is the

Several times, I [am blessed by being able to] offer salaam. My health is, with Allah's grace, good and my bowel movements are in order.

Tuesday, 26 March

We were invited to a meal after Zuhr by Abu Saud, the muallim. An entire roasted *dumba* (a kind of sheep with a thick tail)[1] was placed before us on a platter. On another platter, rice was served. In addition, roti, *saalan*, and chutney[2] were served. The food was in great abundance. But the Arabs do not eat chillies and put very little salt in their food. Hence, we did not particularly enjoy the meal. After the meal, tea was served. Later, after the meal, we went with Doctor Sahib to the house of a certain Madani Sahib, who, once again, offered us food but we had no appetite for it. And so we only had tea. Madani Sahib has young and very pretty daughters. With their pink and rose-like complexions, they look European. His brother-in-law [his wife's sister's husband] is a Hindustani from Bhopal. Although settled in Medina, he still has such 'Hindiyat' left in him. For one, he chews and carries with him a box of paan. He gave us a share of this rare blessing. We stayed at Madani Sahib's house for almost two hours. The time we spent there passed enjoyably.

Wednesday, 27 March

Today, after breakfast, we went to see Koh-e Uhud.[3] A guide named Mohammad accompanied us. He got us a carriage for 3 riyals. The carriage is of the same vintage as the Crakel that once used to be found in Hindustan. It can seat six passengers and if need be, the driver can sit atop the horse. Usually, mules or donkeys are harnessed in these carriages, but ours was horse-drawn. The road is in a very poor condition but the

---

green dome over the centre of the mosque, where the tomb of Mohammad is located. Constructed in 1817 and painted green in 1839, it is known as the Dome of the Prophet.

1 The domestic sheep (ovis) is a woolly ruminant quadruped. It is probably descended from the wild mouflon of South Asia and Southwest Asia.

2 Chutney is a term for a variety of sweet and spicy condiments, originally from South Asia. In India, chutney, both dry or wet, is often made to be eaten fresh, using whatever suitable strongly flavoured ingredients are locally available at the time.

3 Uhud is the name of a mountain near Medina. It was the site of the second battle between Muslim and Meccan forces.

Arab drivers persist in racing over it. We managed to safely reach the foothill of the mountain. During Turkish rule, this used to be a festive place dotted with lots of mosques, wuzoo sites, *hammams*, and hotels. But all you see now are heaps of broken stones. If the houses still have walls, the roofs are missing, and if the roof is there, then some part of the wall is gone. Just as the Muslim victors had defaced the idols by slashing their noses and ears, so too the Nejdis have made the monuments of Koh-e Uhud lame and maimed. There is a hot spring near the grave of Hazrat Syedna Hamza.[1] I performed my ablution from this spring of hot water and offered salaam at the grave (*marqad*) of Syed-ul shuhada.[2] Afterwards, I offered my salaam to all the martyrs at the Battle of Uhud.[3] Soon after the fateha, the spectacle of the helpless death of the martyrs in the battle of Uhud flashed before my eyes and my heart was overwhelmed with emotions. I was especially reminded of those ladies who had lost their fathers and brothers in this battle. And yet they were concerned with nothing else except to look for the Prophet. They had said that if they reached the Prophet (*huzoor-i- aqdas*) and found him alive, they would care for nothing else. I, my father, brother, husband offer ourselves. O, ruler of our faith, before you, we have no standing.

1 Hamza ibn 'Abd al-Muttalib was the uncle of the Prophet Mohammad. They were raised together as they were almost of the same age. After Hamza's death, the Prophet is recorded to have said that he was 'the lion of God and of His Apostles'. On the magnificence of his tomb, later razed to the ground, see Ali, Nadir (1902), *Miratul Arab yaani Safarnama-i Nadir*, Delhi, p. 73.

2 Literally, 'the greatest among the martyr'. Usually referring to Imam Husain, the great martyr of Karbala.

3 The Battle of Uhud was the second major battle between the Quraysh and the Muslims. Quraysh fought this battle in AH 3 (AD 624) to avenge their defeat at the battle of Badr, one year ago. The Battle of Uhud was fought outside Medina near the mountain of Uhud. At first, Muslims had a quick and easy victory over the Quraysh. Some of the frontline Muslim troops began collecting *mal ghanimah* (war trophies) after the Quraysh fled. Other Muslims, who were deputed at strategic positions in the back, left their positions and joined those who were collecting mal ghanimah, completely ignoring the instructions of the Prophet. The fleeing Quraysh noticed the breach in Muslim defence, regrouped under the leadership of Khalid bin Walid, and attacked Muslims from the back. Muslims almost lost the battle of Uhad due to this fresh attack of the Quraysh. The Prophet was wounded in this battle. After suffering heavy casualties, the Muslims finally succeeded in chasing the Quraysh away.

میں بھی اور باپ بھی شوہر بھی برادر بھی فدا

اے شہ دیں ترے ہوتے ہوئے کیا چیز ہیں ہم

Main bhi aur baap bhi shauhar bhi biradar bhi fida
Ai shah-e din tere hote hue kya cheez hain hum.

I, my father, my companion, my brother offer our devotion
O Faith's saviour, we mean nothing as long as you are there.

We left this sacred spot for Bir-e Ruma. This is the well that Hazrat Usman[1] bought from a Jew and handed over to the Muslims as a waqf. As we had no pail, we were deprived of the water of this sacred well. Masjid-e Qiblatain (mosque having two qiblas) was our next halt. It was in this masjid that the order for changing the direction of the qibla was given. One *mehrab*[2] of this mosque faces the Bait-ul Muqqadas [Jerusalem]; the other faces the Kaaba. Close to it is the spot where the Sahaba-e Muhajirin had their houses. On these holy sites are the Masjid-e Ali, Masjid-e Fatima, Masjid-e Salman Farsi,[3] Masjid-e Abu Bakr Siddiq, and Masjid-e Fatah. Now that Allah, the dearest and the greatest (*buzurg-o-bartar*) has brought me to these holy sites, I hope that I find the company of these worthies on the Day of Judgement and get the *shafaat*, benediction, of the last of the Prophets (*khatim-ul mursaleen*).

After performing the ziyarat [at these sites], we returned home. After Asr, we chanced to go to the Mazhari Inn (Rabbat-e Mazhari). The *mutawalli*, a descendent of the Hazrat Mujaddid Alaf Sani (PBUH),[4] is in Hindustan. The madrasa is closed for now. Two or three students reside here but receive instruction in other schools. A muhajir from

---

1 Usman ibn Affan (580–656), a companion and son-in-law of the Prophet Mohammad, played a major role in early Islamic history, most notably as the third Khalifa of the Rashidun (644 to death) and for his compilation of the Quran.

2 A niche in a mosque, that indicates the qibla (direction of Mecca).

3 Salman al-Farsi mosque is one among 'the five mosques' (Khamsa Masajid). This is at the foot of the mount leading to Masjid-e Fatah at Mecca.

4 Shaikh Ahmad Sirhindi, a scholar and prominent member of the Naqshbandi Sufi order, is regarded as having rejuvenated Islam, due to which he is commonly called 'Mujaddid Alf Thani', meaning 'reviver of the second millennium'. He was born on the 10th of Muharram in the year H 971, in Sirhind near Lahore, now in Pakistan.

Bukhara lives here under somebody's trusteeship.[1] We called on him and benefited from his generosity and kindness (*faiz-o-karam*).[2]

Thursday, 28 March

The air at Medina is extremely favourable. The water is light, cool, and sweet. The weather is pleasant these days. You need a light quilt at night and the mornings are quite cool. The days are not too hot, though the sun is quite warm. The city's inhabitants are modest, courteous and sweet-tongued. The people of Mecca are sterner by temperament. But here you notice submissiveness and humility. However, there is no end to poverty. During Turkish rule, the city's population was more than 80,000; now, it has been reduced to 20,000–25,000. And the majority live in dire straits. There are large lavish houses but no one lives in them. The Nejdis have restored order and peace, so there might be an increase in the population. The bazaars are well-stocked and every foreign-made commodity is available in them. The price of essential commodities is much less than in Mecca. Matbakh cost 8 qarsh in Mecca; it costs 6 here. An egg cost 6 halalla there; here you can get 2 eggs for 6 paise. Ghee costs much less here than in Hindustan. You can get all sorts of sweets in the shops. As in Mecca, you can get dry paan here too. Everything you possibly need is easily and freely found in these shops. In actual fact, Medina is a good place to live in by worldly standards!

Thanks to Qamruddin, the gatekeeper of Baab-e Jibreel, after Zuhr, we went to meet an extremely old gentleman, Sheikh Mohammad Madani. He lives in Ribaat-e Usmani, close to Baab-e Jibreel. He is an Allah-fearing, deeply religious man. He met us and offered us dates grown in Medina. He prayed for our well-being. May his prayers come true and may we be blessed by Allah's munificence! It seems that he has stopped going to the Haram Sharif after the Nejdi occupation. Owing to weakness and old age, he is probably unable to attend the congregational prayers. Occasionally, he goes to offer salaam. He is also a Sheikh-ul Dalail, or guide of the pilgrim's rituals. I sought his permission to call on him one morning with the *Dalailul Khairat* (Proofs of Good Deeds—a book of blessings on the Prophet) and listen to its recitation.

1 Bukhara is the fifth largest city in Uzbekistan. It contains numerous mosques and madaris. The last Amir of Bukhara was Mohammad Alim Khan (1880–1944).

2 In other words, it was an enriching experience to meet him.

Friday, 29 March

Today, I was blessed by being able to offer the Friday namaz in the Haram-ul Nabawi. We performed the wuzoo before reaching the masjid by 4.30 pm so that we could secure a good place. Others had been even more determined; we found a place in the last row of the Rauza Min Riyazul Jannat. The man giving the sermon was a Nejdi. He delivered a provocative speech and termed all those who say, 'May peace be upon you, O Messenger (*Assalamo Alaika Ya Rasool Allah*)[1] as polytheists (*mushrik-o-fasiq*) and sinners. We hear that he had made the same declarations on Id and a pious Egyptian had stood up to engage in a debate with him. But today, except for saying, 'We seek Allah's refuge from such offences/lapses', (*Nauzubillahi min tilkal hafawat*), no one uttered a word of protest. This is a sacred spot worthy of respect (*wajib-ul ehtiram*), and it is sinful to speak a wrong.

One can never say enough about the magnanimity and forgiveness (*hilm-o-afw*) of the Prophet! The Bani Umayya tied horses in the Masjid-e Nabawi. The Abbasids slaughtered the Sadaat one by one. The Qaramita destroyed Medina with their atrocities and cruelties. The traitor Husain laid siege upon the city of Medina for three years and vanquished its people. The Nejdis rained canon balls over the city and traumatized its citizens. And today from the mimbar of the Prophet,[2] a fatwa of infidelity or kufr[3] is being issued to those who sit facing the Kaaba. But there is not a crease on any forehead.[4] The good and bad are similarly dear to the Compassionate and Merciful One.

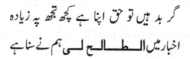

Gar bad hain to haq apna hai kucch tujh pe ziyaada,
akhbaar men 'at-taalihu li' hum ne suna hai.

1 Meaning, 'Peace be upon you, Oh Prophet of Allah'. It is a salutation to Prophet Mohammad.

2 Mimbar is a pulpit in the mosque located to the right of the mehrab, where the Imam (leader of prayer) stands to deliver sermons. The mimbar is often richly ornamented, and usually shaped like a small tower with a pointed roof and stairs leading up to it.

3 To show ungratefulness to Allah and not to believe in Him and His religion

4 *Magar jabin-e mubarak par shikan nahin aati.*

We have heard you say that even the wicked is dear to me
If we are bad then we have more rights over you.

After the Namaz-e Asr, we went to see Arz-e Batha and its groves of date palms planted in pretty rows. Different types of date trees were planted there. The blossoms are just coming out and the trees are being watered. Once upon a time, Medina was famous for these trees and even now, its dates are unmatched for their freshness and sweetness.

I forgot to write that after the Namaz-e Juma the salaam-khwani remained postponed until the Amir of Medina,[1] the Governor, appointed by the Nejdi government, had left the masjid. During his presence in the masjid, salaam-khwani for the Prophet is unlawful. It is permitted everyday after Fajr, Zuhr, Asr, and Maghrib, but not after Isha. It is also ordered that after the salaam, the dua (supplication, prayer or devotional phrases) should be made with one's back to the Prophet's grave because it is considered shirk[2] and bid'at to make a dua while facing the auspicious window that overlooks the grave.

We seek Allah's refuge from such offences.

Saturday, 30 March

After namaz and breakfast, we performed a fresh wuzoo. We got on to a carriage and went to see the Masjid-e Quba[3] along with Jafar Daghistani. Thank Allah, we offered the nafil in the Masjid Ussisa ala Taqwa (literally, 'built-on-the-fear-of-Allah mosque'). We went around this auspicious site where the Prophet's she-camel had sat when he had come to Medina and drank from the water of the well from where the Khatam-e Mustafawi (the Prophet's ring that bore his seal) had fallen from the hands of Hazrat Usman[4] and disappeared in its waters. Allah, in His Infinite mercy, has brought a sinner such as me to these sacred

1 An independent ruler or chieftain (especially in Africa or Arabia). Amir is a title given to a person of high political rank. It is often translated as 'prince'.

2 'Shirk' means associating partners with Allah. Shirk can also encompass any object that a person may hold in regard higher than Allah. It is considered as the most severe of sins.

3 First mosque of Islam, Masjid-e Quba is located just outside Medina Munawwara, Saudi Arabia. Its first stones were positioned by Prophet Mohammad himself on his emigration from Mecca to Medina. He spent more than 20 nights here (after migrating) while waiting for Imam Ali.

4 Usman ibn Affan (c. 580–17 July 656) was a companion and son-in-law of Prophet Mohammad. He played a major role in early Islamic history, most notably as the third of

spots. My request now is that He takes me away from this world with my faith intact and grants me a cup of water from the Spring of Kausar¹ from the Prophet's own hand.

Close to the Masjid-e Quba is the mosque of Syedna Ali. It is not permitted to pray here; in fact, the Nejdis have posted a police force here. In Lucknow, when an old mosque had been turned into a dispensary, the Muslims were angry. Here, it ought to inflame much worse passions to see the Nejdis occupying Hazrat Ali's mosque.² Close to it, there were once several smaller mosques but they have all been destroyed by the Nejdis. Now all you see are heaps of broken stones and no one is allowed to go there. I never used to speak ill of the Saudis before this hajj travel but now it has become impossible to keep one's tongue silent after having witnessed their barbaric actions. May Allah give them better counsel!

(Our Lord) place not in our hearts any rancour towards those who believe. Our Lord, you are full of pity, merciful.

It used to be a densely populated stretch from Quba (the first mosque that was built by the Prophet) to Medina, but now a mere handful of homes are left and of these, most are deserted. A fort from the Ottoman times survives but that too is uninhabited. Groves of dates and pomegranate orchards along the way are bursting with buds. The wheat is almost ready. Close beside the Masjid-e Quba stands a field of wheat ready to be harvested.

After Zuhr, Mohammad Yusuf, Muniruddin and I went to Sheikh Umar Effendi's house. We ate Bukhari biryani and *sheer-e beranj* (a delicacy made from dates). The biryani is considered to be a gourmet's delight; it has more dried fruits than meat. After Asr, we went to the bazaar. I had run out of pages in my diary, so I bought a new one.

the Rightly-Guided Khalifa (644–655). He belonged to the great Meccan family of the Banu Umayya and was responsible for the second and final revision of the Quran.

1 'Spring of Paradise'.

2 Ali ibn Abu Talib, the cousin, son-in-law, and one of the Ahl-i Bait of the Prophet Mohammad, was born in Mecca (17 March 599–28 February 661). When Mohammad reported that he had received a divine revelation, Ali, then only about ten years old, believed him and he was the first male to accept Islam. He also took a leading part in the battle of Khyber. He was married to Fatima, the Prophet's only daughter. The Prophet held him dearly and, according to the Shias, appointed him as the Khalifa. Abu Bakr, it is alleged by the Shias, usurped his right to Khilafat.

Muniruddin Hyderabadi was also with us. He bought a Persian carpet for 8 guineas. The shopkeeper initially asked for 13 guineas but after a lot of bargaining, he agreed to reduce the price to 8 guineas.

Sunday, 31 March

After some investigation, we discovered today that the carpet that had been bought for 8 guineas is worth only 3 guineas. Efforts are underway to persuade the shopkeeper to take it back but there is little hope of success.

This morning after 3 o'clock (according to Arab time), we went to the shop of Abdul Ghani Kathiawari. He trades in tea, sugar and rice. A pious and deeply religious man, he promised to get us a small car at a reasonable rate to take us back to Mecca. I got a 100-rupee note changed at his shop and had 4 guineas and 77 qarsh deposited as an advance so that we would have some money left for our return journey. Carrying cash in one's pockets is unsafe because the poor people and beggars swarm around (us) in such large numbers. May Allah remove the poverty of the inhabitants of Mecca!

Every single inhabitant here cries for the Turks. During their time, Medina was a city of riches. Today, it is the capital of poverty.

After Zuhr, Mir Ghulam Bhik Nairang visited us. A lawyer in Ambala, he is an active member of the Majlis-e Tabligh. He arrived in the ship called *Khusrou* and reached Mecca during Sha'baan. On the 20th of Ramazan, he came to Medina. I had read about his departure from India in the newspapers, and that he had already left for the City of the Prophet before we reached Mecca. I had not seen his face before. In the Masjid-e Nabawi, I had seen a man who looked like he was from Hindustan whom I thought might be Nairang. One day, after plucking my courage, I asked his name as we stood near the door. My guess was confirmed and I discovered that he was, indeed, Mir Nairang. He is staying close to our house. Today, he visited us and talked for a long time. We discovered that he had paid 15.5 guineas for a return fee for the car. This included the cost of the journey from Mecca to Jiddah after the hajj. He intends to leave Medina after the 15th of Zee Qada (the 11th month of the Muslim lunar year). Mir Sahib knew several of my relatives. I enjoyed his company very much.

After Asr, we went to the bazaar. Muniruddin Sahib returned the carpet and took a better one in its place. According to the terms of the agreement, the sale was final. It is an indication of the noble disposition of the dwellers of Mecca that the shopkeeper agreed to the exchange. After finishing this transaction, we went to Abdul Ghani Kathiawari's shop and inspected some samples of dates. From the bazaar, we went straight to the Masjid-e Nabawi and stayed there till Isha.

Monday, 1 April

The caravan of Javanese reached Medina today. We had seen them setting off on camels a day before. How deprived and desolate I had felt then and how helpless too! Alhamdulillah, we had the good fortune to pay our respects ten days before them. Today, there is much excitement among the huge crowds in this exalted city. After 2 p.m., Dr Mohammad Husain Sahib Allahabadi, of whom I have written earlier, visited us. He spoke for half an hour. He has invited us for a meal after Zuhr.

After Maghrib, we met Maulvi Akram Khan Sahib Bangali in the Haram Sharif. He has reached today. At the time of his arrival, I was busy reading my wazifa. So, I couldn't speak to him at length.

Tuesday, 2 April

Today, the second caravan of Javanese reached Medina. Now here too, as in Mecca, you see them everywhere. Many are staying close to our house. They have lent a festive air to the streets. We can now buy all sorts of provisions virtually at our doorstep. My heart was gladdened at the sight of their women going towards the grave of the Prophet for salaam-khwani, wearing shining burqas of *tussar* and satin. In Mecca, I was displeased to see women wearing bright and ostentatious burqas performing tawaf. But in this court of the Rehmatul-Aalameen,[1] I was happy to see them in their Id finery. Id comes every year, twice a year. But this auspicious time is special for these ladies, an occasion that may not come again. May Allah accept their pilgrimage!

How can one compare the archipelago of Java with the lanes of Medina!

رشتۂ در گردِ نم افگنده دوست

می برد هر جا که خاطر خواه اوست

Rishtaee dar-gardanam afgandeh doost
Mi barad har ja ke khatir khwah -e-ust.

1 One of the many attributes of Prophet Mohammad.

The noose of His love is tied around my neck
I move around everywhere at His command.

After Zuhr, we went to Dr Mohammad Husain's house for a meal. We were served the most exquisite and elaborately prepared dishes. We especially enjoyed our hosts' company.

Wednesday, 3 April

This morning, we paid our respects to Maulana Abdul Baqi Sahib Muhajir yet again. For a long time, we discussed the problems of the citizens of Medina. The maulana is extremely angry with the Saudis and is all praise for Turkish rule. Here, as in Mecca, we have still not met anyone who is happy with Nejdi rule.

This year the mosquito menace is great. The maulana told us that earlier there were far less mosquitoes; this year, however, the menace has increased. He also said that the locusts have attacked eight times.

Another caravan of Javanese arrived today. A few Afghans too have turned up. The masjid is now very crowded. Haji Mohammad Noor Sahib Banarasi, who had come with us on the ship, reached Medina last evening. He had left Mecca on Friday with the rest of the Hindustani caravan but had found the journey on camelback disconcerting. With only three halts left for Medina, he decided to travel on foot. Walking all the way, he had reached yesterday after Asr. Today, after Asr, he came to our house and joined us for tea.

The floor of the Masjid-e Nabawi is being repaired. It is said that some trader from Sindh who lives in Mecca has donated a certain sum of money to the government for repairs.

Munshi Mohammad Yusuf Sahib has received a hundi for Rs 300 from Abdullah Obaidullah. Despite his frequent trips to the house of the agent in Medina, he has not been able to recover his money. Today, Haji Abdul Ghani too tried to help, but the agent is bankrupt and unable to pay back the money.

Thursday, 4 April

The Hindustani caravan is expected today. We (Muniruddin Sahib, Haji Noor Mohammad, and I) went to the city gate to welcome it. The caravan is coming in driblets. Hundreds of visitors arrived but not the pilgrims from Neemuch whom I had especially come to meet. We waited for an hour without luck. The camels of the Indians are weak.

They might, therefore, reach tomorrow. The better part of the caravan has arrived today but it has mostly Javanese and Bengalis. The Indians have been left behind.

Today, we saw the Egyptian *langarkhana*. Roti, meat and rice were being distributed among the poor. The Department of *Auqaf* (Endowments) in Egypt is responsible for running it. Food is distributed among the poor throughout the year. The needy are given enough for two meals. The poor, especially the Negroes, subsist on this. May Allah grant mercy to the mutawallis and those who have instituted auqaf!

The door to the chamber housing the Prophet's grave is opened twice a week on Thursdays and Sundays. No one else is allowed to enter except the eunuchs who have been appointed as caretakers.

After Asr, as I sat close to the screen in the Jannat ki Kiyari, reading Durood Sharif, a eunuch entered the grave chamber. He began cleaning it. Thanks to Allah, the dust from that holy site fell on me too. My friend Muniruddin Hyderabadi has made arrangements through Qamaruddin, the gatekeeper of Baab-e Jibreel, to ask a eunuch to keep some rose flowers, *misri*, cardamom, etc. wrapped in a handkerchief under the cover of the grave so that they might be blessed by the sacred air and dust of that holy spot.

Mohammad Yusuf Sahib and I decided to divide these things equally into three and carry them home as gifts. Incidentally, they were placed under the sacred cover in front of my eyes. The eunuch raised the cover slightly and hid these things underneath. Alhamdulillah!

I was reminded of how the Prophet had appreciated the services of Bilal[1] for Allah so much that till this day only Negroes are permitted to serve in the grave chamber. The servitors of this most sacred place are these black eunuchs; all hajjis must respect them.

It is worth remembering that owing to the mischief wrought by the rebellious Husain, the infidel armies had reached Medina during the First World War and laid siege to it. As a result, all the routes for carrying essential supplies were closed. The Turks commanded the citizens of Medina to evacuate the city and migrate to Syria because stocks of essential commodities had been exhausted. Nothing was left for the

---

1 Bilal ibn Rabah was an Ethiopian born in Mecca in the late sixth century, some time between 578 and 582. Prophet Mohammad chose him as his muezzin. The muezzin is a chosen person at the mosque who leads the call (*adhan*) to Friday service and the five daily prayers from one of the mosque's minarets. Bilal was known for his beautiful voice with which he called people to their prayers.

people except dates and water; barely 100–200 people were left behind when all others had either been expelled or had left of their own free will. Among the thousands of servitors of the Rauza-e Sharif, only 40 were left who had refused to leave the Prophet's company; of these 40 servitors, 20 were eunuchs. At such a delicate time, only the compatriots of Bilal had stayed behind to keep the Prophet's grave lit and cleaned. Not a trace of the Syeds and the elites of Mecca remained. That is Allah's favour. He gives it to whomsoever He wishes.

اور امتحاں بغیر تو یہ آپ کا غلام

قائل نہیں ہے قبلہ کسی شیخ و شاب کا

Aur imtihan baghair to yeh aap ka ghulam,
qa'ail nahin hai qibla kisi shaikh-o-shaab ka.

He is your slave without any further tests
The qibla needs neither the old nor the young.

Before namaz, I presented myself for fateha-khwani[1] in the Jannat-ul Baqi and, as always, brought with me a heap of overwhelming emotions.

Friday, 5 April

The caravan from Hindustan reached safely with its bags and baggage. Mir Reham Ali too has come. But I haven't met him yet. The waterman from Neemuch, whom I have mentioned before, walked all the way to Medina. I met him at the Masjid-e Nabawi but couldn't talk to him much at that time.

Medina wears a festive air. The locals say that in the entire year, there are only two Fridays when there is no space left in the Masjid-e Nabawi—one is Friday as today, and the other is the Friday after hajj in the first week of Muharram.[2] After a bath, we reached the mosque at 3.30 p.m. that is, two and a half hours before *zawal* (the time when no namaz can be offered). By then, several rows had already been filled up and just a little before zawal, there wasn't even space for the proverbial seed of sesame to be placed on the floor of the great mosque.

---

1 Prayer for the deceased.

2 Muharram is the first month of the Islamic calendar. The tenth day of Muharram is called Yaum-i 'Ashurah, meaning, 'the tenth day', and it is a day of voluntary fasting.

Due to the fear of the Nejdis, I normally don't read the Dalailul Khairat. But today, I read the entire text. No one objected. The Nejdis don't disallow people from visiting the grave chamber. But, they do not allow pilgrims to read from any book other than the Quran Sharif inside the Haram Sharif. There are special guards to ensure that no one touches the screen around the grave and, at the time of the salaam, no one stands with clasped hands. It is even disallowed to raise one's hands for prayer. The four imams of the mosque have decreed that one must not raise one's hands in prayer after namaz. If one feels the need to make a prayer, one can do so softly under one's breath. However, raising one's hands in prayer after namaz is heresy.

There is no harm if during the namaz, the 'Amen' is said so loudly that others praying beside you are alarmed! But it is sinful to make a prayer after namaz. Such a sin cannot be tolerated.

By now, I have worked out a schedule such that after the Tahajjud namaz, I sit and read from the wazifa, facing the window of the grave enclosure with my back against the wall of the masjid. At such times, one is able to see the mischief worked by the Nejdis. There are two guards on either side of the window whose job it is to stop those pilgrims who stand with folded hands, raise their hands in supplication, or attempt to come close to the screen. Some Punjabi pilgrims argue and Egyptian women hurl the choicest abuses when they are stopped, but the Nejdis are not to be stopped from their headstrong stubbornness and forcefully free the hands that are either folded or raised.

Owing to the financial crisis, there is an acute power shortage. Often, the electricity goes off even when large numbers of pilgrims congregate inside the mosque. At such times, the believers have an unexpectedly good time. They rush towards the screen around the Prophet's grave and, in the darkness, do as they please in accordance with the fatwa of rightness given by the religion of love.

عاشقاں را مذہب و ملّت جداست

Aashiqan ra mazhab-o millat judast

Lovers have different creeds and credos.

But the tragedy is that even in that darkness the Nejdis give no respite to Allah's lovers. They pull and drag away whosoever they manage to grab in the darkness.

بجرمِ عشق تو ام میکشند غوغائیست
تو نیز بر سرِ بام آ کہ خوش تماشائیست

Be jurme ishq to am mikashand ghogha eest
Toa neez bar sare bam aa ke khush tamasha eest

The hinds drag me in crime of love
You come to your balcony to complete the spectacle.

Today, thanks to the sheer number of pilgrims or as a result of some other intevention, the khatib did not deliver a provocative speech. He kept dwelling on the fear of Allah and the notion of purity. He even failed to give the appellation of kafir to those who read the salaam.

Carpets have been laid out in the mosque because of the large numbers of pilgrims. From the time I have been here, the Rauza min Riyazil Jannah has had tattered old rugs and mats. This pathetic sight has immensely pained me. As the number of hajjis increased, the number of mats kept getting fewer and fewer. Old carpets were spread out in their place. Thank Allah, today there is a flooring of carpets all over the mosque. In Hindustan, there is an old saying regarding putting a coarse cotton patch on brocade robes, but here it is a common sight to see cotton darning or a cotton patch on woollen and silk carpets.

Allah-o-Akbar! This is the same Blessed Mosque where during the Turkish rule, there used to be the finest silk carpets laid out on the floors and at night, the mosque would be transformed into a cuppola of radiance from the light of thousands of chandeliers. When, due to the strictness of the rebellious Hussein, Medina fell on hard times, the Turkish Governor had the gold chandeliers and priceless jewels safely transported to Istanbul.[1] When Husain gained control of Medina, he took away all the expensive artefacts kept in the stronghouse of the Rauza-e Mubarak to decorate his own palace in Mecca. The Nejdis ruined the few carpets and floorings that were left behind. Now, in the Mosque of the Prophet once again, you see those tattered sackcloths

---

1 Istanbul, in its long history, served as the capital city of the Roman Empire (330–95), the Byzantine Empire (395–1204 and 1261–1453), the Latin Empire (1204–61), and the Ottoman Empire (1453–1922).

on which once pieces of the royal crown and *durfash kaviyani*[1] were distributed among the Muhajirs and Ansars.[2]

بدأ الاسلام بالغريب و سيعود الى الغريب

Islam began with aliens and will return to aliens.

The Masjid-e Nabawi is being repaired. The honour of restoration has gone to a Sindhi gentleman. It is said that the Huzoor Nizam (of Hyderabad) has pledged ten lakh rupees, but the Nejdis insist that they would carry on the repairs on the condition that the cash be handed over to them. This, quite sensibly, the Nizam refused. I have already recorded my visit to the Masjid Qiblatain. It is a historic site but, unfortunately, not a single door survives. One corner of its wall is in a poor condition, but the Nejdis neither get it repaired themselves nor allow anyone else to do so. Once, a few date palms grew in the courtyard of the Masjid-e Nabawi. Allah knows why those trees were chopped down. Once, a well—*Chah-e-Kausar*—existed on this site.[3] The Nejdis have closed it down, because it is considered bid'at to call a well of this world 'Kausar'.

O Lord, guide my people to the right path, for they know not.

After namaz, I met Maulvi Akram Khan. I learnt that he planned to leave the next day and would reach Mecca after visiting Shuhada-e Badr (Martyrs of Badr, the site of a battle). He came with us to our house. Dinner was served. We had kababs from the bazaar and halwa-e

1 The major conquest of the Persian empire took place in AD 635/AH 14 during the early period of the second Khalifa, Umar. The huge treasures of ancient Persian brought back to Medina included, among other things, 'the crown of the great emperors'.

The ancient Persian legend has it that Kaveh, the blacksmith with a leopard skin around his waist, attacked Zahhak and dethroned him, crowning Faridun instead. Faridun, after having the leopard skin of Kaveh laced with gold, always carried it as a symbol of victory in all his subsequent war adventures. This leopard skin was later referred to as Kavehyani Durfash. The first vowel in 'Durfash' is to be pronounced as 'u' as in 'put'. Four emperors of ancient Persia are described as 'the great', signified by the Persian prefix 'kay' in Kaykhusrow, Kayqabad and Kaykus, and so on. Their crowns are referred to as 'Kiyani Taj'.

2 The term 'Ansar' originally applies to the companions of the Prophet Mohammad. When he left Mecca for Medina, they were the Medinese who aided him and who became his devoted followers, serving in his army.

3 In the Islamic context, the Hauzul-Kausar is the lake of abundance in paradise. See T.P. Hughes (1896), *Dictionary of Islam*, London, p. 449–450, for details.

nakhud,[1] a delicacy made by a *halwai* from Bahawalpur. Maulvi Akram Khan Sahib joined us in this impromptu feast and, for a long time, regaled us with his lively conversation.

After Asr, Munshi Mohammad Yusuf and Muniruddin went to Abdul Ghani Kathiawari's shop and today, after several days of trying, managed to encash the money of the hundi.

Saturday, 6 April

I have not met Maulvi Akram Khan Sahib. It seems that he has left today. I spent the better part of the day sleeping and did little else, except for going to the masjid at the appointed hours.

Sunday, 7 April

Today, we went to meet Dr Mohammad Husain Sahib. Having bought a palatial house here, he has made alterations according to his taste and requirement. He was reading a translation of the Quran to his son-in-law and grandson in a comfortable room on the second floor. We were pleased to see groves of date palms in front of the room. When I praised the ambience in his house, Doctor Sahib took us to the third floor. Here, too, he had a luxurious bedroom. We could see the mountains of Ahud and Sila, and the shrine of Hazrat Amir Hamza, and it pleased us enormously to be up here. Doctor Sahib observed that Ibn Saud had recently gained victory over the rebellious factions among his countrymen, that several chieftains have been arrested, and that the chief of the rebels, a man called Duwesh, was killed. The government rejoiced over this victory; yesterday, the doctor too congratulated the Amir of Medina. He offered us delicious coffee.

Meanwhile, Maulvi Syed Ahmed Faizabadi, who has been mentioned before, arrived. He had brought an ailing guest for treatment. We met him too. Afterwards we returned home.

The *muzawwir* of Rauza-e Sharifa make the pilgrims say salaam after Fajr, Zuhr, Asr and Maghrib. This is a noisy affair. The Amir of Medina has ordered that in future the salaam should be read half an hour after the namaz and be said softly. Too much noise is contrary to the spirit of

---

1 The word 'halwa' is used to describe many distinct types of sweet confection, across the Middle East, Central Asia and South Asia. Halwai is one who makes these sweets, also known as mithai.

courtesy. I, therefore, feel that this order is not inappropriate. But it will cause difficulties to the guides who are, naturally, extremely angry.

It is worth remembering that a Humbali Imam leads the Fajr and Maghrib namaz. During this time, the *iqamat*[1] says takbir twice, once *shahadatain* and once *heelatain* and, after rukoo while in *qauma*[2] when the Imam says, '*Sami allahu liman hamida*, the mukabbir raises the cry of *Rabbana walakal hamd*[3] which has an extra 'w' sound (we say *rabanna lakal hamd*).

A Maliki Imam leads the Zuhr namaz. At that time too the iqamat is like that of the Humbalis. The Asr namaz takes place at a time suited to the Hanafis' belief and there is still time left for Zuhr. The imam is a Shafai. Iqamat is like that of the Humbalis, but in the qauma (rising, in the namaz), the mukabbir also says, 'Sami allahu liman hamida', that is, he does not say, 'Rabana lakal hamd'.

A Hanafi imam leads the Isha namaz. He has a pleasant voice and recites the *qir'at* (recitation of Quran) beautifully. At such times, the iqamat is complete—that is, the takbir is repeated four times, shahadat twice, and heelatain twice. At the time of qauma, he says, 'Rabbana lakal hamd', but the imam is not allowed to raise his hands to perform the dua.

On Thursday, we received the objects placed beneath the cover of the Prophet's grave after Asr. I put them against my eyes. I cannot describe the pleasure and intoxication of that moment.

O Allah, have mercy on the people of Mohammad!

Monday, 8 April

A caravan of Javanese left yesterday. At this point, most hajjis in Haram Sharif are Afghanis and Bengalis. One Afghan takes the place of three Javanese while sitting. And so, despite their departure, the Haram Sharif is as cramped as before. The Afghans are from the poorer classes and don't have the means to rent a house. They sleep on a platform outside the Haram Sharif or on the streets at night. They spend the better part of their day in Rauza Mubarak. There is at least one office in Medina from every Muslim country—except Afghanistan.

---

1 'Iqamah' or 'iqamat' is an Arabic word that refers to the second call for the prayer, which follows the first call (adhan). Iqamah means that the prayer is ready to start.

2 Sitting posture while performing the namaz.

3 Our sustainer all praise is for you; Our sustainer and all praise is for you.

This morning, Mohammad Yusuf, Muniruddin, and I went to the bazaar. We drank tea at a qahwakhana and spent some time at Abdul Ghani's shop. We returned home after a stroll through the city.

After Maghrib, as I sat reading the wazifa in the Jannat ki Kiyari near the holy screen when an Arab girl, who was no more than three years old, asked me a question.[1] I felt extremely sorry for her; the abject poverty of the people of Medina shook me to the core of my being. May the Merciful Allah have mercy on those living in Medina and make them self-sufficient! Girls from Medina are usually extremely beautiful. Little girls, in particular, look like pretty porcelain dolls. Their complexion is like that of the ladies of Europe and their features are similar to those of Hindustani women. It seems as though the blood of Syrians and Turks has got mixed in the blood of the people of Medina. For, in the past, one had not heard of such beauty among the Arabs. Such fair complexion cannot survive in a hot climate.

My heart breaks into pieces when I see these pretty girls begging.
O Allah, have mercy on the people of Mohammad!

A relative of the Nejdi Amir of Medina is blind. He comes occasionally to the Masjid-e Nabawi with the help of an employee. He enters from the Baab-e Jibreel and leaves impertinently from the Muwajah-e Aqdas. He doesn't stay for the salaam. I have seen him in the masjid on several occasions but noticed his insolence today, the reason being that before the morning namaz, I sat, as always, close to the wall of the mosque facing the Muwajah-e Aqdas and an elderly pious-looking Arab follower of Imam Shafai sat close by. Suddenly, I heard the Arab pray, 'May Allah rid this city or country of shurafa of these dogs!'[2] I opened my eyes and saw that the Amir's relative was passing by. I looked towards the Arab. He explained the Nejdi's insolent behaviour and began to pray for him.

May Allah give better counsel to the Nejdis and may they come to honour the Prophet! Already, the foundations of their kingdom are fragile. By wounding the hearts of the people of Medina, it will burst like a bubble.

1 In other words, she was soliciting.
2 Plural of 'sharif', respectable. Commonly referred to the aristocrats or men of upper caste lineage in upper India.

Tuesday, 9 April

Another caravan of Javanese pilgrims has left; now, my mohalla is deserted. Our street wore a festive look over the last few days owing to them. No more does one hear the shopkeepers' cry of 'Marhaba Jaavi! Marhaba Jaavi!' The price of eggs had shot up; it is now down. The look of prosperity on the faces of the shopkeepers is now gone. May Allah give greater strength to the faith of the Javanese and grant them ever more success in both the worlds! They come to Medina and purchase all sorts of things, regardless of whether they are of any use to them. They buy (certain commodities) because they are sacred (holy). Several shops selling *sherbet*[1] and *falooda*[2] had opened in our street. Local boys would forcibly offer sherbet and extract money from the Javanese. They would laugh at them but, unwilling to hurt the feelings of the residents of Medina, drink the sherbet whether they wanted to or not. May Allah bless them for their good disposition and may these residents of far-off islands be granted independence, prosperity and self-rule!

Another caravan of Afghans has arrived. Now, the Pathans are all over the city. Unfortunately, they don't bring much business. They are from among the poorest sections of society. Those requiring assistance cannot possibly be of any help to the others!

An Afghan showed up at my door after the Isha prayer. He lives in Dar-us Saltanat, and speaks correct and fluent Farsi.[3] His name is Mohammad Hanif Ghazi. He was a mujahid in the last war in Afghanistan and had met Dr Abdur Rehman Sahib Mungeri on the ship. And he had reached our house in search of him. The Arabs call the Afghans *haivaan*, barbarians, but Mohammad Hanif is a liberal man. He has complete sympathy for Amanullah Khan. He regrets that the Badshah Ghazi adopted the wrong policy and had wanted to make the country run on the highway of modernity by forsaking religion. Today's news is that Amanullah Khan has set off on a march from Kandahar and moved 40 miles towards Kabul. Mohammad Hanif prayed for Allah to give better counsel to Amanullah Khan and, if the people and religion

1 Sherbet is a traditional cold drink that is not alcoholic.

2 A South Asian refreshment drink made by mixing milk, vermicelli, basil seeds, tutti frutti and sugar along with ice cream. The most popular flavours of falooda include rose, *kesar* (saffron), mango, chocolate and fig. Falooda is very popular throughout north India, and is easily available in hotels and on beach stalls.

3 Means Persian, the language spoken in Iran and nearby countries.

are likely to benefit from his rule, may He grant victory to this fair and just king.

Today, I saw a new *durrie* laid out in the Rauza-e Mubarak in front of Muwajah-e Aqdas. I discovered that the good fortune of this act was destined for a Bohra from India.[1]

A man from Sindh has donated 2,000 guineas for setting up a water engine in the Masjid-e Aqdas. A Memon from Hindustan has arrived to serve the Prophet and has brought Rs 14,000 to help those living here. Today, he has bought bags of cement and distributed them among the labourers so that the repair work, that is currently under way, may be partly paid for.

May Allah bestow the finest reward to them for Islam and Muslims!

Allah, Allah, while the Mussalmans of Hindustan are willing to sacrifice their lives at the Rauza-e Aqdas, the Javanese do all they can for the residents of Medina, and the Afghans cling to the pillars of the mosque and weep. But the government of Hijaz neglects the repair of the Rauza-e Rasool and is intent upon removing the traces of the graves of the sahaba (companions of the Prophet) and *taabieen* (followers of sahaba or companions of the Prophet). It is said that the day when the grave of Hazrat Saiyedatunnisa (that is, Hazrat Fatima) was destroyed, the city mourned. And for three days, the people of Medina did not light fires in their homes.

حسن ز بصره بلال از حبش صهيب از روم
ز خاک مکه ابوجهل ايں چہ بوالعجبی ست

Hasan za Basra Bilal az Habash suhaib az Rome
Za khaak-e-Mecca Abu Jahal een che bul ajabeest.

Hasan from Basra, Bilal from Africa and Suhaib from Rome
How strange that Mecca should be Abu Jahal's home.

Wednesday, 10 April

Today, Saiyed Mohammad Jamal Husaini, former Khatib Masjid-e Nabawi, came to my house and permitted me to recite the *Dua-e Kibreet Ahmar*. Along with the permission came a printed copy of the dua. Alhamdulillah.

---

1 Ismaili Shia; based largely in western India.

سخنہائے نادر نہ باید نہفت

Sukhan hai nader na bayad nehuft

Good works should not hide.

The Nejdis have introduced the practice of fixing a time for women to offer the salaam. The time fixed is an hour after the namaz-e Maghrib. While men are removed from the Muwajah-e Aqdas, women come in freely for salaam and dua in the courtyard in the north-eastern wing. If only such an arrangement existed for the tawaf in Mecca!

I saw two new carpets laid out in the Muwajah-e Aqdas. They, too, have been presented by some Hindustani. For the past two or three days, a short while before Maghrib, Muniruddin Hyderabadi and I have been spending some time in the north courtyard of the mosque. From there, we gaze upon the delightful sight of the Gumbad-e Khizra[1] and Minar-e Bilal. The green dome, the golden finial, the white *minar* please the eye so much that one does not feel like leaving the place. And without any conscious effort, the tongue keeps uttering the Durood Sharif.

آنکھوں کی پتلیاں ہوں تصدق کلس کے گرد

Aaankhon ki putliyan ho tasadduq kalas ke gird

My eyeballs revolve around the tomb's finial.

In the morning I went to meet Hazrat Syed Mohammad Madani, who is staying in the Usmani Inn. He read out half the Dalailul Khairaat.

Thursday, 11 April

Today we finished reading the Dalailul Khairaat and I have been given permission to read it everyday as a wazifa. After Zuhr, we were invited to a meal at Abdul Ghani Kathiawari's house. First, a pleasant-voiced *qaari*[2] read two rukoo from the Holy Quran, then, after reading from the *Panch Ayat*,[3] fateha was recited for the Prophet and his dear ones. Later, the Prophet's genealogy was presented, and his miracles were

1 Masjid-e Nabawi or the Mosque of the Prophet. In the middle of the mosque is the shrine of the Prophet Mohammad, famously known as Gumbad-e Khizra. The original mosque was built by Mohammad, and this is also where his house was.

2 Qaari is the reciter of the Quran.

3 Panch Ayat are Quranic verses.

described. Durood was read. A dastarkhwan was laid out, and biryani and *zarda*[1] were offered to the entire congregation. Almost 40 people were invited. Everyone ate well and thanked Allah. After eating, we went to the house. We were told that a caravan from Hindustan had arrived. It had Maulana Abdul Majid Sahib Daryabadi[2] and Maulvi Abdul Bari Sahib Nadwi.[3] I had previously met the Maulana Sahib but I could not recognize him owing to the stress of the journey, which had wrought such changes on his face and countenance. The Maulana stayed with us for a short while. Then, he went to the Hyderabad Inn; several ladies accompanied him.

After Maghrib, I saw the Maulana in the Haram Sharif near the Musalla-e Nabawi. His voice was frayed and he looked washed out. May Allah accept my hajj thanks to His grace!

آ نا نکہ نزدیک ترامذ حیران ترامذ

Aanaan ke nazdik tarand hairaan tarand
Those closer to you are more perplexed.

Friday, 12 April

As always, we went to Haram Sharif at 3.00. I plucked courage to read the entire Dalailul Khairaat in the Masjid-e Nabawi.

Maulvi Manazir Hasan Sahib,[4] Sheikhul Hadis Jamia Usmania, too, has come with the caravan that reached yesterday with Maulana Abdul

---

1 Rice cooked in sugar and flavoured.

2 معلوم ہوا کہ منشی امیر احمد صاحب علوی کا کوروی (ڈپٹی مجسٹریٹ وڈسٹرکٹ جج بچ چھاؤنی) ہیں جو کئی ماہ قبل سے یہاں مقیم ہیں! اس وقت انکا ملنا نعمتِ غیر مترقبہ تھا، خود مہمان تھے، مگر ہمارے میزبان بن گئے، منشی صاحب اردو کے ایک ممتاز ادیب اور اہلِ قلم ہیں، اور متعدد دادِ بی کتابوں کے مصنف، لیکن یہ کم لوگوں کو معلوم ہوگا کہ محض "اہلِ قلم" نہیں "اہلِ دل" بھی ہیں۔

3 Maulana Abdul Bari Nadwi (1889–1976), son of Maulana Abdul Khaliq, was educated at Lucknow's Nadwatul Ulama. For a while he taught at the Osmania University, Hyderabad. He joined the Tabligh movement under the influence of Maulana Mohammad Ilyas and Mohammad Yusuf Kandhalvi. He performed the hajj in 1928 in the company of Abdul Majid Daryabadi and Syed Manazir Ahsan Geelani. See Syed Mahmud Hasan Hasani Nadwi (2009), *Hayat Abdul Bari*, Lucknow.

4 An Islamic scholar from Deoband, he wrote many books in Urdu language some of which are: *Musalmano ka Nizame Taleem-o-Tarbiat, Islami Muashiyaat, Imam Abu Hanifa ki Siasi Zindagi, Tadween-e-Hadith, Ad-deenul Qayyim, Tadween-e-Quran, Tadween-e-*

Majid Sahib. This interesting gentleman is staying with Madani Sahib, who lives close to our house. After Isha, he kept us engaged in lively conversation. Maulvi Sahib, a man of good faith, is learned too.

Saturday, 13 April

A large caravan of Hindustanis departed from Medina today. A large contingent of Afghans also left. Mir Reham Ali Sahib too has gone to Mecca with his companions. The crowds have dwindled in the Haram Sharif. Now remain only those travelling by cars or the ones going back on foot. A few cars come each day from Mecca, bringing in fresh pilgrims. There is no appreciable difference in the city's population itself. Today, after Zuhr, we were invited yet again for a meal at Abu Sayeed, the muallim's house. Once again, an entire dumba was placed before us.

A little before Maghrib, I met Maulvi Abdul Majid Sahib Daryabadi in the courtyard of Masjid-e Aqdas. We talked at length about Medina's pitiable state. The Maulana has moved out of Hyderabad Inn. With the efforts of Maulvi Saiyed Ahmad Faizabadi, he has found a house close to the Baab-un Nisa.

Sunday, 14 April

I saw a lot of pilgrims from the Bohra community in the Masjid-e Aqdas. They come here with utmost devotion. Praying with folded hands, they spend most of their time reading the Quran in the Rauza-e Jannat. In the evening, finding the coast clear, a Bohra kissed the screen and then looked fearfully in case a Nejdi might descend upon him with a cane.

In our country, the Afghans are considered to be barbarians. Here, too, most people refer to them as haivaan.[1] The fact is that, in their respect for the Prophet's Rauza, they are no less than any intellectual. They are strong and well-built; it is only the awe of the Prophet's grave that keeps them silent. As soon as they nudge closer to the screen, the Nejdi soldiers drag them away and they slink away quietly with their heads bent low. However, outside the Haram Sharif, if someone so much as presses their finger they are ready to wring their necks; clearly,

---

Fiqh, Maqalaat-e-Ahsani, Tafseer-e-Soora-e-Kahf, Tazkara-e-Shah Waliullah, Musalmano ki Firqabandio ka Afsaana, Rehmatun lil-Aalameen. He was born in September 1892.

1 Barbarians.

it is the grandeur and sanctity of this sacred spot that renders them speechless for they don't even look up at the Nejdis.

I went to meet Sheikh-ud Dalail, Maulana Abdul Fattah Qari, to seek his permission to read the Dalailul Khairaat. He commanded me to appear before him for an entire week without fail and read one section everyday to him; only then would he grant the permission. I agreed to his terms. Today, I read the Asma Sharif and the preliminary verses. From tomorrow, I shall read the first section.

Monday, 15 April

With Sheikh Abdul Fattah, I recited a section of the Dalailul Khairaat this morning. This will now continue for a week. So, I need not record this everyday.

There is a change in the prayer timings. The morning namaz begins at 10.10 a.m.; I get back home in 20 minutes. The sun rises at 11.30 a.m. After 12.30 p.m., I spend half an hour with Maulana Abdul Fattah. I kill time at home from 1.00 p.m. to 4.00 p.m. This period passes most slowly. After this, I go to Haram Sharif and keep myself busy reading the Quran till it is Zuhr time. The azaan for Zuhr is before 6.00 p.m. I return home after the namaz 15 minutes later. I eat and rest for a while. At 9.00 p.m., I go once again to the Haram Sharif. The Asr namaz begins at 9.30 p.m. I return home to drink tea. I go again to the Haram Sharif at 11.00 p.m. I spend some time gazing at the Green Dome and do duroodkhwani before offering Namaz-e Maghrib in the Jannat ki Kiyaari. Later, I read the wazifa till Isha. After Isha, I drink 2–3 cups of milk or tea and then go to sleep. By about 8 o'clock, I get up, perform wuzoo, and go to the Haram Sharif. I offer the tahajjud namaz and then read wazifa in the Muwajahe Aqdas until it is time for the Fajr namaz. Afterwards, I return home and drink tea. On some days, I eat a light breakfast too. And then the same schedule starts all over again. Thank Allah the days are passing well! Allah willing, may I continue to present myself in the mosque for the congregational prayer even upon returning home though, naturally, there is not much hope of that!

And that is no great matter for Allah. (Quran: Abraham 20)

I had left home [Kakori] two months ago. I haven't received any letter since reaching Medina. Thus, I have no knowledge of the well-being of my near and dear ones. Last night, I saw my youngest and dearest son, Nawab, in my dream. I pray to Allah that he is well and not missing me too much. I expect letters from home to be waiting at Nawab Ali Qutubi's shop in Mecca. I shall reach Mecca in fiften to twenty days. Hopefully, I shall get my letters then. May Allah grant peace to my restless heart and may He drown me so in His love as to dissolve all worldly ties!

O Lord make your love dearer to me than my family, my money, and cold water.

A large caravan of Indian pilgrims has arrived. They have all come in cars. Today, I spotted more Turks and Egyptians than usual in the Haram Sharif. A couple of new rugs have been laid out in the Jannat ki Kiyaari. The blessing of this too rests with some Hindi.

May Allah give him the best reward.

Tuesday, 16 April

Returning from Shaikhud Dalail's house this morning, I went to the Hyderabad Inn to meet Maulvi Abdul Bari Nadwi and his father. I took a copy of *Tajreedul Bukhari*[1] to read, because I have nothing to keep me occupied from 1.00 p.m. till 4.00 p.m., and that's the time when I feel most restless. Dr Abdur Rehman Sahib is surrounded by scores of patients; Yusuf Sahib spends a lot of time with him. Muniruddin Sahib sleeps during those hours or walks around in the bazaar. I find myself sitting idle. I take no more than ten minutes to write this diary. And it becomes difficult to stretch time till 4.00 p.m. Now that I have laid my hands on this sacred book, I hope it will keep me occupied.

It is being said that many Hindustani pilgrims have arrived on the cars but I doubt if I know any one of them.

A dispute has arisen in our circle over the time of departure for Mecca. Dr Sahib and Mohammad Yusuf Sahib believe that we should leave on 3rd Zul Hijja. I believe that we should leave during 20–25 Zul Qadah. It looks like our difference of opinion will prevent us from travelling together.

1 Imam Bukhari was born at Bukhara (now in Central Asia), into a family of Persian origin. At the age of 16, he made the pilgrimage to Mecca and then stayed in Medina in order to hear the famous scholars of tradition. During the years he visited the centres of learning in Egypt, Palestine, Syria, Iraq and Persia, collecting as well as transmitting traditions. The title of al-Bukhari's collection of traditions, *Sahih*, refers to his precept of including only traditions (*hadiths*), which he considered as being of certain authenticity according to his own rigid criteria.

A big crowd had assembled in the Haram Sharif during Maghrib. There were Indians on all sides. Unfortunately, I did not spot a single acquaintance of mine.

Wednesday, 17 April

In the morning, we learnt that Maulvi Abdul Majid Sahib Daryabadi's wife is suffering from diarrhoea. Dr Abdur Rehman Sahib and I called upon them. We found that the lady's health had improved. The diarrhoea had lessened. She was being treated by Maulvi Syed Ahmad Sahib Faizabadi. His treatment had brought much relief to her.

Two things worry me: first, can the ihram be changed if it becomes impure; second, can those pilgrims who have reached Mecca during Ramazan and reached Medina during Shawwal[1] do tamattu[2] or qiran?[3] We decided to discuss these issues with Maulvi Syed Ahmad Sahib. So, accompanied by Maulvi Abdul Majid, I set out to meet him. He gave a straight and simple answer to the first question: it is permitted to change an ihram that is impure but not the one that is simply soiled or dirty.

On the second issue, he said that it is better to be on the safer side and to do the niyat for Hajj-i Mufrad. I asked why it was permitted by the Sahibain and disallowed by the Hanafi. The question, then, was on whose ruling was the fatwa to be issued? The Maulana said that he did not know, but it was safer not to combine the two and do the niyat only for the hajj. In that case, I had to wear the same ihram and then do the Hajj-i Mufrad. Afterwards, the conversation veered towards the Afghanistan affair. He offered us milky tea. I took leave from him, stopped by at Sheikh Abdul Fattah's place, and returned home.

I was told that my mutawwif Abdul Qadir Sikandar had come to Medina yesterday. I had been upset with his lawyer in Mecca. I mentioned this to Abdul Majid Sahib. We decided to describe the entire state of affairs to Abdul Qadir and to lodge a complaint against the lawyer.

1 Shawwal is the tenth month on the Lunar Islamic calendar. The first day of Shawwal is celebrated as Id.

2 Tamattu means wearing the ihram with the intention of performing umrah during the hajj season. Anyone intending to perform a tamattu hajj should declare his intention for umrah when approaching the miqat. The pilgrim should say, 'Labbayk-Allahumma labbayka bi'umrah!' or 'Labbayka 'Umratan!', meaning 'O Allah! I answer Your call to perform umrah.'

3 Qiran is the performance of hajj and umrah together in a single ihram from the miqaat. This is applicable only to persons who live within a radius of 16 farsakh or 48 miles of Mecca.

Sultan Ibn Saud, the King of Hijaz, is shortly expected here. Preparations are under way to receive him. He shall stay in the Darul Hukumat near the old Hijaz railway station. Poles have been dug up at short intervals from there till the Haram Sharif. Flags will be strung on them and gates erected. I don't know whether similar arrangements were made to receive the first four Khulafa. No doubt when Hazrat Umar Farooq[1] had visited the Baitul Muqaddas, the same sort of arrangement would have been made! Or else why would the Nejdi government permit such a terrible bid'at in imitation of the foreigners and infidels?

It is allowed for the learned, not allowed for the illiterate.

After Maghrib, Abdul Qadir came looking for me in the Haram Sharif. For a long time, he kept apologizing on behalf of his lawyer. It seems that Abdul Majid Sahib has already narrated my tale of woes to him. It has been only 19 days since Abdul Qadir Sahib left Lucknow. He brought me greetings from some of the elderly men back home. They are known to me. Today, I fully appreciate their greetings. I also learnt that two or three pilgrims from Kakori were shortly expected to arrive. May Allah give my brothers the good fortune to be here!

Thursday, 18 April

This morning after paying my respects in the company of Sheikhud Dalail, I went to meet Maulana Abdul Baqi Sahib Firangi Mahali Summal Madani at his residence, along with Dr Abdur Rehman and Mohammad Yusuf. The Maulana keeps poor health; Doctor Sahib has offered to send him some medicine.

I sought Maulana Abdul Baqi Sahib's counsel on those subjects which I discussed yesterday with Syed Ahmad Sahib. He felt that it was permitted to change the ihram to remove impurity. I said that I have seen in the *Juziyaat* (a book of *maslai-masail*: literally, a book on the rituals and hajj codes) that washing an ihram was not permitted if it had become impure. However, washing one that has become soiled or dirty was in order. In such a case, it would not be permissible to change the

---

1 Umar ibn al-Khattab (c. 584–7 November 644), was an early Muslim convert from the Banu Adi clan of the Quraysh tribe, and a companion of Mohammad. Umar is also referred to as ʿUmar al-Faruq and Farooq-e-Azam. He became the second Khalifa (634–44) following the death of Abu Bakr.

ihram for the sake of impurity. The Maulana referred to Manasik Mulla Ali Qari.[1] It is not permitted to wash the ihram to rid it of lice, etc., but it is not wrong to wash it to remove dirt. Therefore, it was alright to change the ihram.

On the second issue, too, he differed with Maulvi Syed Ahmad Sahib and said that the fatwa depends upon the *qaul*, sayings, of the Sahibain. If an outsider sights the Id moon in Mecca and then goes far away from the city, he can do tamattu provided his companions are not in the Masjidul Haram. I said that Maulvi Syed Ahmad Sahib had—to err on the side of caution—suggested that one should do the hajj-i Afrad, that is, a kind of hajj which does not include umara. Maulvi Sahib said that for a Meccan, the miqaat is Masjid-e Haram and not *Zul Hulaifa* and, if you are not a Meccan, there is nothing better than tamattu and qiran. I asked again if he was ready to give a fatwa that, under my present circumstance, I should do the tamattu and qiran. He said that I should do so, but should also give *dum*.[2] I was pleased by this facility. Inshaallah, I shall now avail of the facility of tamattu. *Addin usr:* 'Religion is ease'.

I went to Jannat-ul Baqi in the interval between Asr and Maghrib, and sought eternal blessings. A large contingent of Bohra pilgrims reached today. I also spotted some Javanese, but the masjid is largely full of Indians. With Allah's grace, I completed one reading of the Quran in the Masjid-e Nabawi.

Friday, 19 April

Most houses in Medina are three-storied, though you can see some two and four storied ones as well. My house is three-storeyed. I have taken over one room in the middle floor. A well is attached to the house. It is constructed in such a way that the occupants can draw water from it from every floor. Each floor has separate toilets. There are no sweepers.

---

1 Mulla 'Ali al-Qari (d. AH 1014) the erudite scholar, is renowned as one of the Hanafi masters of hadith and imams of fiqh, Quranic commentary, language, history, and *tasawwuf*. He authored several commentaries such as *al-Mirqat* on Mishkat al-masabih in several volumes, a two-volume commentary on Qadi 'Iyad's *al-Shifa'*, and a two-volume commentary on Ghazali's abridgment of the Ihya entitled *'Ayn al-'ilm wa zayn al-hilm* (The spring of knowledge and the adornment of understanding). His book, *al-Hizb al-a'zam* (The supreme daily *dhikr*) forms the basis of Imam al-Jazuli's celebrated manual of dhikr, Dalailul Khairaat, which along with the Quran, is recited by many pious Muslims around the world.

2 An amount given either as penalty for a transgression or in thanksgiving.

A deep pit is dug in every house where the sewage is collected and after some time, its stench is removed with the help of salt and other chemicals. While there are separate toilet seats for every floor, all of them are connected to the same septic tank. Traditionally, the people here live on the topmost floor during the cold months and on the ground floor during the summer season when it is cool during the days. At night, most people sleep on the open roof.

The summer is setting in now. It is unbearably hot in my room during the early part of the night. The roof is being used by other travellers, but we are quite comfortable during the day. A group from Hyderabad has been staying on the ground floor for the past three to four days. They are being troubled by mosquitoes that multiply because of the well and the septic tank. Travellers are advised to stay on the middle floors when they visit Medina, and, if it gets hot, they are required to seek permission to sleep on the roof.

It is either a sign of the people's trust and honesty or the fear of the Saudi government that shopkeepers leave their shops unattended during namaz. Nothing is ever stolen from anyone's shop. Every street has jewellers' shops. There are at least four to five of them stretching from my house until the Haram Sharif. Their tables are strewn with *halal*, qarsh, riyal, *asharfiyan* (gold coins) and notes. No passer-by would ever think of picking up even one. A jeweller whose shop is closest to the masjid is the most heedless of them all. I have often noticed that he is away from his shop even outside the namaz timings, and his table stays unattended by the roadside. But I have not heard anyone dare pick up a handful of asharfiyan or a bundle of currency notes. During Turkish rule, it was unsafe to walk alone even as far as Jannat-ul Baqi, but now cash and gold lie unattended. No one dare look at it with ill-intent. Nejdi rule will be remembered for ushering in peace and prosperity.

خوش درخشید و لے دولت مستعجل بود

Khush darakhsheed wale daulat mustaajil bud.

It shone bright though soon passed out of sight.

Today I have offered the Namaz-e Juma for the fourth time in the Masjid-e Nabawi.

Fal hamdo lillahe ala zaalika.

So, all praises be to Allah for this bounty bestowed upon.

Saturday, 20 April

Some passengers from Delhi and Muzaffarnagar returned to Mecca on the 40 guinea-roundtrip ride in the cars. It has been heard that the car fare will increase after 15 Zul Qadah. Muniruddin Sahib and I are trying to leave for Mecca by Friday or Saturday.

Preparations are underway for the arrival of Sultan Ibn Saud, but he has yet to come. In the evening, I met Mir Nairang in the masjid's courtyard. He too is planning to leave next Friday.

Sunday, 21 April

It has been cloudy all morning. The rain started by about 3.00 and an hour before zawal, it turned into a torrential downpour. As always, I was in the masjid from 4.00 onwards. The rain fell heavily; the devout bathed under the spout of the Green Dome. Thanks to Munshi Muniruddin Sahib's generosity, I too got a bowl full of this sacred water. It kept raining till the evening. The pennants that had been put up to welcome the Sultan in front of Baab-e Salaam were ruined. The wind became chilly and the night turned cold. After sunset, the skies cleared and the stars appeared.

Monday, 22 April

For the first time after reaching Medina, I went to the mosque with my ears covered and a chadar wrapped around me. The cold revived an old ailment. I had to urinate several times from the morning till afternoon. Before zawal, when I was busy reading the Quran, I had the urge to urinate. There is a clean toilet inside the Haram Sharif. Next to it is the place for wuzoo as well. I used the toilet and prayed for those who had thought of building one. It too is a reminder of the poor Turks. May Allah give them a second life!

It was cold again at night. Despite the day being filled with sunlight, at night I had to sleep with the windows closed. Still, I slept with a bedsheet and that too, after midnight.

Tuesday, 23 April

Today, I obtained permission for reciting the Dalailul Khairaat from Maulana Abdul Fattah. For the past eight days, I have been going to his house daily without fail. That mercifully is over. The Maulana is well versed in qirat. Apart from reading the Dalailul Khairaat, he teaches students how to recite the Quran. He has a fine voice and his manner of reading the Quran brings great joy. He allows the reading of *Hisn-e Haseen* (a compendium or book of prayers). Unfortunately, I have left my own copy in Mecca or else I too would have taken permission to read from the *Hisn-e Haseen*.

Yesterday, Munshi Mohammad Yusuf informed that Munshi Abdul Hadi Khan Sahib Shahjahanpuri has arrived and is staying near the Baab-e Salaam. I had previously met him and he too was well acquainted with some of my relatives. Therefore, Munshi Sahib and I went to meet Khan Sahib a little before one o'clock at his lodging. He has availed pension from his employment as a deputy collector. His face has changed so much that I could recognize him with some difficulty. When I mentioned my name, he got up to embrace me. For an hour, we talked about matters related to Hindustan and the time passed pleasurably.

Khan Sahib will return to Mecca on Friday or Saturday. From there, he shall proceed to Taif. If I meet him in Mecca and my budget permits, I would like to accompany him to Taif.

It is 2.30 p.m. now—that is, it is over three hours since sunrise but it is still extremely cold. The fingers don't work fully because of the chilly winds. After Zuhr, I had laid down for a while when Hakim Sahib Dehalwi, who had come with us in the car from Mecca, arrived. He told us that several motors had returned empty. Everyone plans to go back after the next Friday. As a result, the car fee is expected to increase and we should, therefore, arrange for our return at the earliest. It was decided that after Asr, Muniruddin Sahib would go to Abdul Ghani Kathiawari to finalize the arrangements for the car.

We wasted a lot of time in this discussion. My sleep was disturbed and my head felt heavy. Muniruddin Sahib left after Asr to arrange for the car, but no decision could be taken. I was feeling somewhat listless after Maghrib and felt ferevrish. After Isha, I returned to the house and drank two bowls of milk. The night was cold. This was caused by the rains day before yesterday.

Wednesday, 24 April

It is 12.30 p.m. The sun has been up for over an hour but it is still severely cold. I am lying covered with a sheet as I pen these lines. It was very cold at the time of tahajjud. My resolve weakened, as I thought of keeping away from the Haram and sleeping till the morning. But Allah's help came to my rescue. Somehow, I managed to get up and make my way to the Masjid-e Nabawi wrapped and covered up. There, I was at peace and the chill left me.

I slept after breakfast and felt better after a couple of hours. After Zuhr, we were invited to the home of Abdullah, Sheikhul Bawwabeen, the head of all the sentries of the various gates,[1] and the *durban* (guard) of Baab-e Rehmat. I was accompanied by my friends. We were amazed by the opulence and extravagance of the house. The Sheikh receives only one guinea per month as a salary and he doesn't get much of an extra income from the pilgrims; yet, thanks to the finesse of the people of Medina and the skills of their women, they manage to maintain such grand homes which one will not find even amongst the courtly and rich in India. The Sheikh has been a durban in the house of the Prophet. When Medina was occupied by the wickedness of the Sharif and its occupants were banished, he too was asked to migrate to Syria. But he chose not to forsake the house of the Prophet and continued living there through both good and bad times.

The Sheikh served us delicious food and excellent tea, but I was saddened to hear him say that, after the World War, the Syrians and Egyptians had tried, Allah forbid, to turn Medina into Cairo and Paris! He didn't explain the exact situation clearly but indirectly acknowledged that some *juhala* (plural of *jahil* or ignorant)[2] here had begun to worship the devil. Women eager to have a child would play tambourines for Satan[3] and sacrifice goats. The name of Allah was not taken, and the sacrifice was, therefore, meant for Satan. This evil practice continued. The Nejdis declared that the juhala of Medina have become polytheists and idolators, and have lost their faith. They put an end to such ill practices and rid this holy city of shirk and kufr. May Allah bless them for this *islah* (reform/correction)!

According to a hadith, doomsday shall not come till the women of Medina are once again engaged in idol worship. Their wrong-doing turned Medina into the victim of a mini calamity (*qayamat-e sughra*). It is difficult to describe the trauma of its inhabitants during the siege of

---

1 The gates at Masjidul Haram are nineteen in number, and are distributed about it, without any order or symmetry.

2 *Jahiliyah* or *jahilia* is an Islamic concept of 'ignorance of divine guidance' or 'the state of ignorance of the guidance from Allah' referring to the condition in which Arabs found themselves in pre-Islamic Arabian society prior to the revelation of the Quran. By extension, it means the state of anyone not following Islam and the Quran.

3 *Shaitan* or devil is the equivalent of Satan in Islam.

Medina. They are still not freed from the claws of poverty and want. The essence of the truth (*ghairat-i haq*) is that there should be no wrong-doing in the house of the Prophet or a *futoor*[1] should arise in the faith of the people of Medina. *Inna lilla he wa inna ilaihi rajioon.*

Thursday, 25 April

Last night's experience was a memorable one. I was graced by being present all night long in the Haram Sharif, and a sinner such as me experienced such blessings from Him who gives refuge to the poorest and the most desperate asylum seekers. I cannot describe my experience in these pages. All I can say is that the pilgrim who visits Medina but does not stay in the Masjid-e Nabawi at night shall remain untouched by the limitless blessings of this place. After the Fajr namaz I returned home. My eyes were filled with a sleepless night. I slept deeply for three hours. I ate breakfast after 1.30 p.m., drank tea, and now at 3.00 p.m. in the morning, I sat down to write this memoir. My health, thank Allah, is good and there isn't the slightest discomfort from staying awake all night.

The car has finally been booked. The fare has been fixed at four and a half guinea. We shall leave day after tomorrow at 2.00 p.m.

The Masjid Sharif is crowded. A lot of Egyptians and Turks have arrived. And a lot of Bengalis too are present. I offered the Maghrib namaz in the courtyard. I met an Egyptian who came today. He is a railway engineer. We spoke in English for a long time. Later, I regretted speaking English inside the Haram Sharif. From tomorrow the crowds will lessen and in a week or ten days you won't see anyone except the locals and the *muhajirin*. Thank Allah I would have gone by then and spared of witnessing this sad spectacle!

پھولا ہی پھلا چھوڑ کے اٹھ جاؤں چمن سے

اللہ دکھائے مجھے عالم نہ خزاں کا

Phoola hi phala chhod ke uth jaoon chaman se
Allah dikhaye mujhe aalam na khizaan ka.

May I pass out of the garden while in full bloom.
May God never show me autumn's gloom.

---

1 From the word *fitna*. It has several meanings, such as rebellion and disturbance.

Friday, 26 April

I went to meet Maulana Abdul Baqi Sahib for the last time. On my return, I took a bath and presented myself in the Haram Sharif between 3.00 p.m. and 4.00 p.m. according to the Arab time. Thank Allah I have been blessed by being able to finish the Quran in the Masjid-e Nabawi for the second time. A little before *Nisf-un Nahar* (noon), the son of Hakim Sahib Dehalvi, with whose help Muniruddin Sahib had arranged for the car, came to see me. He told me that we would have to leave Medina today itself because the car driver was being called to return to Mecca. The news saddened me. I was hoping to spend one more night here; the news shook my heart.

After namaz we returned home, finished eating, and Muniruddin Sahib went to persuade the car driver to take us on Saturday and let us stay one more night. But the driver made such promises and lured us with such temptations that Muniruddin ended up by agreeing on our behalf to leave after Asr. Now, we had no option but to leave. We packed our belongings and, heeding Allah's command, agreed to move on.

Dr Abdur Rehman and Munshi Mohammad Yusuf will stay and return only after sighting the Baqr Id[1] moon. They have arranged for their transport through Dr Mohammad Husain Sahib Allahabadi whose son-in-law and others are going to Mecca for hajj. My two friends shall go in the same car. We, Muniruddin Sahib, the Sufis from Delhi and the hakims[2] included, shall leave today.

I had already taken my bath in the morning. After wuzoo, I wore the ihram and went to the Masjid-e Nabawi for the last salaam. After two rakat-i nafil, I made the niyat for ihram, and then came to Muwajahe Aqdas for the last time. I cannot describe the sadness I felt at that time. Tears coursed down my cheeks heedlessly and it was beyond my control to stem them. I would say the salaam and feel as though my heart would pop out with every word.

---

1 The Muslim religious festival Id al-Adha, also called Baqr Id, is celebrated on the 10th of Zul Hijjah as a commemoration of Prophet Ibrahim's (Abraham's) willingness to sacrifice his son Ismael for Allah. On this day, animals such as the goat and sheep are sacrificed in the name of Allah.

2 It means wise man or physician (notably *unani* doctors), usually practitioners of herbal medicine.

حیف در چشم زدن صحبت یار آخر شد

روئے گل سیر ندیدیم و بہار آخر شد

Haif dar chashm zadan suhbat-e yar akhir shud
Ru-e gul sair nadeedeem wa bahar akhir shud.

Alas! In the bat of an eyelid, my love's company came to an end
Even before I could admire the garden, the spring came to an end.

Even after spending 35 days in Medina, I could not fully appreciate its unending bounty. I have little hope of ever returning here.

عرفی اگر بگر یہ میسر شدے وصال

صد سال می تواں بہ تمنا گریستن

Urfi agar begeryeh mayassar shude wisal
Sad saal mi tawaan be tumanna gereestan.

O Urfi! If reunion could be achieved by shedding tears
I am willing to lament for hundreds of years for my desire to come true.

Thank Allah I was able to offer 171 prayers in the Haram-e Nabawi —and in the name of Allah the benevolent—always with the entire congregation and not once was I late when the imam gave the call for *Takbir-e Ula*.[1]

And continue talking about the bounties of your Lord. (Quran: Duha 11)

After the Asr namaz I took leave of the Masjid-e Aqdas with moist eyes and a heavy heart (*ba-chashm-e giryaan wa seena-e buryaan*). I went to the lodging, collected my luggage, and walked in the direction of the car station. Munshi Muhammad Yusuf walked along to see us off. After some time, Dr Abdur Rehman Sahib too came to bid us farewell.

A large caravan of cars is ready to depart. Some were returning empty because a group of pilgrims were waiting to board them at Jiddah. We loaded our luggage in an empty car. I along with Muniruddin, the Dehalawi gentlemen, four other persons, the Hyderabadi gentleman who was accompanied by two women and two children who had come with us from Mecca got into one vehicle. Dr Sahib and Mohammad Yusuf bid us farewell and left. Our car set off about half an hour after them. At the time, some of my co-passengers prayed that Allah may

---

1 First takbir during the prayer.

allow us one day to visit this holy city once again. I joined in this prayer. As the car left the city limits, I felt as though I was leaving my heart behind in that holy compound and only my lifeless body was placed on the car to carry it to its journey's end. Till the Green Dome—may a thousand blessings of Allah be on its owner—stayed in sight, I kept turning and craning my head to catch its glimpse. When the hills hid that blessed sight from view my life suddenly seemed a waste.

سیر کی خوب پھرے پھول چنے شاد رہے

باغباں جاتے ہیں گلشن تیرا آباد رہے

Sair kee khoob phire phool chune shaad rahe
Baaghbaan jaate hain gulshan tera aabaad rahe.

We have enjoyed, wandered, picked flowers and cherished
O Gardener, we depart, may Your garden flourish.

One stage beyond Medina, at Zul Hulaifa, used to be the miqat for the residents of Medina. Now there is a post called Bir Ali close to it. We offered our Maghrib namaz here and some of our co-passengers tied the ihram. After namaz when we set off again, our car broke down. It stopped after every 10 to 15 minutes and the driver got off and set it right. Other cars left us far behind; finally, our car lost its speed as we climbed up a hill. And instead of going up, it began to roll down rapidly. The driver did not apply the brakes and we looked set to overturn down the incline. There was a sharp drop beside the road. Had the car fallen over, it would have broken into smithereens and it would have been difficult to collect the bits and pieces of our bodies. The Merciful Saviour spared us. There was a pile of rocks beside the road. The car bumped against the pile and came to a standstill. This is how we were spared. The car, however, broke down and it was impossible to make it climb the hill. We stood helpless and alone in that deserted hillscape. With two women we saw no means of completing our journey. Once again Divine Providence came to our rescue. A driver coming from Jiddah stopped, fixed our engine, and made our car climb the hill.

یا رب تو کریمی و رسولِ تو کریم

صد شکر کہ ہستیم میانِ دو کریم

Yarab tu kareemi wa rasul-e tu kareem
Sad shukr ke hasteem miyan-e-do karim.

Lord, Thou art benevolent, Prophet, Thou art kind.
Many thanks to Thee, I'm surrounded by Thy munificence.

We left that terrifying landscape in an hour or two and the car, with a great deal of trouble and stopping every few paces, reached Bir-e Darwaish close to midnight. Several cars were parked here, so was the one that carried our luggage. We drank some tea from the qahwa shop and then went to lie down in the car. The night was still not over. We tried sleeping but remained bereft of any sweet dreams. The journey's fatigue didn't leave us.

Saturday, 27 April

Breakfast followed the namaz. We had the apples and *jalebis*[1] with our tea. These we had carried from Medina. The driver, an Arab Bedouin, did not accept that anything was wrong with his car. Some of my co-passengers felt that we should inform the local police and have it changed but I disagreed. I tried to make my fellow passengers see that if the complaint did not bear fruit, then our driver would give us no end of trouble. So I counselled them to stay quiet and bear whatever comes our way. They agreed and, trusting in Allah, we climbed into the same car.

We set off on the road about an hour after sunrise. We don't know when the car had been fixed but now it seemed fine except for the jolts. The morning was nippy but the sun grew strong by the time of zawal. It had rained quite heavily the previous week; hence the air was cool. A stray gust of hot wind would bounce off the hills but it would be followed, almost immediately, by bursts of cool air. And so, the hot wind did not seem unpleasant. The path from Bir-e Darwaish till Rabigh goes through the hills and is in a bad condition. The Hindustani drivers slow down to negotiate these stretches, but our driver was a Bedouin. He raced the car down that bumpy road. The car would jump. The passengers would bump their heads against the roof and get hurt, but the Bedouin couldn't care less. It can be said that he hated those who climbed aboard his car and he was sad that they had forsaken to travel

---

1 Jalebi is a popular sweet in the subcontinent. It is made from deep-fried, syrup-soaked batter and shaped into a large, chaotic pretzel shape, rather like the funnel cake. Jalebis are mostly bright orange in colour.

on camelback and caused a loss of earnings to his tribesmen. He wanted to avenge the loss to his clan.

We were a hardy lot. We managed to reach Rabigh in one piece. There was still time for Zuhr. We did wuzoo and offered namaz. Then we climbed back into the car because the driver wanted us to reach Jiddah the same day. My muallim, Abdul Qadir Sikandar, whom I had met in the Masjid-e Nabawi, was also in Rabigh along with the hajjis with whom he is going to Mecca. He is accompanied by his nephew, Sulaiman. I found out that 35 cars are full of Sikandar's hajjis. Sulaiman has hunted abundant prey in Awadh, just as Hasan has in Bombay. They have managed to trap a large contingent of poor hapless pilgrims in their net. May Allah have mercy on their poor victims!

In accordance with a government order, the cars in Rabigh are checked and the number of passengers counted in order to ensure that they do not avoid the tax, called *koshan*. By the time the inspection took place, it was time for the Asr namaz. Close to the place where our car was to be inspected was a close platform. We wanted to offer our prayer on it but its owner demanded one qirsh per person. We were not willing to pay for offering namaz. So we prayed in the open on the rocks. We left this place three hours before sunset.

My head ached because of the jalebis I had had for breakfast unlike my usual practice, tolerating the afternoon sun, staying up all night, and taking the knocks in the car all day. It became worse after we left Rabigh. The road runs beside the seashore. The sun is not so strong now. I was hoping the balmy air would make my headache go away. The car drivers had assured us that we would reach Jiddah in four to five hours. But, after a few miles, we had to cross a water channel and all the cars got stuck in the mud one after the other. The flood had caused the sea water to flow onto the road. The passage had caused deep ruts on the road where the cars would get stuck.

We had to get off and walk through the water. Women, too, had to get off the vehicles and, with a great deal of difficulty, cross the watery stretch. The drivers helped each other. The pilgrims too pitched in. By sunset, the cars were pulled out of that quicksand. Our feet were encrusted with mud. It was difficult to get rid of it. We tried removing the mud as best as we could and did wuzoo with the same water before offering the Maghrib prayer.

My headache was very bad by now. When the car set off again, its jolts worsened my condition. When the headache became intolerable,

I prepared my fellow travellers to stop at the nearest halting post. We pleaded with the driver. We were exhausted by the troubles of the day and the toil of the quicksands. He agreed. He stopped the car at the next post. I thanked Allah for this mercy. I drank tea from the qahwakhana, offered the Isha prayer, took two tablets of quinine to stop the fever, and slept in a secluded corner which was well covered to protect me from the cold wind. My body ached. I slept soundly and sweated profusely.

Sunday, 28 April

I was up early. I felt better, though my body still ached from the previous night. The headache had nearly gone. I drank tea and took some more quinine. I was now ready for the onward journey. I discovered that one of the cars from our caravan was still stuck in the mud and the driver had left it behind because at night they could not rescue it. Now, following a good night's sleep, the driver went back to retrieve the car, leaving all of us in the qahwakhana. As it was taking a while for them to return, I sat beside Abdul Qadir Sikandar. I talked to him for a long time. After a while, I lay down on his carpet just to straighten my back, and went off to sleep. I felt a lot better after an hour without a trace of yesterday's troubles. The colour of my urine was, however, red and so the recurrence of fever was still a possibility.

The water at the qahwakhana was extremely dirty. The tea was tasteless. I felt thirsty. Muniruddin Sahib bought a watermelon. I gingerly took a few wedges and ate. It rid me of my thirst and I felt a lot better. The drivers returned after rescuing the car from the mud by the afternoon and we left this place. We offered the Zuhr and Asr namaz on the way and reached Jiddah a little before Maghrib. Along the route, the cool sea breeze gave us immense pleasure.

We had travelled on the Saudia Company car. Its cars were parked in the same compound where the Netherland Trading Company had its office and bank. In Jiddah, we were told that we would have to halt because the cars that had brought us were to return to Medina right away with a fresh lot of pilgrims. We were to be provided with another fleet of cars to transport us to Mecca. The number of pilgrims in Mecca is such that the company has raised the return fee to 17 guineas per head and the pilgrims are ready to pay the amount.

We thought we wouldn't get enough sleep if we were to spend the night in this compound, and that the journey's fatigue would stay with us. Therefore, Muniruddin Sahib went to Abdur Razzaq, the lawyer's house, and brought him to the car garage. The lawyer willingly and happily let us stay and had our luggage carried to his house by porters. Once we reached, I felt better. After a bit of rest, I offered my Isha namaz. Then we set out in search of food in the bazaar because I had eaten nothing save a few wedges of watermelon since yesterday morning. We bought rice and *shorba* but my taste buds were awry. I could barely eat a few morsels. I wanted to taste something sweet, so I ate a little *shirni*[1] and went to the qahwakhana for tea. Later I returned to Abdur Razzaq's house and went to sleep on a towel I had laid out on the floor.

Monday, 29 April

I woke up to discover that there was no water for wuzoo. The mosque close to the house was locked. I had no option but to go to the Jama Masjid for wuzoo and namaz. After finishing the wazaif, I had tea at a qahwakhana and returned to Abdur Razzaq's house. The night had passed comfortably and the exhaustion of the previous day's journey had gone. For two hours, I talked to the Sufi gentlemen, Muniruddin, and others. Then, I went to the car garage with Abdur Razzaq. Muniruddin Sahib had left his extra baggage so that he wouldn't need to lug it all the way to Mecca and back. A box belonging to Mohammad Yusuf, which had come with us, was handed to Abdur Razzaq's care for safe-keeping.

Reaching the car garage, I discovered that we would have to wait. The Netherland Trading Company opened its office at 4.00 p.m. according to the Arab time. I went to meet the agent along with Abdur Razzaq and retrieved the money that he owed against my hundi. The hundi papers had become soiled during the course of the journey and the discomfort of the ihram. I was worried that they would be completely destroyed by the time of the hajj and that retrieving the money would be difficult. Razzaq had helped me to recover my money back and so I gave him five rupees. He wouldn't accept it, but I put it in his pocket. There are good and bad people everywhere. There is Abdur Razzaq, who is willing to do all sorts of things for us without expecting a cowrie in return and demurs when money is offered to him. On the other hand, there is my muallim Abdul Qadir Sikandar and his son, who will not hesitate to pull the skin off the backs of the hajjis.

---

1 Meaning 'wet sweets' or sweets dipped in syrup.

All the cars belonging to the Saudia Company have returned to Medina. Cars were brought for us on loan from some other company. At long last, we left Jiddah a little before noon.

It is a distance of a mere three hours from Jiddah till Mecca but the intensity of the heat made us a pathetic lot. Thanks to Allah's mercy, the *loo*[1] hasn't begun as yet but even this heat is unbearable. The car stopped at a couple of posts on the way but I didn't have the strength to get off and go to a qahwakhana. Thanks to Muniruddin Sahib, I was able to drink tea in the car. We left Behra and stopped at Shamsiya. The latter is the same village that was once called Hudaibiya where the famous treaty was signed with the infidel Quraysh.[2] Close by, there is the site where the incident of Baitul Rizwan took place under a tree.[3] A mosque is built on that spot. Due to the heat, I didn't have the courage to walk till the mosque and offer two rakat namaz, even though I could see the mosque directly in front and was a bare 40–50 steps from the road.

It was almost past the time for the Zuhr namaz when we reached the outskirts of Mecca and, according to the rules, we were dropped off. I bought water from an Arab, did my wuzoo, and offered the Zuhr namaz. I loaded my luggage on a porter's head and entered the city on foot. The sun was still hot but I immediately felt better as I set foot in Mecca. I went to my old lodging at Mohammad Hanif Zardoz's. Muniruddin Sahib showed me the way. The house is close to the Junagadh Inn but my condition was such that I had even forgotten the name of Junagadh. I was looking for the Tonk Inn. Anyhow, we reached the house by late

1 Hot winds.

2 The powerful and prominent tribe in all of Arabia in Mohammad's era. The Quraysh were the keepers of the Kaaba and, therefore, one of the wealthiest and most powerful tribes. When Mohammad started to preach the religion of Allah, the Quraysh violently persecuted him and his followers.

3 *Bayah* (Pledge of Allegiance): Rizwan Bayah is a famous pledge that the sahaba (companions) of Prophet Mohammad undertook with him at the Hudaybiyah, a place near Mecca where Muslims and the Quraysh entered into a very important treaty. It occurred in the year 6H (Hijrah) (AD 629), when Mohammad decided to go for umrah with 3,000 of his companions, and they were stopped by armed Quraysh riders at Hudaybiyah. The Quraysh told the Muslims that they would not allow them to travel to Mecca for umrah. Mohammad sent Usman bin Affan to Mecca to discuss the situation with the Quraysh leaders. Muslims became uneasy when he did not return within the stipulated time. They suspected foul play and feared for the safety of Usman. They took a bayah to Mohammad who was sitting under a tree. This bayah is known as Bayah Rizwan. Quraysh entered into a treaty with Muslims and allowed them to enter Mecca for umrah the year after the treaty at Hudaybiyah.

afternoon. The lady owners welcomed us and gave us cold water to drink. Mohammad Hanif Sahib is yet to return from Hindustan, but is expected shortly. Four ships are on their way from India. Possibly, Hanif Sahib is on one of them.

We rested for an hour and refreshed our wuzoo. Then we arrived in the Haram. By the time we had completed tawaf and namaz, it was Maghrib time. It seemed unlikely that we would finish the saii from Safa to Marwa before the azaan. So we postponed the saii. In order to keep myself occupied, I went to Nawab Ali Qutbi's shop near the Baab-e Salaam. There, I met Nawab Ali Sahib and his munshi. A pile of letters awaited me. I gathered them but could not read them without my spectacles. After namaz, I did the saii between Safa and Marwa and had a lock of my hair snipped. I thanked Allah that I had completed my umrah. While returning to the Masjidul Haram, I came across a shop selling sherbet on the way. I was surprised to see slabs of ice there. I had not imagined that one could buy ice in Mecca. Muniruddin Sahib and I each had a bottle of lemonade with ice. We felt instantly energized. Alhamdulillah. When it was time to pay for it, we were a little surprised. For, we were charged only 2 qirsh for each bottle of lemonade and ice. Sometimes, we have to pay more than this back home. Here even 8 qirsh would not have been excessive.

I offered the Isha namaz with the jamaat and returned home. I began to read the letters excitedly. Each letter carried a complaint against my lack of response. My elders had written to say that they had not received any letter from me since I had left Karachi. The letters were till 21 March and till then, the letters I had posted from Qamran, Jiddah and Mecca had not reached. They may have reached after 21 March. Anyhow, it was good to know that the near and dear ones were well. Our hostesses served us potato curry. Muniruddin Sahib and I set out our bedding and went to sleep.

Tuesday, 30 April

I took off the ihram and wore stitched clothes and went to the Masjidul Haram (in Mecca) for Fajr namaz. My body ached all over due to fatigue. I didn't have the strength to perform the nafil tawaf. I finished the namaz and hurried back. Muniruddin Sahib bought harisa and tea from the bazaar. We ate and gave our soiled clothes to the washerman close to our house. After some time, we went to the house of Akbar Umar Sahib. The father and son met us with great civility. We spent an enjoyable hour talking. By the time we returned, the intensity of the sun had increased. Muniruddin Sahib set off towards his lodging at the Hyderabad Inn and I came home to sleep. I got up in the afternoon, ate, and lay down again. I felt so unwell that I didn't have the courage to present myself in the Haram Sharif. A little before Asr when I felt somewhat better, I went to the mosque and till the time for Isha, as was my habit in the past, stayed there.

The weather has now turned warm and it is impossible to sleep inside the house at night. Through the good offices of my hostesses, I have rented a chair from a qahwakhana. I slept outside in the verandah. These chairs are a bit like an Indian bed; one has to pay 2 qirsh per night.

Wednesday, 1 May

I slept in an open space under the sky. The dullness that had dogged me so far was finally over. I offered the Fajr namaz in the Masjidul Haram before eating harisa with Muniruddin. Then, I bought gifts for my family back home and spent almost a 100 rupees shopping. The sun had become strong by the time I returned home. I didn't have the courage to step out all day. I went to the Haram Sharif at Asr, met Nawab Ali Sahib, and returned after Isha. It took very long for the chair to be brought from the qahwakhana. The chair came after 4.00 p.m., according to the Arab time. I lay down but sleep was long in coming.

Thursday, 2 May

I went again to Akbar Umar Sahib's house and arranged with him to have my luggage sent to Abdur Razzaq's house in Jiddah so that we need not worry about lugging it back after the hajj. He agreed. I returned home and packed. Muniruddin Sahib put some of his own stuff in my box and then carried it to Akbar Umar's house. May Allah take them safely till Jiddah!

The sun was strong all day long. It was difficult to step out of the house. I stayed in Haram Sharif from Asr till Isha and, for that duration, remained comfortable.

Friday, 3 May

After several days, I was blessed by being able to offer a nafil tawaf before the Fajr namaz. By Arab time, I had taken a bath and left for the masjid by 3.00 p.m. I stayed till the Juma namaz.[1] The Masjidul Haram was very crowded today. Due to Allah's mercy, clouds appeared by the time of the Juma prayer and within two hours it turned dark with rain. Lifeless bodies were revived. I felt listless after the namaz, because I had had too much to eat. The kababs did not probably suit me. By Asr, I had a slight headache and both my feet were heavy. I could perform just a single tawaf after Maghrib, and that too with difficulty. After Isha, I came home, took some *namak suleimani* (salt used for indigestion), and went to sleep.

Saturday, 4 May

I slept but the listlessness didn't go. I got up with a heavy head. I took some more namak suleimani. This is the first time after reaching Mecca that I offered the Fajr namaz at home and lost out on the jamaat. By Arab time, it is 3.00 p.m. now, but my temper is not too good. May Allah keep me in good health because sickness during travel is such a terrible thing that nobody wants it![2] By the afternoon, I felt somewhat better. My house becomes very hot during the day. The room is like an oven. Muniruddin Sahib has suggested that I rest in his lodge during the day. I went to the Haram Sharif at Asr and met Nawab Ali Qutbi. I found out that Sultan Ibn Saud has reached Medina and is expected to come here shortly.

A postcard written on 17 April from an elderly relative from my watan[3] brought news of my family's well-being. Surprisingly, the letter mentioned [complained] that I had not written to them. The fact is that I had sent scores of letters from Medina to my people. I don't know where they went and how they were destroyed.

A little before Isha I saw a black-clad Bedouin woman standing in front of the Kaaba. She had her body hidden in a black dress from head

1 A weekly congregational prayer held by Muslims every Friday just after noon. It replaces the Zuhr prayer performed on other days of the week.

2 No great improvement was in place in the sanitary conditions of the towns of Jiddah and Mecca or in the public medical services provided by the Hijaz government. Conservancy was practically an unknown art, and it was more or less recognized as a sentence of death to be sent into the Hedjaz government's hospital at Jiddah. Private medical practitioners did exist in Jiddah, Mecca and Medina, but they are not well-qualified. For this reason, the Government of India provided, on a limited scale, medical assistance for the benefit of its pilgrims. One qualified doctor was permanently attached to the Consulate at Jiddah and lived in Mecca as the pilgrims gathered there.

3 Refers to a mother country.

to toe. On her head, she carried a small *dol* (pitcher), which was probably filled with Aab-e zumzum. She stood at this sacred spot, Allah knows, with much *khuloos* and *niyaz*.[1] The sight was overwhelming. I was engaged in tawaf. By the time I reached the spot, the woman had disappeared. But the effect of her grace is still in my heart. After Isha, I returned home, and, as always, the chair came from the qahwakhana. I spread out my bedding and prepared for sleep, but I couldn't sleep till midnight.

Sunday, 5 May

I woke up at the time for Tahajjud, performed the wuzoo, and reached the Haram Sharif. I performed the tawaf, completed my namaz, and returned home. I had brought *sattu*,[2] which I mixed with milk, and ate it with a spoon. It turned out to be an excellent breakfast. For the next few days, I shall have the same breakfast and stay away from 'hot' dishes like harisa. I shall also avoid drinking tea in late afternoon.

The city is preparing to welcome the Sultan. Poles have been dug at short intervals to hang flags and pennants. Gates and arched doorways have been erected at scores of places all along the road from the city outskirts to the Haram Sharif and Baab-ul Hukumat. Preparations have been on all night because the Sultan is expected during the next couple of days. Thousands of rupees are being spent on these gates, but in the eyes of the Indians, all this pomp and ceremony is worth nothing.

There is a single roof over my head. That is why it becomes so unbearably hot during the day. After tolerating the harsh heat for the past few days, I decided to go to the Hyderabad Inn and stay with Muniruddin Sahib till Asr. I lunched with him and slept well in the lower rooms of the Inn. Thank Allah I was spared of the heat and sun!

As always, I reached the Haram Sharif at Asr time. After meeting Nawab Ali Sahib, I returned home after Isha. The chair came from the qahwakhana and I went to sleep on it.

Monday, 6 May

I offered the Fajr namaz in the Haram Sharif and returned home, ate sattu and sipped milky tea. I had just begun to write a letter when Abdul

---

1 Khuloos and niyaz mean sincerity and devotion, respectively.

2 Sattu is made from the flour of fried grams; coarsely ground mixture of *jau* (barley). There are many other dishes, which are made from sattu like *litti*, sattu ki roti, and so on.

Qadir Sikandar's son, Hasan, arrived with a jar of zumzum water. He stayed and talked for a long time. He was remorseful about the lawyers' poor behaviour. I handed him a sum of Rs 60 for the muallim's duties, and for the zumzum and other things. Their details are as follows:

1. Muallim's fee (even though he hasn't done a single thing for me so far): Rs 15
2. Towards the Zubaida canal: Re 1
3. Cleaning: 12 annas
4. Zumzum: Rs 3
5. Tent in Arafat: Rs 4
6. Rent for house in Mina: Rs 7 and 8 annas
7. For the camel and its *howdah* (from 8–12 Zul Hijja): Rs 27
8. Miscellaneous expenses: Re 1 and 12 annas
Grand Total: Rs 60

فائق بے حیا چو ہجوم گفت   دلِ من سوخت سوخت سوختہ بہ

صلہ اش پنج روپیہ دادم   دہنِ سگ بہ لقمہ دوختہ بہ

Faeq-e-behaya chu hojuam goft,
dil-e-man sookht sookht sookhteh beh
Sile ash panj rupye dadam,
dahan-e-sag be luqmah dookhteh beh

When some eminent person criticizes me in my dishonour, my heart is stricken
And in such a circumstance, it is only natural.
I gave him five rupees as a reward
For it is best to close a dog's mouth with a morsel.

I learnt from Hasan that the muallim's nephew, whom I met on the way from Medina at Rabigh, is a blatant liar. He had told us that 35 of his cars filled with hajjis were expected from Medina, but today I learnt that Sikandar has only 103 hajjis so far. Of them only one-third could afford the journey by car. The nephew is called Ismail, and not Sulaiman as I had previously recorded in these pages.

Muniruddin Sahib came after Hasan had left. I went with him to the Hyderabad Inn where I rested for an hour and then went to the Haram Sharif. I read the Quran till Zuhr. Afterwards, I came home. Our hostesses sent us food. I had lunch and, thereafter, left for the Hyderabad Inn. Here, I stayed till the late afternoon. I offered the Asr namaz in Haram Sharif and remained there till Isha. I went Nawab Ali's shop and bought a small book of prayers for tawaf and saii for 1.5 qirsh.

Unfortunately, I hadn't thought of buying this inexpensive book earlier or else I would have memorized the prayers by now.

The sky has been slightly clouded all day and the sun has been less fierce. At night, it turned hot and the mosquitoes became a menace. I couldn't get much sleep.

Tuesday, 7 May

I wrote letters home. I doubt if I shall have the time to send them from here again. After all, only 11 to 12 days are left for the hajj to take place.

The city is, *Mashallah* (with the grace of Allah), bustling. The people of Mecca are busy getting rich. People from all parts of the world are present in the Haram at this time. The Egyptians outnumber the Javanese now. It is a great pity that their women have completely disowned the purdah,[1] and that they go around unveiled as they do during tawaf. Some of them are so wretched that they joke and tease as they perform the tawaf and also laugh and giggle. May Allah grant them better sense and make their men *ghairat-mand*![2]

As always, I offered the Fajr namaz in the Haram. I returned home for breakfast, which was a gruel of sattu made of jau,[3] mixed with a little milk. I couldn't get much sleep last night owing to mosquitoes. I took a tablet of quinine and drank tea. I went to the Inn after 2.00 pm. Having spent an hour talking to Muniruddin and reading the *Tafseer Azizi* (an explanation of the Quran Sharif), I went to the Haram at 4.30 pm and read the Quran till Zuhr. After namaz, I came home, ate lunch, and left for the Inn at 7.00 p.m., where I slept for some time. I stayed in the Haram from 10.30 p.m. onward, until Isha. These daily occurrences need not be recorded everyday.

It is difficult to exit from the Baab-e Ibrahim after the Isha prayer. The crowd has swelled so much that you can no longer find the space to even breathe inside the gate. It was especially difficult today because Sultan Ibn Saud is expected. Two rows of policemen are lined along the road and no one is allowed to pass by. The footpath is extremely narrow and all the hajjis must walk on it. With a lot of trouble, I reached my lodging, drank tea, and talked to Muniruddin Sahib for a while. The

1 The system of keeping women from public view. Purdah exists in various forms in the Islamic world and among Hindu women in parts of India.

2 Self-respecting.

3 Barley is an annual cereal grain, which serves as a major animal feed crop, with smaller amounts used for malting and in health foods.

chair came from the qahwakhana. Muniruddin went to his Inn and I spread out my bedding and went to sleep. A few Egyptians have come to stay in my neighbourhood, and they too spread their beddings close to my chair on the ground and slept beside me.

Wednesday, 8 May

While returning from the Haram after namaz, I discovered that Mohammad Hanif Zardoz, in whose house I've been staying, has returned from Hindustan and had gone, in my absence, for tawaf–e umrah. After some time, my hostesses began to cry. At first, I thought that they had lost some relative in Hindustan and Mohammad Hanif Sahib had brought the bad news, and hence this mourning. An Indian woman from the neighbourhood solved the mystery when she told us that Hanif Sahib had, Mashallah, come with a third wife! And now she accompanied her husband to perform tawaf. The two wives were, on the other hand, mournful. I was saddened by this news. Hanif is about 60 years old. He already has two wives, of whom one is barely 15–16 years old, and the third who has now come is, I am told, the prettiest of them all, and apparently even younger than 15! I don't know what the parents thought of when they married their young and pretty daughter to such a decrepit old man.

Sultan Abdul Aziz bin Saud, the ruler of Hijaz and Nejd, arrived in Mecca last night. He is one-eyed but the Hindustanis should not mistake him for *Dajjal*[1] because, according to the Hadis *Sahih*,[2] Dajjal cannot enter Mecca and Medina. Boys from the madrasa are going in little groups with their teachers, flags in hand, to greet the Sultan. Shops have been decorated with green pennants. Thousands of rupees have been spent on decorating the gates and arches but nothing can be considered against the Shariat because the people of Mecca are the fountainhead of *Sunnah*![3]

1 Dajjal (The Deceiver/Impostor), also known as the False Messiah. An evil figure in Islamic eschatology, he is to appear at a time in the future, before the Judgement Day.

2 Sahih is an Islamic term meaning authentic. It is commonly used to describe the authenticity of a Hadis. The authentic collection *al-Jaami al-Sahih* or popularly al-Bukhari's authentic *Sahih al-Bukhari* is one of the six major Hadis collections. Most Sunni Muslims view this as their most trusted collection.

3 Sunnah means 'the way of the Prophet Mohammad'. In general, the word Sunnah means habit, practice, customary procedure, or action, norm and usage sanctioned by tradition. It refers to Mohammad's sayings, practices, and living habits.

Yusuf, Abdul Qadir Sikandar's employee, came to meet me on the *Rehmani S.S.* He came looking for me twice yesterday but we could not meet. He heaped abuses on Abdul Qadir Sikandar for a long time and listed his malicious and spiteful behaviour. He said that Abdul Qadir will not take proper care of me in Mina and Arafat and, as is his wont, trouble the hajjis no end. Yusuf has promised that if he goes to Arafat he will look after me.

Mohammad Hanif Sahib returned from the Haram Sharif after umrah and talked about Hindustan for a long time. He is very critical of Sikandar. Unfortunately, I did not know of his bad ways in Hindustan or else I would have stayed free of the claws of this tyrant.

الـخيـر في ما وقع

Whatever happened must be fine (for us).

Hanif Sahib's elder wife is intelligent and obedient. There was a hue and cry in the house till he had not returned from the Haram Sharif and all the neighbours were trooping in to offer their condolences. But when Hanif returned and his new wife entered the house with him, her sorrows disappeared. She became solicitous towards her husband. In fact, an outsider would not have known that this was, until half an hour ago, a house of tears and mourning.

Thursday, 9 May

Today, I took a bath at Muniruddin Sahib's inn. I changed and felt lighter all day, and cooler too. According to the almanac, the solar eclipse will occur today. It will be sighted in Mecca between 8.00 and 9.00 a.m. According to the Arab time, it would be between 2.00 and 3.00 p.m. The eclipse couldn't be seen but with the temperature going down, I suspect that is when the eclipse will take place.

After Asr, Sultan Ibn Saud appeared for tawaf in the Haram. I too caught a glimpse of him. He is a tall man with a charismatic face. The mosque was packed with a lakh and a half people, and everyone stood up to see him. Eunuchs cleared the way by calling out *Tarriqu* ('Give way') as the Sultan went around circumambulating in the tawaf. Because of his height and build, he was head and shoulders above the others who milled about him. May Allah increase his renown! The peace in Hijaz is because of him; it has come after several centuries.

After Maghrib, I met Abdul Qadir in the Haram. We made plans for the journey to Arafat and Mina. Hasan promised that he would arrange for a car to take me to Jiddah well in time. Let us see what fruit his promises bear.

دل افگندیم بسم الله مجریها و مرسها

Dil afgandeem Bismillahi Majreha wa Mursaha

We have given our heart to him
In the name of Allah, it shall set sail and cast anchor.

Letters came from Hindustan today. I received a lot of them from my relatives and elders. Thank Allah, all is well at home. Or at least, all was well till 24 April as I've received letters till that date.

Friday, 10 May

I went to the Hyderabad Inn at 10.00 a.m. I took a bath and went to the Haram Sharif at 10.30 a.m., accompanied by Muniruddin Sahib. Thousands had gathered in the mosque by then. By 4.00 p.m., there wasn't an inch of shaded place in the entire complex. The azan was heard at 5.20 p.m. and the khutba began ten minutes later. What can I tell you about the crowd—I don't think that there will be a bigger Juma congregation this year! After namaz, I left the mosque. It was difficult to get out. Everyone was in a hurry; nobody thought twice before pushing and shoving. A young woman virtually fell at my feet in the melee and no one stopped to pick her up. I reached home by 6.00 p.m.

Hanif Sahib had gone for the Friday namaz with his new wife. He hasn't returned yet. His old wives offered me lunch and bemoaned their misfortune. I had eaten before going to the Hyderabad Inn and before Hanif Sahib's return. As always, I rested till Asr. In the evening I met Maulvi Khalilun Nabi Rampuri at Nawab Ali's shop. From him, I learnt that, according to some people, today itself is the first of Zul Hijja, and that the new moon had been sighted last night. According to this, hajj would take place on Saturday.

والغیب عندالله

(But) only Allah knows transcendental things, invisible things.

Sitting near the Maqam-e Ibrahim at the time of Maghrib, I spotted the hajj moon. The crescent was a mere sliver but it was so high up in the sky that I could see it. Allah alone knows better if it is new or a day old. The Qazi Sahib has yet to make the announcement. The matter shall be resolved in a couple of days. I have sent my bags to Jiddah in the care of the muallim, Umar Khayyam. I hear from him that I have to pay 4 riyals as tax for transportation. I shall pay after borrowing some cash from Abdul Jabbar's shop.

Saturday, 11 May

Experience tells me that there is no better way to beat the heat in Mecca than to bathe every day. Watermelons are available in plenty. One feels a lot better by eating one of them and bathing regularly with cold water. Or else the terrible heat becomes intolerable. Despite my best efforts I could not procure water for my bath. As a result, I did not feel as good as I did yesterday and the day before.

After Zuhr, I returned from the masjid, baking and broiling in the heat and the blistering hot loo wind. As I reached close to my home, I spotted khus[1] curtains on the lower floor of the Junagadh Inn. They were being drenched with sprinklers. The smell of khus maddened my senses; its coolness could be felt even by those who walked on the road. Ignorance is a terrible thing. I have brought all sorts of perfectly useless things from Hindustan but it did not occur to me to pack two curtains of khus. How much comfort they would have given me here! And they would have been useful in Arafat too.

Indian hajjis write travelogues without providing any useful information. You don't need to bring anything to Mecca and Medina because every single commodity in the world is accessible. One could do with 4–5 stitched sets of clothes, a small bedroll, and enough money with you, in guineas or notes—that is all you need, though, yes, if one is used to the good life, one must remember to pack two curtains made of khus as long as hajj falls during the hot season. They will be a source of immense comfort. Hajj falls in the middle of May this year. For the next five years, one will have to stay in Arafat during the hot months and the khus curtains will prove to be an incomparable blessing.

Owing to my ignorance, I have committed a couple of errors. The first was to have considered Munshi Mohammad Yusuf Sahib Allahabadi as my friend and companion on this journey without thought or

---

1 The dried root fibres of a type of grass, often woven into mats and screens to give shade from the sun in warmer climates.

regard to the fact that his muallim is different from mine. How, then, would he and I stay together? The muallimin here don't let the hajjis in their charge meet each other during the hajj, and in Arafat or Mina one is definitely separated. Because of this mistake I have had to incur additional expenses and it looks as if my difficulties shall not end unitl my return to Jiddah. The other mistake is that I fixed the rent for Mohammad Hanif Zardoz's house after meeting him in Jiddah without checking or consulting anyone. Once I reached here, I discovered that the Rs 150 we paid as rent was excessive. We could have found a far better place for 5–6 guinea, that too one that would have afforded us some respite from the terrible heat. May Allah bless Muniruddin Sahib for keeping me at his inn all day for if I had had to spend 15 days in this house in this inferno, my health would have surely given up. There is no provision for a fan in this house and the roof too is in no condition to have a fan installed. I have spent a great deal of money on this pilgrimage but due to the sorry state of this house, I have not been able to do anything about a fan, though it does not cost much and brings such comfort.

My third mistake has been that I did not buy dry paan from Bombay. I could have bought a wad of them for a paisa or a paisa and a half; each wad has 12–13 paan. The same costs 6 paise and 2 annas. In fact, in Medina we even bought them for 4 annas per wad. I have eaten at least Rs 25 worth of paan during the past three months though by Bombay prices, would cost no more Rs 3–4. In Hindustan, I had never even looked at dry paan nor did I know that they were plentifully sold in the shops of Bombay. Here, for the past three months, I have been subsisting on dry paan and have got used to them by now. They are immersed in water and later the dirt is rubbed off them with a dry cloth, and then *katechu* and lime paste is rubbed on them. Munshi Muniruddin Sahib has been doing this for me ever since we reached Jiddah. May Allah bless him!

After Asr, I went to Abdul Jabbar's shop and recovered the money that he owed me (that is Rs 300). Today, I received Rs 13 and 11 anna for a guinea. There are plenty of jewellery shops here which do a roaring business of *lootmaar*.[1] They take a cut of 4 annas on every 10-rupee note. It is surprising that even when exchanging a Saudi riyal, they deduct 1 qirsh. As far as possible, they don't give you the hallal. They only give

1 'Robbery' or 'act of a dacoit', especially in unprotected buildings and shops.

one qirsh or half a qirsh. If you insist on taking the hallal, due to you, they say, 'This man is such a traitor and so miserly that he is not willing to spend even an anna or two; in fact he wants to get by with using just a paisa.' And if they do give you a hallal after heaping many curses upon you, they will still deduct 2–3 qirsh for every riyal.

Before the Maghrib namaz, I went to meet Umar Khayyat in the Haram Sharif. He wasn't there but I met his son. I handed over the 4 riyals for the transport tax. He told me that my luggage had reached Jiddah and that he had the receipt of its safe arrival. Alhamdulillah!

The employees of Dr Andur Rehman Sahib who had come from Medina on camel have arrived safely tonight. They are staying at Hyderabad Inn.

All day long, we waited for Maulvi Abdul Majid Sahib Daryabadi and his friends, but they haven't yet turned up.

The city is abuzz with the rumour that today is the 2nd of Zul Hijja and the moon was sighted on the 29th. One still doesn't know what the Qazi Sahib has announced.

Sunday, 12 May

The Hanafi imam leads the Isha prayer. At that time, the full *iqamat*[1] is recited. The rest of the time the iqamat is recited only once. As I have recorded earlier, the incidents in Medina, the mukabbirin (he who recites the takbir) here do not say, 'Rabbana walakal hamd'; instead they recite, 'Rabbana Lakal hamd'. At the time of the Maghrib, Isha and Fajr namaz, the Imam stands right beside the Baab-ul Kaaba. The stones in the masjid are so fiercely hot that it is impossible to step on them. Even then the creatures of Allah perform tawaf. Bare-head, bare-foot, wearing the ihram, they are intent upon tawaf. I can barely walk a few steps. There is no shade from the Baab-e Reham to the mosque and I find myself in a sorry state whenever I walk that short distance. The people's faith is so strong that they sit on these burning stones to offer namaz and walk on them for tawaf. The Shariat of Islam has not given any injunction to tolerate such a harsh regimen.

There is no monasticism in Islam.

Be not cast by your own hands to ruin. (Quran: Al-Baqara 195)

---

1 The call for takbir—Allah-o-Akbar—is recited twice before the congregation starts the prayer.

Thanks to Muniruddin Sahib, I was able to secure water for a bath today. As a result, I felt good all day long.

Monday 13 May

While returning home after the morning namaz at the masjid, I met the waterman from Neemuch. He told me that Mir Reham Ali, the man who wrote complaints (*araiz-navis*), died yesterday and was buried in the Jannat-ul Moalla.[1] I had not even heard of his illness; the news of his death saddened me. May Allah show clemency to him! His wife, too, is said to be unwell. May Allah have mercy on her!

I went to the Jannat-ul Moalla at 1.00 p.m.. Hazrat Khadija Al-Kubra, Abdullah bin Zubair,[2] and their companions are buried here. I had the good fortune to offer fateha at unmarked, unknown graves. The state of this holy burial ground is worse than that of Jannat-ul Baqi. There are such illustrious elders of the faith buried here that if the dirt from their shoes were to fall on the saints and holy men of India, they would consider it a source of good fortune. But the tyrants have not allowed even the traces of their graves to remain. This graveyard was once reserved for the Muslims, but now it is said that the government realizes Rs 15–20 from the families of the dead. I saw three dead bodies being brought to the graveyard. It seems as though they were poor or those without family or kin. They were bathed in one corner of the graveyard and wrapped in a shroud before being placed in the earth. The pits were already dug, the dead bodies were placed in them, and the earth was levelled. The body decomposes very rapidly in the burning sand and is reduced, in the next 2–3 days, to nothing. The bones disintegrate and the same grave is ready for the next occupant.

Those who are buried here are probably released from the torments of the grave due to the proximity of the illustrious elders buried nearby and their blessed spirits perchance find a resting place in the Jannatul

---

1 On the disposal effects of Indian pilgrims who died in the Hijaz, see L/PJ/8/76, 1943–44, IOLR.

2 Abu 'Abd Allah Zubayr ibn al-Awwam (624–692) was a companion of Mohammad. After the death of Husain at Karbala, Ibn Zubayr returned to the Hijaz where he declared himself the righteous Khalifa, and consolidated his power by sending a governor to Kufa. Ibn Zubayr established his power in Iraq, southern Arabia, and in the greater part of Syria, and parts of Egypt.

Firdaus.[1] But the bodies of those who die are not treated very well. A man's body is treated like that of an animal. If the dead man is wealthy, and his friends and relatives are present at the time of the burial, then he is bathed with due care, wrapped in a shroud, and placed in front of the Baabul Kaaba, where the congregation offers the Namaz-e Janaza and the corpse is taken out by way of Baab-e Salaam and then buried in the Jannat-ul Moalla. If the dead person has no heirs or near and dear ones, then two labourers carry the body on a cot and bring it to Jannat-ul Moalla and bury it under a curtain of soil after the barest of ritual baths. Only Allah knows what happens in the grave but we have enough faith in His mercy to know that the dead would certainly be at peace in the other world.

The world is a prison for the believers and paradise for infidels.

May Allah grant release to Mir Reham Ali and grant him a place in Jannatul Firdaus by virtue of his being buried in the Jannat-ul Moalla! But his body (*naash*) was subjected to the same treatment that is meted out to the kinless. Two labourers carried him till the graveyard and handed him over to the earth. Except for the waterman, who has been repeatedly mentioned in these pages, there was no friend to accompany the dead body to the grave.

At least it is still better here than Arafat and Mina where, it is said, that the dead don't even merit a grave or a piece of cloth. In fact, it is far better to die at Medina.

O Lord, grant me death in the city of your Messenger.

Today, I was blessed by the sight of that hallowed ground for the first time. On a particular date, this site, that is, the spot at which the Prophet was born had become even more sacred than the Kaaba. And this piece of ground had become as high as the loftiest of skies. Muslims the world over are devoted to the name of their Prophet and take pride that no other ummat has loved their Prophet as dearly or as well. From Adam till Jesus, there is no known record of the exact spot of the birth of any of the Prophets and even the Christians revere the spot where the Prophet of Islam was born. However, in the words of the late Khwaja Hali:

---

1 The highest level of heaven, Firdaus, is said to be the place where the prophets, the martyrs, and the most truthful and pious people will dwell.

مومنوں پر کشادہ ہیں راہیں

Mominon par kushadah hain raahein

The paths are wide open for the Believers

The Muslims don't feel the need to keep this place clean or pure, a place where their religious history began, and where that esteemed personage came to life who was to turn the tide of the world.

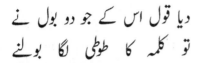

Diya qaul uske jo do bol ne
To kalme ka tooti laga bolne

His words brought forth such convictions
The Statement of Faith spread near and far

Today, old utensils and old clothes are sold on this sacred spot. Rags are auctioned. Such is the fate of the self-esteem of the Muslims. Their ancestors had martyred the hungry and thirsty cherished ones of the Prophet within 50–60 years of his death. And had tied horses near the Prophet's grave. And now after 1,300 years, if rubbish has been heaped upon his place of birth, then is there any reason for surprise? Wonderful!

ہم طالبِ شہرت ہیں ہمیں ننگ سے کیا کام

بد نام اگر ہوں گے تو کیا نام نہ ہوگا

Ham talib-e shohrat hain hame nang se kya kaam
Badnaam agar honge to kya naam na hoga

I seek fame, I care not for disgrace
After all, infamy brings fame along

I recited durood at this sacred spot and wept. My friend Muniruddin did a tawaf of the auction house and with a great deal of difficulty we could stop our tongues from speaking ill of those brutish savages who have reduced this historic site to such a sorry state. During Turkish times, there used to be a grand monument here. Thousands of chandeliers would be lit at night and several sers of ambergris perfumed the place. But the Nejdis got rid of every trace of those buildings, and levelled the ground. Today, the place is used as an auction house.

So learn a lesson, O ye who have eyes. (Quran: Al-Hashr-2)

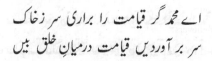

Ae Mohammad gar qayamat ra bar aari sar ze khak
Sar barawar wain qayamat darmiyan-e-khalq been

O Prophet if you'll raise one from dust to fame on Doomsday
Show a spectacle of it to the creation suffering like Doomsday situation.

We reached the Hyderabad Inn at about 3.00, carrying with us the scars of horror and amazement. A caravan of pilgrims arrived from Hyderabad and the Inn is very crowded now. Muniruddin has had to leave the top floor and leave his room for the others. After 4.00, the two of us, as always, went to Masjidul Haram and stayed there till the Zuhr namaz. Afterwards, I went to my lodging, ate and went to sleep. It was hot but the Hyderabad Inn is so crowded that I would probably have found no respite there too. It became cool by 9.00. Muniruddin Sahib too arrived and at Asr, as always, we presented ourselves in the Haram Sharif.

After Maghrib, we met Abdul Qadir and his son, Hasan. We reminded him about the car and enquired about the camels and the howdahs. Muniruddin Sahib, like me, had become the prey of an ace hunter in India. His muallim is still enjoying himself in Hyderabad. He is not willing to bear the heat and dust of Mecca. The muallim's lawyer did not get Muniruddin to do the tawaf, nor made him drink zumzum, nor ever bothered to check on his well-being. But when he was leaving for Medina, he showed up to demand his share—just like mine had! And till he had extracted Rs 20 as his fee for muallimi and giving zumzum, he did not let Muniruddin leave for Medina. Muniruddin had, after a great deal of trouble, finally obtained a receipt for the money he had paid to the lawyer and now he is free to make his own arrangements for the trip to Arafat and for the car to take him to Jiddah. My muallim has made arrangements for him to be taken by camel. He and I shall share a camel. I hope, Inshaallah, to benefit enormously from his company. Neither Mohammad Yunus Sahib nor the caravan of Maulvi Abdul Majid Sahib has arrived from Medina. I don't know the reason for their delay.

Tuesday, 14 May

My stock of sattu was exhausted yesterday, and I ate harisa for breakfast after a very long time. May Allah save me from the terrible discomfort caused by the heat during the day! It is 2.00 in the morning and I am feeling fine.

After making the above entry, I went to the Hyderabad Inn and stayed there talking to Muniruddin Sahib for two hours. Later I proceeded towards Masjidul Haram. Thank Allah I have completed reciting the Quran in the Haram Sharif. The ihram has been tied around the Kaaba, that is because its cover had become tattered and the wall of the sanctuary could be seen naked through it. A white cloth has been tied all around from the ground till the height of a grown man. Later, I found out that every year, an ihram is tied around the House of Allah. I don't know how the Nejdis have permitted this to continue. Now it has been decided that today is the 5th of Zul Hijja and the hajj shall be on Saturday, Inshaallah.

After Zuhr, I returned to my lodging. It was extremely hot. After 9.00, the heat lessened somewhat. Muniruddin Sahib arrived after some time. I went with him to the masjid for the Asr prayer and, as always, stayed till Isha.

Mecca's population has increased so much that it is difficult to get out of the mosque or to walk on the streets. It is Allah's grace that despite such a large crowd, the shops are stocked with groceries and essential commodities. Green vegetables and fresh fruits are found to be in abundance. There is no shortage of either water or food. Inflation too is not very high. Excessive heat is the only problem. From 2.00 in the morning till 9.00 in the evening, it is as difficult to pass the time as to dig for a canal of milk as Farhad did.[1] May Allah keep me in good health and make my hajj be accepted in the grace of Allah!

---

1 A legendary character in love with Shirin, the wife of Khusrau II of Persia. The romance of Farhad and Shirin is a classic text of Persian literature. The poet Nizami created the romance for a local ruler in northwest Iran in 1184 and from the fifteenth century manuscripts containing the poem were often illustrated with miniature paintings.

Wednesday, 15 May

I avoided eating harisa owing to the hot weather. Instead, I mixed English biscuits with milk for breakfast. At Asr, I drank the sherbet made of *imli*.[1] From 2.00 in the morning till 4.00, I stayed with Muniruddin in the Hyderabad Inn. Later, I presented myself in the Masjidul Haram. After Zuhr, I returned to my lodging. As always, I tolerated the terrible heat from 7.00 to 9.00. Today, a large caravan of Egyptians and Javanese set off for Mina. From morning till evening, a long row of camels headed towards Mina. In Masjidul Haram, there was a great deal of commotion in connection with the rites of tawaf and ramal. The muallims normally make the pilgrims in their charge do saii of Safa-Marwa before the tawaf-uz ziyarat (a tawaf done for thanksgiving). Therefore, all day long people performed the tawaf and saii. Perhaps it will be the same tomorrow.

Maulvi Abdul Majid Sahib Daryabadi arrived with his entourage a little before Maghrib. I spotted him from a distance in the Masjidul Haram but did not get the chance to speak to him. I have heard that Dr Abdur Rehman Sahib too has arrived, but I haven't met him yet.

Munshi Mohammad Yusuf Sahib has still not arrived. The news is that he might come in the same caravan as Dr Mohammad Husain Allahabadi.

I returned to the lodging after Isha. I did not sleep too well last night.

Thursday, 16 May

Today is the 7th of Zul Hijja. I will tie the ihram after a bath at Asr, and perform the tawaf-e nafil and saii of Safa and Marwa. Abdul Qadir Sikandar's caravan shall set out for Mina after Isha; I too shall go with it. Muniruddin Sahib too shall give me company.

This book of memories shall not go with me. And so the writing of this diary will be postponed for the next 3–4 days. If I return safe and sound from Arafat, I shall record my impressions later.

I went to Hyderabad Inn after writing the above account. I met Maulvi Abdul Majid Sahib Daryabadi and his friends and fellow travellers. From them I learnt that it was extremely difficult for them to find a car in

---

1 The tamarind, the hard green pulp of a young fruit, very tart and acidic, is most often used as a component of savoury dishes. The ripened fruit is sweeter, yet still distinctively sour, and can be used in desserts and sweetened drinks, or as a snack.

Medina. Therefore, they were delayed in reaching Mecca. Their fellow travellers experienced great difficulties during the journey. Obviously, if 26 people get into one car along with their bags and baggage, there will be some discomfort even on a good road; and the road from Medina is a tortuous one. I thank Allah I left Medina at the appropriate time, or else I would have experienced even greater difficulties than the Maulana because at least he had a return ticket and the car company had to make sure that he returned to Mecca. No company, on the other hand, was responsible for seeing me back in Mecca, because I had travelled on a one-way ticket. The mercy of the Beneficent One is such that I managed to reach Mecca with the utmost ease and here too I was able to present myself in the Haram Sharif to my heart's content. Alhamdulillah Ala Zalik.

Dr Abdur Rehman Sahib came in the morning but I wasn't home. I met him at the Inn at 4.00 p.m. He too found it extremely difficult to find a car for the return journey. Hence the delay in reaching Mecca. I learnt that Munshi Mohammad Yusuf Sahib was expected this evening. He would not travel with Dr Mohammad Husain Allahabadi's relatives but with Abdul Ghani Kathiawari. May Allah bring him here safely and may he not lose out on the hajj!

In Medina, I often heard that Munshi Muhammad Yusuf Sahib was keen to get married. I treated this as a joke and did not consider it worthwhile recording such idle talk in my diary. Today, I learnt that he had indeed got married to an Arab's daughter in Medina. It is said that he paid 50 guineas in hard cash as *mehr* and that some extra money would have to be paid after hajj. The girl is, reportedly, extremely beautiful and educated. Yusuf Sahib is said to be completely infatuated by his 'Zulaikha' and he has even adopted the Arab dress.[1] The people of Medina opposed this marriage, but the girl's parents had accepted the match because they were poor. May Allah bless their marriage and may it turn out well. May it not come in the way of his hajj!

As always, I presented myself in the Haram Sharif. Today, the khutba was not read at the time of Zuhr even though, according to tradition, there used to be a khutba on the 7th of Zul Hijja. After namaz, I returned to my lodging, ate, and went to sleep. I woke up at 8.00 p.m. The sky is slightly overcast and the heat of the sun is less oppressive. It is

---

1 This refers to the Quranic verse of Yusuf (Joseph) and Zulaikha.

8.30 now and Muniruddin Sahib has arrived. I shall bathe before I put on the ihram.

O my friend, diary, I take your leave for the next four days. We shall meet again if I get back safe and sound from Arafat. *Khuda Hafiz.*[1]

Wednesday, 22 May

I have been blessed by being able to offer hajj. Yesterday, I returned from Mina after Maghrib. I had hurt my foot on the day after Id, so I was in some pain. I have been well in all other respects. I shall examine my foot at my leisure when I have the time to do so on board the ship back home. For now, I want to secure the events that I witnessed in Mina. It is enough to say that it is precisely due to Allah's grace that one returns safe and sound from Mina and Arafat, or else the lotus-eaters and idlers from India should go straight to heaven from those holy spots.

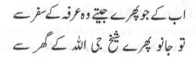

Abke jo phire jeete woh arafa ke safar se
To jaano phire sheikh ji Allah ke ghar se

If Sheikh returns alive from hajj this time
Take it as his return from God's house.

I could not go to the Haram Sharif in the morning due to the injury to my foot. I offered the Fajr namaz at home. Muniruddin Sahib arrived. I ate harisa for breakfast and drank tea. Dr Abdur Rehman Sahib also arrived. He gave me a new medicine for my wound. After some time, came Abdul Qadir Sikandar. I cleared his account and gave him some extra money as tip. In the afternoon, Mohammad Hanif Sahib treated Muniruddin, Mohammad Yusuf and me to lunch. He offered us delicious *pulau*[2] and zarda. I ate well after several days. I went to the Masjidul Haram after Asr and performed tawaf. I also met Nawab Ali. From him, I learnt that the mail hadn't yet arrived from India. After Maghrib, I went to meet Hasan bin Abdul Qadir Sikandar. He apologized

---

1 'May Allah protect you'. It is used in the subcontinent either when leaving or at the end of a telephonic conversation.

2 A dish of rice cooked with meat or vegetable.

for his mistakes. I offered the Isha namaz and returned to the lodgings where I drank tea and sent for the chair from the qahwakhana and went to sleep. My wounded foot hurts exceedingly but I am choosing to ignore it.

Thursday, 23 May

Due to my injury, I prayed at home in the morning. The car has yet to be arranged for Jiddah, though efforts are underway through Umar Akbar, the muallim. The fare for the car—Rs 10 and 8 annas per head—has been handed over to him. If the government allows the cars to set off today, I shall leave today, or else tomorrow. Munshi Muniruddin bought harisa from the market. We had it for breakfast and drank tea. After some time, we heard that permission had been given for the cars and we should prepare for the journey. We performed wuzoo and went to the Masjidul Haram to perform the tawaf al-Wada. While others were going into the Khana-e Kaaba, I could not enter the crowds due to my injured foot. In actual fact, I was in no state to enter that sacred site.

I finished the tawaful-Wada and returned to the lodging.

I waited for Umar Akbar till the afternoon. At the time of zawal, as I was engaged in the wuzoo for the Zuhr namaz, Umar Sahib arrived, riding his donkey. He asked us to leave right away. I demurred by saying that I hadn't eaten yet; I would leave after an hour. I offered my namaz and ate lunch. Today, we were invited to a farewell meal at Mohammad Hanif Sahib's house. His guests had still not arrived because normally people come by 8 o'clock. Mohammad Yusuf Sahib, Muniruddin, and I ate, then we dressed, and set out for the journey. By 7.00 p.m., Umar Sahib came again. Black porters were sent to carry our luggage. They argued and asked for half a riyal per head. Umar Sahib thought that this was too steep; he then ordered a donkey cart. Our bags were loaded on it and we walked beside it. As a result, we ended up paying 3 riyals instead of the half riyal per head!

The sun was extremely strong. I am unaccustomed to walking about under such a strong sun. Apart from this, my foot was still swollen. It was therefore agonizing to cover the distance of a mile from the city till the car depot. I reached the depot with a great deal of difficulty. There, we waited for an hour for Umar. At long last, he arrived; our luggage was loaded on a car. We had barely gotten on board and moved a few steps when we discovered that the car was not fit to travel to Jiddah. We returned to the car depot, unloaded our luggage, and put it in another vehicle. We wasted an hour or two in this.

Having got on board the second car and reached as far as the road, we heard that the government had banned the cars from carrying heavy loads, as this caused injury to the trade of the camel drivers. The order was to off-load all heavy bags. These were to be handed over to the muallims so that they could have them loaded on camels and sent to Jiddah.

The fee has been doubled; now one will have to pay 2 guineas per camel of which 1 guinea will go to the government as tax. I had no heavy bags. I had already sent my trunks to Jiddah, but Mohammad Yusuf Sahib had not. He had to leave behind one of his boxes. It was almost time for Maghrib while all these difficulties were being sorted out. We left the depot after sunset. The car was stopped again at the toll booth because the passengers had to be checked one by one and their bags examined. We wasted another two hours before leaving Mecca at 2.00 in the night.

I felt depressed after the travails of the last 7–8 hours. On top of that, the road was terrible. The car's wheels kept getting stuck in the sand every now and then. Ten or fifteen times, the driver urged the passengers to stop over in Bahra for the night and leave for Jiddah in the morning. But we declined. As we left, the rubber tube burst in one of the wheels forcing us to get off the car. A chilly breeze was blowing off the sea, the sand was cool, and moonlight was sprinkled all about. So far we hadn't had the good fortune to lie on the sands of Arabia; we got the chance to do so now. My friends and I lay down on the sands and went off to sleep owing to our sheer fatigue.

The car was repaired after an hour and we left on our onward journey. Jiddah was nearby. We reached the city gate at 8.00 in the night. The car driver had told us that the gate closes after midnight and we would have to stay outside but he was wrong. We entered the city and reached near the office of the Sharikatul Hijaziya al-Nejdiya (that is the office of the car company) where we got off. There were no coolies to carry our luggage, which was dropped off beside the road where we spread out our sheets and lay down. There wasn't much time to sleep but the exhaustion of the journey put us to sleep. We were unaware of the world around us.

Friday, 24 May

I woke up early in the morning. Close to the car depot was a masjid where I performed wuzoo from a saltwater tank and offered the morning prayer. Afterwards, Muniruddin and I went looking for Abdur Razzaq, the lawyer. We located his house easily. He very kindly gave us a room to stay in and went with Muniruddin Sahib to fetch our bags. The first task was to retrieve our return tickets from the British Consul office where they had been forcibly kept at the time of our arrival. We handed over our receipts for the tickets and our passports to Abdur Razzaq, and requested him to get back our tickets. He went off with the receipts, but all day long there was no trace of him. We were all hopeful of getting back our tickets by the evening but

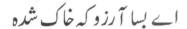

Ae basa aarezoo ke khak shudeh

Alas ! many wishes have turned to dust.

In the afternoon we went for lunch in a hotel. The food was inedible, the place extremely hot. Our bodies were drenched in sweat and we found no joy in eating. My tooth has been hurting since yesterday; it is aching quite a lot today and I had to smoke a cheroot. Thank Allah my teeth gave me no trouble at the Haramain Sharifain and I stayed safely away from cheroots while I was there. Today, this trouble has recurred in Jiddah. The cheroot dulled the pain but did not root out the cause. By the evening, my gums had swollen. I can neither eat paan nor digest food. There is a vast courtyard in front of the room where pilgrims from the Punjab are also staying. They do not let a stranger step foot beside them. Our room is hot and I have become accustomed to sleeping under the open sky. I had been up the previous night and the strain of the journey was troubling me. Yet I went to sleep despite the heat and was soon oblivious to everything around.

Saturday, 25 May

I got up in the morning. My gums were still swollen but the swelling was a little less now. After sunrise, I met Abdur Razzaq. From him, I learnt that the tickets for Mohammad Yusuf and Muniruddin had been retrieved but not mine. Apparently, misfortune dogged me, thanks to my muallim, Abdul Qadir Sikandar. My ticket had been deposited at Jiddah upon my arrival from Hindustan under the name of Swaleh Bisyoni but I had stayed in the house of Abdur Razzaq, the lawyer. When Razzaq presented the receipt for the ticket, the people at the office objected saying that Amir Ahmad was a client of Swaleh Bisyoni and his ticket could be obtained only through Swaleh. I was extremely worried to hear this. Had Abdur Razzaq mentioned this to me yesterday, I would have managed to get the ticket returned through Swaleh. The delay of 24 hours is a setback. It now looks like I may not get a berth on the first ship leaving Jiddah.

I also learnt that the *Rehmani* will be the first to leave, one of the finest ships of the Mogul Company which will sail direct to Bombay. The ship is scheduled to depart on the 27th of May, followed by *The Shujah* to Karachi and on the third or fourth day *The Khusrou* to Bombay.

I requested Abdur Razzaq to give my receipt to Bisyoni and entreat him to retrieve my ticket. It is possible that there may still be a place left in the first class and my ticket would be accepted for the *Rehmani*. Abdur Razzaq agreed to do so but I remained doubtful and worried. At 1.00 in the morning, I went to the Mogul Company and tried meeting Munshi Azizuddin. I learnt that he hadn't reached the office. Then I went to Munshi Ehsanullah Sahib's house only to learn that he was having breakfast.

By chance, Razzaq told me that he had passed on my ticket receipt to Swaleh. I returned to the lodging. After an hour, I went again to the Mogul Company and met Munshi Azizuddin. Although busy, he was extremely courteous. I narrated my tale of woes. He told me that there were enough seats left in the first class but that the final word rested with Munshi Ehsanullah and the Hajj Committee. They allotted the passage for those whose names are sent across to them; the Company was not authorized to do any more. I was a trifle disappointed and so we went to knock at the door of Munshi Ehsanullah. He met us warmly. We repeated our narration and described Abdur Razzaq's mistake. By chance, Razzaq too showed up. He agreed with my story. Munshi Sahib summoned Swaleh Bisyoni on the telephone and said something to him which I could not understand. Meanwhile Munshi Mohammad Akram Khan Sahib Bangali arrived. I learnt that he had reached today itself. He had a second class ticket and had come with me on the *Rehmani*. Munshi Sahib knew Mohammad Akram Khan quite well and seemed kindly disposed towards him. I began to hope that if Akram Khan could find a berth in the second class, then there is no valid reason why I cannot find one in the first class even though I have been here for a day before him. Munshi Ehsanullah Sahib too said that there were still some seats in the first class, and that I would probably be able to travel. My anxiety lessened somewhat but still my heart was not totally at ease. For a long time, I sat talking to Munshi Sahib. Several influential Indians came to see him and all were in distress. I learnt that there was no room left in the third class of the *Rehmani*, while passengers from second and first class could still travel—provided Munshi Sahib was kindly disposed towards them.

Jiddah is a difficult place. Thousands of pilgrims are lying in the streets. They tolerate the morning heat and the night dew. The religious zeal had made these hardships tolerable in Arafat and Mina, but not in Jiddah. Heaps of rubbish lie everywhere. There are no garbage disposal systems here. More than half the pilgrims are ill. If they have to stay here any longer, it is doubtful if any will reach the ship in a healthy state.

Our Lord, save us from the fires of Hell.

I returned to my lodging. I was in no condition to eat because of my aching tooth. Muniruddin Sahib set out in vain to get some milk for me. I dunked some biscuit in sherbet and ate a little. Then, I lay back patiently. The injury to my foot made it difficult to walk; so I could not get around. Somehow, the day passed. By evening, I got a little milk which I drank and thanked Allah. The Punjabis occupied the courtyard. The room had no air. All night long I suffered due to the heat and could not sleep soundly for even one hour.

Praise be to Allah in all circumstances.

Sunday, 26 May

I finished namaz and the wazifa in the morning. There was a hotel nearby, where I had tea with milk. The discomfort of the night abated somewhat. By 2.00 p.m., Mohammad Yusuf Sahib and I went to the house of Munshi Ehsanullah. There we met Maulana Abdul Majid Daryabadi. I learnt that his ticket had been submitted that very day. But, he was hopeful of getting a berth on the *Rehmani* because of Munshi Ehsanullah's kindness. Munshi Sahib said that there was place in the first class, and assured me that I would be able to travel on this ship. Comforted, I returned to my lodging. My tooth was better. I decided to eat something substantial. By the afternoon, Mohammad Yusuf, Muniruddin and I went to an Arab hotel beside the seashore and had lunch. After the Zuhr namaz, I went to the Mogul Company with Mohammad Yusuf Sahib. There, we met Munshi Azizuddin. He had a lot of work at hand. The tickets were being counted and Munshi Sahib was busy discharging his duties. After some time, he showed us the approved list of passengers. Mohammad Yusuf Sahib's name was on it, but not mine. Munshi Sahib said that there were still 6–7 berths in the first class of the *Rehmani*. If my ticket were to come through right now, he could still confirm my passage. The ticket is in the control of Munshi Ehsanullah and till he returns it, the Company's employees could do nothing.

In sheer desperation, I decided to go to Munshi Ehsanullah's office. The sun was severe, my foot injured, and my heart heavy. Mohammad Yusuf Sahib accompanied me. Despite the odds, I reached the Consul office where we met Abdur Razzaq. He told us that Munshi Sahib had gone away for lunch and would return after some time.

The Consulate's grand building is situated on the seashore. The room we sat in was filled with sea breeze. We were no longer bothered by the heat, but by now I was so severely depressed that I could not fully enjoy the balmy sea air.

After about half an hour Munshi Ehsanullah showed up. Mohammad Yusuf Sahib plucked the courage to describe my situation to him. I expressed surprise that my name had not yet reached the shipping company's office, but Munshi Sahib said quite bluntly that he had made no promise of sending me on the *Rehmani*. The departures would be strictly on a first-come-first served basis. If my number had not come, I could not travel on this ship.[1]

Meanwhile, Swaleh Bisyoni's employee, a man called Mustafa, showed up. Munshi Sahib asked him about me. The man said that my ticket had been handed to him only yesterday and so it was not submitted for the departure listing of the *Rehmani*. Fearing that Abdul Qadir may have plotted my detention, I felt very angry. Munshi Ehsanullah said that there were still ten berths in the first class of the *Rehmani*, but that he had a list of those hoping to travel on it. If there were the slightest possibility of accommodating me, he would have me in mind. Saying this,

---

1 Ultimately, the names of the pilgrims were recorded at the Consulate in the order of their arrival and they were provided with shipping accordingly.

he prepared to leave for home. I sought permission to meet him at his residence, which he very kindly granted. Munshi Sahib was surrounded by scores of pilgrims and each one was asking for his ticket, but Munshi Sahib gave everyone the same answer: 'You will be given your ticket when your number comes.' An old man fell at Munshi Sahib's feet and began to cry piteously and asked for his ticket, but he too received the same response. The poor man was forcibly evicted from the spot.

Depressed and disconsolate, I walked back from the Consulate. All this walking hurt terribly. Heartbroken, I prayed to Allah Almighty that He might grant me leave to travel by the *Rehmani*. If detained in Jiddah, I shall suffer grievously. I shall lose the company of my dear friends. The injured foot will add to my trouble. I had tried everything I could possibly do; nothing had borne fruit. Now I depend on Allah's grace.

I confide my cause unto Allah, verily Allah is seeing of His slaves. (Quran: Al-Momin 44)

It seems as though I prayed at a time when prayers are meant to be answered. By the time I reached Munshi Ehsanullah's house, I found Swaleh Bisyoni there and noticed Munshi Sahib being so kindly disposed towards me. Now, it became clear that the receipt for my ticket had been submitted only today. Munshi Sahib's clerk produced a wad of tickets. My return ticket—which I had brought from Bombay and which had been forcibly taken away from me—was on top of the pile.

A Chaudhry Sahib from Rudauli[1] was present there. He was also Bisyoni's client. Ehsanullah was favourably disposed towards him. He had brought him in his car all the way from the Consulate till his home. My name was ahead of Chaudhry Sahib's in the list submitted by Bisyoni. Therefore, I expected Munshi Ehsanullah to let me leave owing to the Chaudhry's intervention. Surely, a person whose name is listed after me cannot be allowed to leave before me.

Briefly, after going through the papers for some time, Munshi Ehsanullah decided that all our names would be approved for departure. Chaudhry Sahib and some of his friends from Rudauli were travelling third class. They too managed to get in because of Chaudhry Sahib and they too were allowed to travel on the *Rehmani*.

---

1 A town in Barabanki district. Even after the abolition of zamindari, it remained a centre of Awadhi tehzeeb and helped nourish the cultural supremacy it acquired over the last couple of centuries.

شنیدم کہ در روز امید و بیم

بداں را بہ نیکاں بخشد کریم

Shunidam ke dar rooz-e-umeed-o-beem
Badan ra be neekan bebakhshad kareem.

I heard on the day of Hope and Despair
The merciful God would pardon the sinner along with the pious one.

I have fully understood the real meaning of this verse. Thank Allah I have finally been released from this terrible dilemma. I begin to hope that I might be able to board the ship along with my friends tomorrow. Swaleh Bisyoni promised that he would have my ticket sent to Abdur Razzaq's house. I thanked him for his kindness and returned to the lodging along with Mohammad Yusuf.

رسیدہ بود بلائے ولے بخیر گذشت

Rasideh bud balai wale bakhair guzasht.

Trouble had come but it has passed away

The sadness has left me now and I feel a lot better. I went to the seashore to get some fresh air. A caravan of Javanese had come from Mecca this morning. And they were now going towards the shore to board a ship. The Dutch Consulate is very well organized. The Javanese are not forced to surrender their tickets at the Consulate; the pilgrims carried their tickets with them. They reached in the morning, and the shipping companies stamped their tickets and asked them to board. As simple as that! All this trouble and toil is only for us poor Hindustanis, who have had to hang around Jiddah for the past three days and are in danger of losing their lives. But the Consulate could not care less for our welfare. I have eaten the salt of the British Empire, obtained an English-medium education, and purchased a first class ticket. I have spent a great deal of money on the hajj travel; at this time I have a lot of money still left with me. Yet, I have faced such immense hardships in getting back [to India]. How can I possibly narrate the troubles faced by those poor illiterate souls who are lying by the roadside and don't even have the courage to approach their rulers?

I offered the Maghrib namaz at a mosque, a short distance from the shore near the bazaar, and returned to the lodging. We drank the milk brought by Muniruddin Sahib. This was our diet for the night. The heat began to trouble us and sleep were unable to. After about two hours, Swaleh Bisyoni's employee, Mustafa, appeared and announced the glad tidings of my departure. I thanked the Merciful Allah whose intervention saved a situation that was going awry and instilled hope in a hopeless situation. Mustafa said that the lawyers in Jiddah are paid a fee to retrieve the ticket and a sum of Rs 2 per head has been fixed. What a pity that I was troubled for two days over such a trifling sum of money! I would have gladly paid Rs 20 if I had somehow been saved from the terrible trouble caused by the anxiety and strain. Anyhow, I now presented Rs 5 to Mustafa and secured the ticket safely away in my box.

I cannot describe my happiness at this moment. I could not sleep till midnight out of sheer joy. The distress caused by the heat disappeared as though by magic and we laughed and talked amongst ourselves. We went to sleep past midnight.

Monday, 27 May

A new worry began to bother me since the morning—Swaleh Bisyoni's employee gave me my return ticket but not my passport. Even though I'm unlikely to need the passport back in India, I nonetheless anticipate some difficulty in Bombay. I, therefore, thought it best to retrieve my passport from the lawyer. My friends were busy transporting their baggage from the house till the seashore. I waited for them to finish so that I could take them along to Swaleh Bisyoni.

A cart came to carry the bags and I had to go with mine till the dockyard. As a result, I could not find the time to go to Bisyoni's house. By chance, however, I met him on the way. I asked him for my passport. He said he would have it sent immediately. It is against all good sense to trust the word of lawyers and muallims; and I left Jiddah whereas the passport never reached me. May Allah allow the outcome to be satisfactory and may I not face any trouble in Bombay!

I had to stay on the seashore for almost two hours.

Abdur Razzaq asked me to pay Rs 24 as fee for the boatride till the ship, whereas the fee for the 12 people who were on board the boat with me should have been only Rs 12.

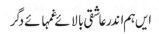

En hum andar ashiqi bala-e-ghamha-e-degar

In love, this sorrow too is above all other sorrows

At long last, the boat left the shore of Jiddah and we safely boarded the *Rehmani*. Maulana Abdul Majid Daryabadi and his 15 fellow travellers and Chaudhry Mohammad Ali Rudaulvi, along with his friends, had occupied the best rooms in the first class. I got the last room that lay vacant. I thanked Allah for finally freeing me from the clutches of the muallim and the lawyers of Arabia.

Even though the Mussalmans of Hindustan are slaves of foreign rulers as a punishment for their own misdeeds and they do nothing else but blindly follow the others, I think it is far better to suck up to the coolies on board than to tolerate the forceful rule of the Arabs.

The ship is quite full. There is no place in the first and second class. A few Afghans too have boarded the ship due to an oversight on the part of the Shipping Company's office and they have taken over the prime location on the deck meant for the first class passengers to move about and breathe freely. As a result, they have impeded our easy passage on the deck, if not blocked it altogether.

By the late afternoon, Munshi Ehsanullah and Munshi Azizuddin came to see off the ship. They met the Captain and tried to persuade the Afghans to get off this ship, which was headed for Bombay and not Karachi. But they refused and stayed put on their own Khyber Pass![1]

The ship pulled anchor at 5.30 in the evening and within an hour we had left the shore of Jiddah far away.

I corrected the time in my watch after three months and matched it with the ship's clock.

It was very hot in my cabin but I was able to sleep because of the electric fan and spent the night fairly comfortably. Alhamdulillah!

Tuesday, 28 May

The first morning on board dawned. I got out of bed at 4.00, offered the namaz, and read the wazifa. My room was hot; so I went up on the deck to be with Maulana Abdul Bari, Maulvi Manazir Ahsan and others. The running around during the past few days has made my injured foot

---

1 The mountain pass that now links Pakistan and Afghanistan. Throughout history, it has been an important trade route between Central Asia and South Asia, and a strategic military location.

sore. Today, it was swollen too. Dr Abdul Rehman Sahib Mungeri's medicine was with me. I put it on my wound and bandaged it. With hardly any place to move about on the ship in any case, the wound further incapacitated me. I went up on the topmost deck in the evening where Maulana Abdul Majid Sahib was present along with his entire entourage. Chaudhry Sahib, as the host, had arranged for some tea to be sent from the English Hotel. It was decided that we'd take turns to host such teas one by one. Tomorrow, Inshaallah, will be my turn.

I returned to my room by Maghrib. Munshi Muniruddin Sahib is also staying in the same room, even though his travelling cost was taken off the car when we were leaving Mecca and had been handed over to Akbar Umar, the muallim, so that he may have it sent to Jiddah by camel. But thanks to the muallim Sahib's kindness, the travelling cot on which was wrapped Muniruddin Sahib's ja-namaz (prayer mat), ended up being buried in the sacred sands of Mecca. It had still not reached Jiddah at the time of our departure. Munshi Muniruddin is very upset becuase his cot is lost. If he had the bed, he could have set it out on the deck and enjoyed the fresh sea breeze. But now he has to perforce sleep on the floor in my room and endure the terrible heat. This is yet another small miracle that can be attributed to the many blessings of the Arabs!

Mohammad Akram Khan Sahib is travelling second class but his cabin in intolerably hot. So he spends the better part of the day in our room and keeps us engrossed in his enjoyable conversation.

Today, a Malabari youth died of pneumonia. The people from the ship's dispensary put his body in the sea without the ritual bath and prayer. We came to know about it when it was too late. We felt sad that all the Muslim passengers on board were collectively guilty of this major lapse.

Wednesday, 29 May

Thank Allah all is well. My foot is a lot better, but not entirely satisfactory. The Muslim Hotel on the ship provides meals that taste good, but the quantity of the food has been reduced.

Today, it was much less hot. I slept well in the afternoon but the wind died down in the evening and the weather turned still and suffocating. Again, a tea party was held on the topmost deck but here too there was no breeze. At night I couldn't sleep much because of the heat. We passed the island of Piram at 2.30 a.m. but our ship didn't sail anywhere close to the harbour.

Thursday, 30 May

Today the sky is a little overcast. The wind had picked up duirng the morning. The ship has changed direction so that we are heading east. I went back to sleep after breakfast at 10.00 and woke up only after noon. Meanwhile, our ship crossed Aden.

As always, there was a tea party on the top deck. Today, it was Mohammad Yusuf Sahib's turn to play host. An hour passed in enjoyment. The sun set at about 6.30 p.m. The ship's clock has been set forward by 15 minutes; I set my watch accordingly. The night was cool; I slept very well.

Friday, 31 May

The weather had been very pleasant in the morning but by 10.00 it began to get warm. Our ship is approaching the Socotra River. Here the sea is very turbulent. Some people are beginning to suffer from sea sickness. The stock of coals had caught fire and the ship's employees have been engaged in putting out the fire for the past two or three days. A lot of water was used to extinguish the fire but a lot of smoke is still coming out. Clearly, the fire has still not been fully extinguished. Today, the ship's employees are trying to remove the coals with the help of a crane. Its rumbling causes a great deal of discomfort to the hajjis.

By the evening, the waves rose higher and it became difficult to walk on the deck without support. Thank Allah for the cool night. I slept well.

Saturday, 1 June

Today, the sea is so turbulent that the ship rocks violently and disturbingly. I lay on my bed all morning till 10.00 a.m., because sitting up makes my head spin. The ship's employees say the sea will be choppy like this all the way till Bombay. In fact, it is possible that storms may set in too and add to our difficulties. May Allah have mercy on us!

The ship's clock was set forward by 20 minutes yesterday; today, it was increased by 25 minutes. The sun set at 6.45. The turbulence increased at night and I could not sleep for several hours.

Sunday, 2 June

The rocking of the sea has made it impossible to walk about. I offered my namaz in a seated position because my feet falter when I try to stand.

Sufi Sahib Pir Ji Reham Bakhsh, the Sufi from Delhi, who was with us on the journey to Medina and had travelled with us from Mecca to Jiddah in the same car, departed for his heavenly abode this morning. He had fallen ill two days before hajj. He performed hajj in his state of illness. He was made to do the tawaf on a stretcher. The heat on the ship worsened his condition. Munshi Mohammad Yusuf Sahib tried his best and got him admitted in the ship's dispensary.[1] Yesterday, he was conscious but that was probably just a false recovery before death claimed him. Today, he has found a grave in the sea. The Turkish Compounder in the Dispensary gave him the ritual *ghusl*,[2] for which he received Rs 10 as a fee. Six or seven men recited the Namaz-i Janaza. Then they placed his body on a plank and dropped it into the sea. May Allah grant him maghfarat!

I felt listless all day. I spent a few enjoyable hours on the deck in the evening but my heart remained stricken with fear. The ship's clock has been set forward by another 20 minutes. The sun set at 6.45. I couldn't sleep till about 11.00 p.m.; thereafter, I fell fast asleep.

Monday, 3 June

The turbulence is said to be a little less than yesterday but the lethargy plaguing me continues unabated. May Allah let me reach the shore safely! There is nothing in particular to report.

Tuesday, 4 June

We were expecting to reach Bombay tomorrow, but today we've discovered that there is no hope of getting off this ship before the day after tomorrow. The sea is a little less rough now. My foot is better, though it still pains. The ship's clock was set forward by 15 minutes. The sun set by 6.45. We spent some pleasant time on the deck in the evening. Again, I did not sleep very well.

Wednesday, 5 June

Today, the ship's clock was not set forward. Its speed has slackened during the past two days. During the past 24 hours, it has covered a mere 147 miles. It rained heavily in the morning, accompanied by thunder and lightning. The passengers were stricken with fear. The storm abated

1 *Shafakhana.*
2 Purification bath or total ablution.

after an hour. May Allah let us reach our homes safely! It is being said that we shall be able to sight Bombay by the evening, though our ship will enter the harbour only tomorrow. I have been feeling so depressed and listless for the past one week that I don't even feel like writing my diary. I force myself to write a few lines.

7

Arafat and Mina

[The account of Arafat and Mina ought to be have been recorded before Wednesday, 22 May (p. 114 of the Urdu original), but because it was penned later, it is being recorded here as a separate chapter.]

Thursday, 16 May to Tuesday, 21 May (7 Zul Hijja to 12 Zul Hijja AH 1347)

I took a bath on Thursday, 7 Zul Hijja, three and a half hours before sunset, tied the ihram and went to the Masjidul Haram to offer two rakat namaz. I did the niyat for ihram hajj, performed tawaf nafil, and offered two rakat namaz close to the Maqam-e Ibrahim. Then, touching the Hajjr-e-Aswad, I set off to complete the last rounds of the saii of Safa and Marwa. In the last leg, I suddenly spotted Mohammad Yusuf Sahib. I discovered that he had just arrived from Medina. He wore the ihram for qiran and performed the umra at that time. We did not have the time to converse. After the saii, I entered the Masjid-e Sharif through the Baab-e Salaam. There, I offered two rakat namaz-e nafil, and then the Asr namaz.

I stayed in the masjid till sunset. After namaz, Muniruddin Sahib and I went to Mohammad Hanif's house. We drank tea and left for Hyderabad Inn with our belongings. Muniruddin collected his things and the two of us went to Abdul Qadir Sikandar's house, which was quite close to the Bait-ul Haram. There, we met Hasan bin Sikandar who told us that the camel caravan would leave after two hours, though those travelling by foot could leave right away. We left our belongings in the sitting room and went to the Haram Sharif for the Asr namaz. Afterwards, we again went to Abdul Qadir's house.

The camels belonging to the other muallims were already leaving but there was no sign of Qadir's camels. For an hour or two, I sat on a chair next to the door. Finally, we got up and went to a nearby qahwakhana. A pleasant breeze was blowing. We drank tea and I sat talking with Muniruddin. Half the night passed in this manner and still there was no sign of our camels. Hasan left with those heading for Mina on foot. Qadir went in hiding, and there was no one to take care of us. If an employee of the muallims chanced our way and we pounced eagerly on him to ask when the camels would come, we were told, with the utmost casualness, that they would arrive shortly. Like me, there were several other clients who were similarly troubled. All of them had been told that the camels would leave by Isha and all had been waiting with their bags packed and ready. The entire night was spent in this fretful waiting. A little before the morning azaan, the camels were brought. By then, we were so short of time that we were not even allowed to offer our Fajr prayer in the Haram Sharif. We lost out on a night's sleep as well as the morning's jamaat and the sunnat of leaving before the morning of 8 Zul Hijja was also lost to us. Inna lillahe wa inna ilaihi rajioon.

The distance from Mecca to Mina is no more than three miles. If I had had the courage to walk, I would probably have reached easily. We reached our destination an hour after sunrise. Hasan was in Mina but he disappeared the moment he saw our caravan. As I had already paid the rent for the house in Mina, the muallim was bound to give me a place to stay. But he and his son had disappeared. Now, who would get me the house and where would I complain? Hasan had promised to organize meals in Mina and Arafat and I had trusted him. As a result, I did not carry much provisions. In the absence of Hasan, who would now take care of my meals?

I carried some halwa for breakfast. I ate that, drank some water, and sat atop the camel's saddle because there was no other place for me to go to. When the sun became strong and the saddle provided no shelter, I went over with Muniruddin Sahib to the caravan from Hyderabad. A fine house has been rented by the Nizam of Hyderabad for the people of that state and Muniruddin Sahib is entitled to stay there. Thanks to him, I found a roof over my head and spent the terrible hours of the hot afternoon in its shade. I bought a watermelon from the bazaar and ate it because there seemed to be nothing else by way of food. Moreover, I was extremely thirsty. In the afternoon, I learnt that the Nejdi government needs this house for its soldiers and the people of the caravan shall have to vacate it. Some of the soldiers entered the building forcibly and compelled the Hyderabadis to leave. Every effort was made to explain to them that the State of Hyderabad had taken this house on rent and it would cause immense difficulty to the hajjis if they were forced to leave at short notice. But those barbarians would not listen. Muniruddin and I collected our bags and went back to the shaqdaf (camel saddles).

It was late afternoon by now. The sun was no longer so fierce. We sat in the shade of the saddles till the evening. There was a mosque nearby which the locals call Masjid Inna Aataina and say that the *Sura-i Kausar* was revealed at this very spot.[1] But this belief is probably wrong because the sura belongs to the Medina section and was not revealed in Mina. The masjid is now in such a state that the *mutawalli* charges Rs 2 per head for the boarding of the hajjis. With fires being lit for cooking makeshift meals, the place is in a shambles. There is a small tank in the courtyard, which the mutawalli uses to store precious water. He sells the water to the hajjis at exorbitant rates. Anyhow, there was no other place to offer prayers except this mosque and we had to perforce offer our Asr and Maghrib namaz here.

After namaz, we heard that Maulana Abdul Majid Daryabadi had arrived but was caught in the tyrannical clutches of Abdul Qadir Sikandar. He was, like us, without a house or a tent. And he too was lying in a shaqdaf. I went to meet him and ask about his health. The muallim had been giving him trouble for the past several days, bringing him to Mina in severe heat. We decided to lodge a complaint against Sikandar with the government. To let him go is tantamount to being unfair to the denizens of Awadh. Abdul Qadir lives in Lucknow. With his flattery and sweet words, he entices people so that everyone setting off for hajj from Awadh appoints him as their muallim. But he turns his eyes away like a parrot the moment one steps in Mecca. That is when one realizes his deceitfulness and fraudulence.

I talked to the maulana for some time and then returned to my own shaqdaf. Having starved all day, there was still no arrangement for dinner in sight. I survived on whatever meagre snacks I carried with me. Then, I lay down in my shaqdaf and went to sleep.

---

1 Muslim scholars divide the Quran's 114 suras, or chapters, into those revealed at Mecca, during the first phase of Mohammad's Prophethood, and those revealed at Medina in the second.

Past midnight, the camel drivers began to create a din; they forced us to vacate their shaqdaf. We left this place an hour before the morning namaz. Again, we lost the second sunnat too; we could not fulfil the obligatory namaz in Mina. Inna lillahe wa inna ilaihi rajioon.

On Saturday, 18 May, two hours after sunrise, our caravan arrived in Arafat. We forgot the hardships of this long journey. The distance from Mina to Arafat is no more than 6–7 miles and there is an excellent place to rest *en route*. Had this journey been undertaken on a bicycle instead of camelback, it would have been a lot more convenient. A lot of people have the stamina to travel on foot; most travel on mules and donkeys. This year, several hajjis used donkey carts. Those used to riding a bicycle should carry one from Hindustan; they would find the journey to Arafat easy. I didn't know about this earlier or I could have hired a bicycle from Jiddah or Mecca. I think even the journey to Medina can be undertaken on a bicycle. You can buy one and bring it on the ship from Bombay within the same fee that you give for the car to take you from Mecca to Medina and, moreover, you can earn your freedom from the tyrannical rule of the muallimin.

مشتے کہ بعد از جنگ یاد آید برکلہ شود باید زد

Mushti ke baad az jang yad aayed bar kalleh kuhd bayed zad.

The blow that is remembered after the war should be struck on one's own head.

The Arabs object that it is against the sunnat not to travel by camel, but the Hindi hajjis do not take up the cause of the sunnat at such a time; they prefer to use the shaqdaf, which was unheard of during the Prophet's time. Moreover, the muallims force scores of other sunnat upon the hajjis. At least by riding the bicycles, the hajji shall be free. He can come and go as he pleases and rest where he wants. He can leave Mecca on the 8th of Zul Hijja after Fajr, offer five namaz in Mina, and start the journey to Arafat after sunrise. He might lose out on the sunnat of riding on camelback but will benefit from observing many other important sunnat.

Maulvi Khalilul Nabi Sahib Rampuri was staying in a tent with his entourage. I too went to stay with him. The tent belonged to Abdul Qadir Sikandar and it had a thin roof. The fear of the afternoon sun and the fierce loo wind was with me but there was no other haven except this. Khalilul Nabi Sahib also has a gentleman called Shah Sahib Rampuri along with a coterie of disciples and followers staying with him. None of them objected to my presence in their midst. Muniruddin and I occupied a corner of the tent. Shah Sahib very kindly offered us sattu to drink and sweets to eat. We had bought some *peda* (made from sweet milk flavoured with cardamom and pistachio) in Mecca to bring along with us; we turned them into sherbet and drank that. Our camel driver came to our tent to ask for *bakhshish* (tip, mostly given in cash for services performed).

We sent him to a qahwakhana to fetch some tea. The tea proved to be eminently efficacious in alleviating the terrible heat and also served to slake our thirst. We had already decided to forego lunch; now, given the disorderly state of affairs, there seemed no way of procuring provisions for a meal.

Today, thank Allah there has been no *loo* wind and we found the strength to endure the heat. The company was enjoyable. I remained engrossed in interesting conversations. That's how the afternoon passed somehow. After zawal, we did the wuzoo and offered the Zuhr namaz in a congregation. Our tent is far away from the Masjid-e Nimrah[1] and Jabal-e Rehmat.[2] It is said that the government has put an end to the khutba that was always read out during the hajj. Now, no khutba is read in the Masjid-e Nimra during the Zuhr namaz. Therefore, we did not gather the strength to go all the way to the Masjid. Later, we found out that the khutba was actually delivered and that a congregation had offered the Zuhr and Asr namaz there. Anyhow, we spent some time in *isteghfar* (forgiveness) and dua after the Zuhr namaz. Shah Sahib was a respectable elderly gentleman whose presence moved us all. And for the moment, the pleasure of being in Arafat was magnified for all of us.

کہتے ہوئے ساقی سے حیا آتی ہے ورنہ

ہے یوں کہ مجھے دردِ تہِ جام بہت ہے

Kehte hue saqi se haya aati hai varna
Hai yon ke mujhe durde tahe jaam bahut hai.

I am ashamed to admit it before the *saqi*
The truth is that the leftovers in the cup are enough for me.

---

1 Masjid-e Nimrah is closed for the entire year except during hajj.
2 The Mountain of Mercy: the mountain in Arafat on which the Prophet Mohammad preached his famous sermon, known as the Farewell Sermon during his hajj.

We felt very emotional after the dua and, for a long time, engaged in the zikr of Allah and His Prophet. At Asr, we offered namaz in a congregation and spent some time in dua and isteghfar.

Shah Sahib had learnt by the afternoon that Abdul Qadir and his son had troubled me a lot and that I had made up my mind to complain on the day of Id. Being Qadir's well-wisher, he let the muallim know of my intentions. After Asr, when I was busy with my dua and there was barely an hour or two left for sunset, Qadir came and apologized for his mistakes. I remained silent for some time, but did not like his insistence. Finally, we ended up exchanging harsh words. Later, I was reminded of this *ayat* from the Quran[1] and made up with the muallim on the following conditions: that he write my decree of freedom, provide me with a house to stay in Mina upon my return from Arafat whose rent he has already extracted from me, and let me make my own arrangement for a car to take me from Mecca to Jiddah. This was necessary because, according to the government rules, no one could hire a car or camel or leave Mecca without the muallim's permission. While this was going on, Hasan bin Sikandar showed up and he tried his best to prevent me from getting the letter of freedom, but Allah's mercy was with me. Qadir had the letter announcing my freedom written out and signed. He handed the document to me.

The business of the muallim was sorted out, but I felt extremely saddened that, on the day of the hajj in the field of Arafat at the time of Asr, I had a verbal duel with my muallim. I turned towards Jabl-e Rehmat and sought pardon for my wrongs with the utmost humility and sincerity. And the truth is that the clear heart with which I sought forgiveness was even better than what I had experienced earlier in the day after the Zuhr namaz.

A little while before Asr, a swarm of locusts appeared in the field of Arafat but they did not fall to the ground. People say that they came from the Masjid-e Nimrah and went towards Jabl-e Rehmat. Those of easy faith among the pilgrims began to say that they weren't locusts but angels or djinns,[2] who were sent to make up the shortfall among the hajjis. Half an hour before sunset, a severe storm blew, which was

1 The pilgrimage is (in) the well-known months, and whoever is minded to perform the pilgrimage therein (let him remember) ... 'there is (to be) no lewdness nor abuse nor angry conversation on the pilgrimage'. (Quran: Al Baqara, 197)

2 The word *jinn* literally means anything which has the connotation of concealment, invisibility, seclusion and remoteness. In pre-Islamic Arabian folklore and in Islamic

followed by a heavy downpour. It rained so heavily that every thirst was slaked. It is said that the rain symbolizes Allah's acceptance of hajj. Alhamdulillah *ala kulle haal*.[1]

We left Arafat an hour after sunset. We did not offer the Maghrib namaz here, because hajjis must offer their namaz at Muzdalifa on the 9th of Zul Hijja.[2]

It takes almost two hours to cover the distance between Arafat and Muzdalifa. We dismounted in a field close to the Mashar-ul Haram. I performed wuzoo and offered the Maghrib and Isha namaz. Then, we turned to food because we hadn't eaten properly for two whole days. Muniruddin and I set out in search of roti but after some time we realized that we might lose our bearings if we go any further. And if we lose our way, we will end up wandering in this wilderness all night. There was no qahwakhana in sight where we could have some tea. Perforce, we returned to our lodging. A few biscuits were left in our tiffin. We ate those, drank some water, and lay down in the shaqdaf. I was tired after a long day and so I went to sleep.

On Sunday, 19 May, after the Fajr namaz, I collected pebbles for the Rami Jimaar and left Muzdalifa after sunrise. Thousands of camels came in the direction of Mina. Shaqdafs would bang against each other. A few hajjis sustained injuries. I stayed unharmed, thank Allah!

Abdul Qadir had rented a house near Jamratus Sughra (the Small Satan). As a consequence of yesterday's quarrel, he insisted that I go to a room the moment we set foot there. I left my belongings on the shaqdaf to enter the house with Muniruddin. The house was small with almost a hundred guests staying there. Maulvi Khalilun Nabi, along with Shah Sahib Rampuri and his entourage, were staying in one room. Shah Sahib very kindly offered me a space near his bedding. Muniruddin Sahib brought whatever was necessary from the shaqdaf, and we set out our bedding in that cramped space.

Having got that behind us, we left the house and drank tea in a qahwakhana and went to throw pebbles at the Jamratul Uqba (the Big

---

culture, a jinni (also 'djinni' or 'djini') was generally thought to be a race of supernatural creatures.

1 Sign or indication that the hajj has been accepted by Allah.

2 Muzdalifa is an open, level area near Mecca in Saudi Arabia. It lies just southeast of Mina on the route between Mina and Arafat. Hajj pilgrims visit Muzdalifa and collect pebbles to be thrown in the stoning of the Jamarat ritual in Mina.

Satan). We had been hungry for two days but still found nothing suitable to eat. We returned to the house, rested for some time, and then went out to buy an animal for *qurbani*. The place was almost a mile away from the house. But till we had finished the qurbani, we could not take off our ihram. And so we set out towards the qurbani spot in that heat. Due to Allah's mercy, we did not face any trouble purchasing the animals. I bought three goats for Rs 6 each; Muniruddin Sahib bought two. I bought three goats because one was for the ordinary Baqr Id, the second for the *dam-e-tasha Kkur-e-tamattu* (see earlier in entry for Thursday, 18 April), and the third for *dum ehteyati* (just like that!).

We bought animals from a place close to our place. The butcher charged a fee of 2 anna per animal and sacrificed them in our presence. A few Tikroni Negroes and Arabs appeared and collected the animals along with their skins. Earlier, the sacrificial animals were put in a cave. But this year, the government has arranged that the meat and skin of the dumba and the skin of the goat be sold according to its specifications. Hopefully, this scheme will fetch a lot of money to the government, and the lakhs of skins that go waste would be put to some use.

There was no policeman nearby when we performed our qurbani, and the Arabs took away the animals we had sacrificed intact. They would eat the meat and sell the skins. They said all this was *sadaqa* (alms-giving). We agreed.

Having finished this necessary obligation, we were reminded of our hunger and thirst. On the way back, we helped ourselves to some watermelons in the market. This brought us immense satisfaction. Later, we dined in a hotel. But one look at the gravy made us queasy. We ordered roti and dal. The dal was so atrocious that we could not swallow more than a few mouthfuls. At best, it gave us the excuse to gulp some water. In the afternoon, we ran into a barber from India. Having shaved our heads, we were finally freed of the ihram. We put on our own clothes and thanked Allah for having let us perform the obligatory hajj rites. Now only the tawafuz-ziyarat (thankgiving for the visit) remained to be undertaken. Once that is done, we can claim to have completed the hajj.

It was intolerably hot in the room, but there was no way out. Somehow or the other we spent the afternoon. After Asr, we planned to leave for Mecca but could not find any transport. Abdul Qadir promised to arrange transport by tomorrow, because Maulvi Abdul Majid Sahib had planned to leave for the tawaf along with his entourage. I could go along with him. Sikandar said that 2 riyals had been fixed for the to and fro journey, and that we could leave tomorrow morning after the Fajr namaz. I thanked him.

By the evening it was impossible to stay alive in that room. Muniruddin Sahib and I went towards the mountain and then to a qahwakhana near our lodging. Here, we hired a chair for half a riyal per head, spread our beddings on the chair, and spent the night on it. The air was cool. The ease of the night erased the day's discomfort.

On Monday, 20 May, after namaz and wazifa, I went towards Mecca for the tawaful ziyarat. We drove on a donkey cart along with Muniruddin, Maulvi Abdul Majid, and his relative. Abdul Majid's friends rode on another one; Abdul Qadir was mounted on a donkey. The driver joked with his friends on the way. He left the cart and moved away. The donkey turned restless and the cart overturned. My fellow travellers fell, but thank Allah they escaped injury. My foot got entangled in the iron wheel and, for almost five minutes, it stayed stuck. I had lost hope of retrieving it intact. When my companions got to their feet and set the cart upright, I extracted my foot with a great deal of difficulty. Due to Allah's mercy, my bone was not fractured. Moreover, the wound was superficial. My head swam as we emerged from under the wheel of the cart and I stood on my feet. I had become very weak after starving for the past several days. When Maulvi Abdul Majid complained about the driver to Abdul Majid Sikandar, the esteemed muallim said that such things happen; clearly, my pain and discomfort mattered little to him.

Anyhow, I reached Mecca on the same cart. My foot hurt but I immediately performed the duty of tawaful-ziyarat at the end of the hajj. Any further delay, I feared, would cause my foot to swell and prevent me from performing the tawaf. Thank Allah that I have fulfilled each one of the hajj rites.

After the tawaf, I poured a bowl of the water of zumzum over my feet. As a result of its barakat, my pain subsided greatly. Then, I drank tea in a qahwakhana near the masjid and ate matbakh. There seemed to be no option of staying any longer in Mecca because my host, Mohammad Hanif Zardoz, was in Mina and his house was locked. Perforce, I returned to Mina. The sun was fierce and the sand hot. That made it all the more difficult to prod the donkeys to move faster. We reached Mina only after stopping at several places en route. With much difficulty, I reached my lodging and lay down on the bed.

We were told that we would have to pay 2 riyals per head for the donkey cart, but we decided to pay 4 riyals per head. As a result, we had to pay twice the amount that we had bargained for.

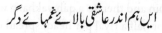

Ein ham andar aashqi baalaa-e-gham haae digar.

For all the other sorrows in love, there is this too.

On reaching Mina, Muniruddin Sahib went to Dr Abdur Rehman's house and brought a medicine for my wounded foot. Dr Sahib is a homoeopath and his medicines are very efficacious. The pain lessened the moment I tied the bandage, though walking about was still difficult. Munshi Mohammad Yusuf Sahib came to enquire after my health in the late afternoon. He is staying in Akbar Umar's tent. After some time, Dr Abdur Rehman Sahib too came to see me. We spent the time in my room till the evening. At night, I again hired a chair from the qahwakhana, and at the cost of half a riyal managed to make my life bearable.

Thank Allah, I could walk on my own feet and take part in the stoning ritual. While wearing a shoe was impossible, walking was not too painful.

On Tuesday, 21 May 1929, after zawal, I was blessed by being able to perform the stoning ritual for the third time. By now, I have successfully completed all the rituals associated with the hajj. After Asr, I returned to Mecca. Although I feared that I might find it difficult to mount and dismount from the shaqdaf, by Allah's grace I was able to do so without too much strain.

It is extremely dangerous for thousands of camels to move out of the narrow alleys of Mina. At such times, the shaqdaf often collide, and the hajjis sustain injuries. But thank Allah I reached Mecca safely. I dismounted at the gate of the Masjidul Haram and walked till my lodging. Hanif Sahib offered me food. After eating a substantial meal after three days, I felt immensely better. Yusuf Sahib had reached before Asr. Again, I had the chair sent for from the qahwakhana, and went off to sleep.

8

End of a Journey

The last lines of this diary were recorded in the afternoon of Wednesday, 5 June 1929. The sea was stormy that day. Waves were mounting attacks upon the ship from all sides and at every instant we feared that it would collapse at the next onslaught. Several factors combined to add to my worries. On a deck close to my room, a young man from the Frontier had died of pneumonia and his corpse lay directly in front of me. The previous night I had seen a disturbing dream, which, briefly, translated meant that my dearest son, Nawab, had died.

The storm in the sea was such that it was impossible to walk two steps. The rumbling clouds and the flash of lightning and thunder struck terror. The ship would constantly blow its siren for danger and I was steadily losing hope of ever reaching the shore.

Apart from all this, another worry burdened my heart: my passport had been left behind in Jiddah. I shuddered to think of the difficulties I would face upon landing in Bombay. I offered the Zuhr namaz seated and prayed for the storm to subside. Only then did I finally find some solace. I set off in search of Maulana Abdul Majid and told him about my missing passport. The Maulana said that the unique thing about this blessed journey is that at every step, the difficulties encountered by the pilgrim tend to disappear on their own. He told me to stop worrying because there would be no dearth of his acquaintances in Bombay who would be able to identify him. He also said that as a government employee, I should have no fear of being without a passport. The Maulana's words brought comfort and I returned to my room. I sent a wireless through the ship's telegram to Syed Samiuddin Sahib's son, who is employed in the Railways, and hoped that he might come to the dock to help in the identification process. Also, I had made him write my ticket number at the time of my departure from Bombay. I had also left behind some of my excess luggage.

Although we spotted the electric lights of Bombay after sunset, a dark cloud of worry hung over my head. Even the sight of those lights failed to dispel the gloom in my heart. At about 10.00 in the night, the ship suddenly dropped anchor. We learnt that we would stay here all night and enter the harbour during the day. The rain had let up by now and the turbulence had died down. I spent the last night on the ship fairly comfortably. I woke up before dawn and began to look longingly towards the shore.

A steady stream of doctors and officials began visiting the ship after sunrise. After a while, it began to move gradually towards the harbour. I came out of my room, stood at the deck, and watched the goings on at the shore with interest. As the ship approached its berth, my eyes began searching for Syed Samiuddin Sahib's son but in vain. But I saw somebody who I had not thought of seeing here. For some time, I doubted but soon convinced myself that my son-in-law—Hakim Syed Zaheer Ali— stood at the platform. I cannot describe my happiness. We exchanged greetings through gestures, and again through gestures, we performed the rituals of enquiring about each other's well-being. He informed me loudly that my son Hafiz Nasr Ahmad had also come from Aurangabad, but had only just gone out of the platform. This news delighted me even more.

Meanwhile, the ship came to a standstill at the deck. Syed (*sic*) Shaukat Ali Sahib, the father of the Khilafat movement, and other Hajj Committee members were present to welcome us. One after the other, they climbed on board and began to embrace Abdul Majid Sahib. I overheard the Maulana ask an Englishman, who was probably an employee of the Mogul Company, whether we would be required to submit our passport. He said that it would not be necessary. This brought immense relief to me: instantly, a major worry was over.

My fellow traveller, Muniruddin Hyderabadi, Allah alone knows how, managed to send for fresh paan and I was able to partake of this blessing of Hindustan even before stepping off the ship. After about an hour, I got off the ship's stairs and set foot on the dock. My two sons, Hafiz Nasr Ahmad and Ahmad Mohsin, had come from Aurangabad. They leapt to fall at my feet. I picked them up and cradled their heads against my chest and prayed for their well-being. After this, I embraced Syed Zaheer Ali and blessed him too. They had found out the date of arrival of the *Rehmani* from the company's office and had arrived a day before to welcome me in Bombay. May Allah grant them sufficient recompense for their *shauq* and *zauq*![1]

My foot has not healed fully. It is still bandaged and so I could not walk around too much. Entrusting the task of looking after the luggage to Muniruddin Sahib, I went off towards the custom house with my sons. My heart was still fearful about my other son, Nawab, and so I asked no questions about the others back home. I kept describing my wounded foot.

It took us almost an hour at the custom house. I had a canister of dates from Medina. I had to pay duty for that. The other things were cursorily examined and allowed to pass. I did not experience the same difficulty that I encountered in Jiddah.

When this hurdle too was behind me and I had stepped out of the dockyard's boundary and set foot on the road, I finally began to feel that the long journey was behind me and I had reached home now. Even though happiness danced inside me and the desire to see my near and dear ones rose uncontrollably, the fear for Nawab's well-being lurked inside me. My happiness was, indeed, not complete.

Syed Zaheer Ali took me to the guest house of the Bohras and settled me in his friend's room. Once there, I finally asked about the state of affairs at Kakori. The boys said that all was well. I still didn't have the courage to ask about everyone's welfare by name and the brief answer given by the boys brought scant comfort. Zaheer Ali insisted that I go with him to Aurangabad first before proceeding to Kakori. I was in a dilemma. If I were to refuse, I would hurt Zaheer and if I were to tarry for leaving for Kakori then my heart would grow increasingly restless. My suspicions about Nawab were strengthened by their insistence that I visit Aurangabad first. I was scared that if I asked about Nawab outright, they may not give me the correct answer. At the same time, if they gave me the bad news right here, the shock would be so great that I may not be able to endure the journey to Kakori.

I was wrestling with this dilemma when breakfast was served. I helped myself to a few morsels and then went to the bazaar with the boys. I spent some time chatting with Munshi Muniruddin and Mohammad Akram Sahib Bengali, who were staying at a modest hotel. The steady rain flooded the streets of Bombay. In that state, I went to the Victoria

---

1 Desire and enthusiasm.

Terminus and sent telegrams to my family back home informing them that I would 'Reach Lucknow Day after Morning'. I decided to put up with Zaheer's disappointment. I bought a second class ticket in the night express train and reserved a seat for Lucknow. Having done so, I returned to the Bohra guest house. Syed Samiuddin Sahib's son and Saeed Qureshi Sahib had traced me to this location. On Thursday, the 14 February, I had bid adieu to these gentlemen and now I was meeting these very kind people once again on a Thursday, on 6 June. They stayed to talk for some time before returning to their offices. They promised to come again to see me off at the station.

For the remainder of the day and from Maghrib till Isha, I rested in the guest house. After Isha, I boarded the train without any difficulty though the rain kept coming down. Zaheer and my two sons too left with me. These people shall change a train at Manmarh to go to Aurangabad and I shall proceed straight to Lucknow. As promised, Saeed Qureshi Sahib and others who had been my hosts here in Bombay were at the station. They stayed with me till the train pulled away.

We spent Friday night on the train admiring the beautiful landscape of central India. It kept drizzling and so the heat did not trouble us; this part of the journey was eminently enjoyable. The train reached Kanpur station early on Saturday morning. I sent for tea from a hotel. I had just begun to sip it when I spotted my relative, Maulvi Hamid Hasan Alawi, on the platform. I left the tea to embrace him. I prayed for his success and well-being. I learnt that he had come all this way to welcome me. I made him sit in the compartment with me. He had a ticket with him. We spoke animatedly all the way but the state of my heart was such that I did not even take Nawab's name in his presence.

After an hour or two, the train reached Lucknow. My brothers, sons, relatives, and friends were waiting for me at the platform. I also saw my Nawab standing among them. I lost all control, when I set eyes on him. Tears began to flow uncontrollably. I left the train in a violent hurry. I reached Nawab after meeting all the assembled relatives. I hugged him and began to cry like a baby. May Allah forgive this worldly love! The barakat of this sacred journey was annihilated in this love.

The train for Kakori waited on the platform. Even though it had only a few minutes to leave, my friends advised me to leave on this very train. Maulvi Hamid Hasan purchased my ticket, while some of my relatives got on the train without one. Later, they gladly paid the fine to the ticket collector.

I got off today on the 8th of June at the Kakori station after four and a quarter months. My homeland's breeze gladdened my heart. Such happiness surged deep within my heart that the journey's troubles and toils disappeared, as though by magic. Friends and relatives had gathered to see me at the station. I walked with them till my house. I entered only after offering two rakat nafil as thanksgiving in the neighbourhood mosque. I touched my mother's feet and placed my hand on my daughters' heads. Friends and relatives were happy, but I was happier than all of them. But, in the words of Abdul Majid Daryabadi, the colour of a mother's happiness is different from all others. Indeed, it is beyond every word and every form of worship.

Epilogue

This daily record of the journey to Hijaz has been shown to some of my friends and relatives. Everyone thought it deserved to be published, but I demurred because in this recollection most of my personal experiences have been recorded which can be of little interest to the public at large. Apart from these, I had recorded my views on the government of Hijaz and the muallims of Mecca, and I was not willing to have these publicized.

From the literary point of view, this diary has virtually no standing because I have expressed my heartfelt feelings and observations in a broken work-a-day sort of way without any artifice or sophistication. As compared to my other publications, these pages are jumbled up and far from coherently written. But Maulana Zafarul Mulk Sahib Alawi,[1] the owner of Al-Nazir Press, took the material away to study and kept it with him for two years. I became so preoccupied after returning to my job and to worldly affairs that I lost the *barakat* of the hajj.

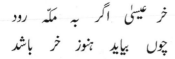

Khar-e Issa agar be Mecca rawad
ehun beaayed hunooz khar bashad

If Christ's donkey goes to Mecca
Remains a donkey even when he returns.

---

1 A journalist-politician (d. 1947) from the United Provinces who took part in the Khilafat movement, supported non-cooperation, founded the Awadh Khilafat Committee and edited several journals including *Haqiqat* and *an-Nazr*.

I had forgotten all about this travelogue. Everyday I would think of devising new ways to punish the wrongdoers. How could I remember the journey to Hijaz undertaken by this old sinner! Last Thursday, I had taken leave and gone home where I met Zafarul Mulk Sahib, who told me that a copy of my travelogue had been written. Soon, it would be published. I should write the epilogue soon and send it to him.

Compelled to do so by his insistence, I have finished writing these pages this morning. I am now sending them off to him. My humble request to the Almighty Allah is that—as a *sadaqa* (literally, 'charity') for the beloved Prophet—may this sinner have the good fortune to present himself in the Most Blessed of Houses once more and may I stand bareheaded and barefoot at Asr time in the holy ground of Arafat and pray for the atonement of my many sins.

رہ جائیں نہ میرے دل کے ارماں

مشکل سے نہ مشکلیں ہوں آساں

Reh jaain na mere dil ke armaan
Mushkil se na mushkilein hon aasan

May none of my heart's desire remain unquenched
May impediments fail to ease impediments!

Thursday, 10 September 1931

Amir Ahmad Alawi
Deputy Collector
Kothi Nehar
Bhognipur
Zilla Kanpur

The voyage to Jiddah as drawn by Rasheed Ahmad, 1955

Select List of Urdu
Publications on the Hajj

BOOKS

Tayyab Usmani Nadwi (1999), *Safarnama Haramain Sharifain*, Delhi
Yusuf Mirza (1996), *Deeda-i Dil Wa Kare Koi*, Karachi
Waheeduddin Khan (1992), *Safarnama: Ghairmulki Asfaar*, Delhi
Asad Geelani (1986), *Mushahidat-i Haramain*, Delhi
Mohammad Imdad Sabri (1986), *Allah ke Ghar me Baar Baar Hazri: 1953 se lekar 1983 tak ke Hajj ke Safarname*, Vol. 1, Delhi
Mohiuddin Salaqi (1983), *Mera Safarnama-i Hijaz*, Srinagar
Kalim Ahmad Ejaz (1981), *Yahan se Kaaba, Kaaba se Medina tak*, Delhi
Saba Mustafa (1979), *Paharon ke Daman me*, Madras
Sulaiman Salik (1978), *Qatra Samandar me: Ek Safarnama*, Lucknow
Mumtaz Mufti (1975), *Labbaik*, Lahore
Abu Yusuf (1973), *Jalwa-i Haram*, Hyderabad
S. Mahbub Rizvi (1973), *Makatib-i Hijaz*, Delhi
Shorish Kashmiri (1971), *Shabja-i ki Manbudum*, Lahore
Mohammad Reza Ansari (1966), *Hajj ka Safar*, Lucknow
Mohammad Hifzur Rahman (1938), *Rah-i Wafa: Safarnama Bilad-i Islamia*, Aligarh
Manzoor Ali bin Taib (1922), *Haqiqat-i Hajj*, Simla

MAGAZINES/JOURNALS

Istiqamat, Kanpur, Hajj Number, October 1978
Maarif, Azamgarh, November-December 1922, edited by Syed Sulaiman Nadawi (1884–1953)
Misaaq, Lahore, June-December 1959

Glossary

Persons

Alawi: Signifies ancestry from Hazrat Ali ibn Abi Talib, the fourth Khalifa of Islam. The Alawi family can be found in the Middle East and South Asia. Alawis are scattered in the northern Indian state of Uttar Pradesh with their main concentration in Kakori near Lucknow. Alawi of Kakori are referred to as Moulvizadigan (Moulvis) or Makhdoomzadigan (Makhdooms), indicating whether they are descendants of Mullah Abu Bakr Jami Alawi, who settled in Kakori in 1461, or of Qari Amir Saifuddin Alawi, who settled in Kakori in 1552.

Hijazi: A Hijazi is a person who belongs to Hijaz.

Hanbali Imam (780–855): Ahmed ibn Hanbal was a prominent scholar and theologian of Persian background. His full name was Ahmad bin Mohammad bin Hanbal Abu ʿAbd Allah al-Shaybani and he was born at Merv, in Khurasan. He is considered as the founder of the Hanbali School of Fiqh (Islamic jurisprudence).

Husain Ahmad Madni Sahab (1879–1957): He served for decades as the rector of the Darul-ulum Deoband madrasa in northern India and as head of the Deobandi-dominated Jamiyat al-ulama-i Hind. In 1916, after the Ottomans were driven out from the Hijaz, Madni, who, at that time, was residing in Medina as a teacher, was arrested by the British together with Sheikhul-Hind Maulana Mahmud Hasan on the accusation of plotting to overthrow the Raj with the aid of the Ottomans. Upon their return to India, both Sheikhul-Hind and Maulana Madni began to rally Muslim support for the non-violent Non-cooperation movement spearheaded by Gandhi against the British.

Jafar as-Sadiq (699–765): The sixth Imam in the Twelver and Isma'ili traditions of Shia Islam, he was widely respected by the Shias and Sunnis alike for his learning and piety. Jafar as-Sadiq was an influential teacher, theologian, and jurist. Among his students were Abu Hanifa and Malik ibn Anas.

---

* The usage of Arabic and Persian words is quite common in Urdu; hence the difficulty of drawing sharp boundaries. Javed Khan, Associate Professor at the Centre for West Asian Studies, Jamia Millia Islamia, has helped me a great deal in preparing these notes. I hope the inconsistency in spellings and diacritical marks would go unnoticed. Our aim in providing these notes is to simply make the text accessible.

Malik ibn Anas ibn Malik ibn 'Amr al-Asbahi (c. 715–796) (AH 93–AH 179): A scholar of fiqh, he is also known as 'Imam Malik'. Living in Medina gave him access to some of the most learned minds of early Islam. He memorized the Quran in his youth, learning its recitation from Imam Abu Suhail an-Nafi' ibn 'Abd ar-Rahman, from whom he also received his *sanad* or certification and permission to teach others. He studied under Imam Jafar as-Sadiq.

Abdul Majid Daryabadi (1892–1977): He was a famous Indian Muslim writer and exegete of the Quran. He edited the Urdu weekly *Sach* and then *Sidq* (1925–76). Daryabadi was actively associated with the Khilafat movement; Royal Asiatic Society, London; Aligarh Muslim University, Nadwatul Ulama, Lucknow; Shibli Academy, Azamgarh, and several other leading Islamic and literary organizations. In addition to contributing an extensive commentary on the Quran in English, Daryabadi wrote also an independent *Tafsir* in Urdu published as *Tafsir Majidi*.

Maulvi Abdul Bari Nadvi (1878–1926): He is one of the renowned Firangi Mahal scholars. The author of some hundred books, he was a prominent participant in the Khilafat movement as well as in religious organizations such as Jamiat al-ulama-i-Hind.

Maulana Haji Muniruddin: He was a Quranic scholar and a former *khatib* of Mecca Masjid in Hyderabad.

Shaukat Ali: An Indian Muslim and leader of the Khilafat movement, he was the brother of Maulana Mohammad Ali. Shaukat Ali was born in 1873 in Rampur in Uttar Pradesh. He was educated at the Aligarh Muslim University, and served in the civil service of United Provinces of Oudh and Agra from 1896 to 1913.

Places and Institutions

Arabian Sea: The Arabian Sea is a region of the Indian Ocean bounded on the east by India, on the north by Pakistan and Iran, on the west by the Arabian Peninsula, on the south, approximately, by a line between Cape Guardafui, the northeast point of Somalia, Socotra, and Kanyakumari (Cape Comorin) in India.

Awadh: Also known as Oudh, Oundh, or Oude, Awadh is a region in Uttar Pradesh, which was before Independence known as the United Provinces of Oudh and Agra before Independence. The traditional capital of Awadh was Lucknow. It signed a treaty with the British East India Company in 1765, and in the later part of the century, Awadh ceded major parts of its territory to the company. In 1819, it declared independence from the Mughal empire.

Baab-e Jibreel: This is the name of one of the gates at the Haram Sharif at Mecca. Through this gate, Jibreel, the angel, used to visit the Prophet.

Baab-e Ibrahim: This is the name of the one of the gates of Haram Sharif at Mecca.

Bab al-Mandeb: It is the strait separating the continents of Asia (Yemen on the Arabian Peninsula) and Africa, and connecting the Red Sea to the Indian Ocean (Gulf of Aden).

Baab-e Salaam: It is one of the gates used to enter al-Masjid al-Haram (The Sacred Mosque). This gate is located on the stretch between Mount Safa and Marwah.

Baitul Haram: Also known as al-Masjid al-Haram (The Sacred Mosque), Baitul Haram is one of the largest mosques located in Mecca. It surrounds the Kaaba, the place which Muslims turn towards while offering their daily prayers. The mosque is also commonly known as the Haram or Haram Sharif.

Darul-ulum Deoband: The Darul-ulum, located at Deoband, is a madrasa seminary, which was founded in 1866 by several prominent ulama, headed by Maulana Mohammad Qasim Nanotwi. Deoband's curriculum is based on the seventeenth-century Indo-Islamic syllabus known as Dars-e-Nizamiyya.

Firangi Mahal: A well-known house of scholars in Lucknow in the state of Uttar Pradesh. The Firangi Mahal is related to the Ansari family of Sehali or Sihali, which later achieved great renown as the Firangi Mahal family or the Ulama-e-Firangi Mahal. The Dars-i Nizamiyya syllabus was introduced here, which still forms the basis for much of the modern day curriculum in the madrasas (schools) of the Indian sub-continent. Apart from being scholars, the Firangi Mahalis were also Sufis, or mystics.

Ghar-e-Thaur: In this cave, the Prophet stayed for three days at the time of his migration (*hijrat*) from Mecca.

Gulf of Kutch: An inlet of the Arabian Sea along the west coast of India, in the state of Gujarat. It divides the Kutch and Kathiawar peninsula regions of Gujarat.

Hatiim: It is a piece of land surrounded by a wall of a man's height adjacent to Baitullah on the north side. It is called Hatim as well as Ahjar or Hazira. While observing tawaf, it is wajib (obligatory) to include this piece of land. It is a part of Kaaba.

Hijaz: Hijaz is a region in the west of present-day Saudi Arabia. It extends from Haql on the Gulf of Aqaba to Jizan. As a region, Hijaz has significance in the Arab and Islamic historical and political landscape. Its main city is Jeddah, but it is better known for the cities of Mecca and Medina.

Hill: The land beyond the four sides of Haram up to miqat (that is, outside the Haram boundaries but inside the mawaqit) is called Hill, for the things prohibited (haram) in Haram are permissible (halal) here.

Hudaybiyah: It is the name of a place before the precincts of Haram on the way from Jiddah to Mecca. Nowadays, it is known by the name of Sumaisiya. A mosque is situated on this very spot. Here, the Prophet entered into a treaty with the Quraysh.

Jabal-e Quzah: It is a hill in Muzdalifa.

Jabal-e Thabir: It is a hill in Mina.

Jabal-e Uhud: It is a hill outside Medina located at a distance of nearly three miles from where the battle of Uhud was fought.

Jannat-ul Moalla: It is a cemetery in Mecca. Also known as al-Hajun, it is the second holiest graveyard after Jannat-ul Baqi. This is the graveyard where Prophet Mohammad's wife Khadijah, Abdullah Ibn Umar, Abdullah Ibn Zubair, Asma and other great Sahabas and Tabe'een are buried. The grave of Hazrat Haji Imdadullah Muhajir Makki is also located here.

Juhfa: It is a place near Rabigh situated at a distance of three manzils (encampment distances) from Mecca. This is the miqat for those coming from Syria.

Kaaba: The Kaaba, also known as Baitullah, is a sacred house in the centre of the Masjid-e-Haram in Mecca. It is the Qibla of Muslims. It is actually a square stone building in al-Haram mosque in Mecca, which all Muslims in the world turn their faces towards while offering their prayers.

Kakori: Kakori is a town situated 14 kilometres north of Lucknow district in the Indian state of Uttar Pradesh. It has been the centre of the once-flourishing Urdu poetry, literature, and the Qadiriya Qalandari Sufi Order. Kakori is also famous for producing hundreds of civil servants in British India, who served all over the country. It was the leading town in Oudh along with Rudauli and Mahmoodabad, which supplemented the culture of Lucknow.

Mecca: This is the holiest city in the world for Muslims, and is located in western Saudi Arabia.

Marwa: This is the hill on which a pilgrim ends his/her Saii.

Mashar-ul Haram: It is a mosque in Muzdalifa but a hill of Muzdalifa, called Jabal-e-Quzah, is also known as Mashar-ul Haram.

Masjid-e Ali: Masjid Ali is a mosque where Imam Ali led Salatul Jamaat after the Prophet's demise (when he was denied his right to the Khilafa). The mosque is behind Masjid Nabawi, near Masjid Ghamama.

Masjid-e-Bani-Zafar: It is also called Masjid-e-Baghla. It is situated towards the east of Jannat-ul Baqi. The tribe of Bani Zafar used to live here. Once the Prophet honoured this place with his presence and at his desire, one of his companions recited Sura-e-Nisa to him. Near the mosque there is a hoof-mark of the mule of the Prophet and that is why it is also called Masjid-ul-Baghla.

Masjidul Haram: This is the mosque around Kaaba.

Masjid-ul-Ijaba: This mosque is in the northern side of Jannat-ul Baqi. The Holy Prophet had prayed here.

Masjid-ul-Raya: This mosque is on the way to Jannat-ul-Ma'la. On the day of the conquest of Mecca, the Prophet had erected his flag here.

Masjid-e Jumu'ah: Masjid-e-Jumu'ah is the second mosque of Islam where the Prophet Mohammad performed the first Jumu'ah prayer. This place is not to far from Masjid Quba, the first mosque.

Masjid-e Qiblatain: It is a mosque on the hillock near the valley of Aqiq in the northwest of Medina. It has two arches, one towards Bait-ul-Muqaddas, and the other towards the Kaaba. This is the mosque where Prophet Mohammad was commanded to change his qibla from Masjid al-Aqsa (Jerusalem) to the Holy Kaaba at Mecca, Saudi Arabia, an event from which it derives its name.

Mataf: Place around Baitullah in Masjid-e Haram where the tawaf is performed.

Medina Munawwara: Medina, originally known as Yathrib, a city in the Hijaz region of western Saudi Arabia is the burial place of Prophet Mohammad. It is the city to which Prophet Mohammad migrated and which lies about 450 kilometres northeast of Mecca. The city's name was later changed to Al Madinah al Munawwara (meaning 'the enlightened city' or 'the radiant city').

Mina: Mina is a desert location situated between two hills some 5 kilometres to the east of the city of Mecca in Saudi Arabia, and is included in Haram. It is best known for the role it plays during the annual hajj pilgrimage, when its tent cities provide temporary accommodation to hundreds of thousands of visiting pilgrims who stay here for three days. Rami and Sacrifice are also accomplished here. In the valley of Mina lies the Jamarat Bridge, the location of the Stoning of the

Devil ritual, performed between sunrise and sunset on the last day of the Hajj.

Multazam: The wall between Hajar-e-Aswad and the gate of Baitullah is called Multazam. It is *masnon* (prescribed as sunnah of the Prophet) to invoke the blessings of Allah while embracing this wall.

Nadwatul Ulama: This is an Islamic institution in Lucknow, which draws a large number of Muslim students from all over the country. It was founded at Kanpur in 1894 during the first annual convention of the Nadwatul Ulema ('Organization of Scholars') by Shibli Nomani, Mohammad Ali Mongiri, Ashraf Ali Thanwi and Mahmud-ul-Hasan, with the aim of countering the challenge of Western education.

Riyadh: The city and capital of Saudi Arabia, in the Nejd region of the central Arabian Peninsula, Riyadh was chosen as the capital of the Saud dynasty in 1824, and it remained the centre of Saud rule until 1881, when the Rashid family of Ha'il extended its influence over Nejd. In 1902, however, Ibn Saud regained control for his family and used the city as the centre for his conquest of Arabia, which he completed by 1930.

Rauza-e Rasool: Tomb of the Prophet, or the Prophet's Mosque at Mecca.

Safa: This is the hill on which a pilgrim begins his/her Sa'i (walking). It lies about 200 metres southeast of the Kaaba at Mecca.

Taif: In the Mecca Province, it is a resort of pilgrimage.

Tanim: It is a place where, at the time of their stay at Mecca, people wear Ihram for umrah. It is located at a distance of three miles from Mecca and is the nearest place

from the precincts of Haram. There is a mosque named Masjid-e Aisha here.

Terms

Arabic

Afaqi: Afaqi is the person who lives outside the Miqat boundaries.

Ahl-e Haram: The person who lives in the land of Haram; whether in Mecca or outside Mecca within the precincts of Haram is called Ahl-e Haram.

Alaihissalatu Wassalam: 'On Him (Mohammad) are the blessings and the peace of Allah.'

Alim (pl. Ulama): Muslim scholars engaged in the several fields of Islamic studies, and Sharia law. In a broader sense, the term 'ulama' is used to describe the body of Muslim clergy who have completed several years of training and study of Islamic sciences, such as a *mufti*, *qazi, faqih* or *muhaddis*.

Allah: Allah is the standard Arabic word for 'God'. In Islam, Allah is the only deity, transcendent creator of the universe and the judge of humankind.

Ar-Ramal: Ar-Ramal is the ritual where male pilgrims are required to walk briskly with their chests thrust forward and with their shoulders rolling slightly during the first three circuits of Tawaf ul-Qudum (Arrival Tawaf). Ladies are not required to practice *Ramal*.

Ash-hur-e-Hajj: These are the months of hajj, that is, the complete months of Shawwal, Zi-Qada and half of the month of Zul Hijja.

Assalamu-alaika Ya Rasool Allah: 'Peace be upon you, Oh Prophet of Allah'. It is a salutation to Prophet Mohammad that Muslims make by saying specific phrases to compliment the Prophet.

Ayat: This means sign or miracle. The word usually refers to each one of the 6236 verses found in the Quran. Muslims regard each *ayah* of the Quran as a sign from God. The plural of ayah is called ayat, which means miracles.

Ayyam-e-Tashriq: These are the days from the 9th to 13th of Zul Hijja wherein *Takbir-e-Tashriq* is regularly proclaimed.

Zil Qadah (also, Dhu'l-Qa'da): This is the name of the eleventh month in an Islamic calendar. Since the Islamic lunar calendar year is 11 to 12 days shorter than the solar year, Dhu al-Qi'dah migrates throughout the seasons.

Fateha: To do Eessale sawaab to the souls of the deceased. Hazrat Anas asked the Prophet, 'If we send sawaab to the deceased, give sadaqa and khayraat and ask dua from them, does this reach them?' The Prophet said, 'Verily it reaches them. Read salaah for them as you read for yourself and fast for them as you fast for yourself. In other words, do Eessale sawaab of salaah and saum for them.' The meaning of this Hadith Sharif is that we should send the sawaab of our actions to the deceased, since in reality one cannot perform salaah and keep fast for another person or on his behalf, but we can send the sawaab of our actions to them.

Fiqh: This implies Islamic jurisprudence and law deduced and worked out by the various schools of thought from the Quran and the Sunnah.

Hajj: This literally means 'pilgrimage'. In Islam, it refers to the annual pilgrimage to Mecca. Hajj is the fifth pillar of Islam to be performed at least once in a lifetime. There are rules and regulations and specific dress codes to be followed during this pilgrimage. It has to take place during the last month of the lunar calendar called the month of Zul Hijja.

Hajr-e-Aswad: This refers to a black stone or a stone from Paradise. It is fixed in the wall at about a man's height in the southeastern corner of Baitullah. It has a silver frame around it.

Hammams: This is a Middle Eastern style steam bath followed by a dip in cool water and massage. It also refers to an establishment where these facilities are available.

Ihram: This means declaring a thing as haram (forbidden). When a hajj pilgrim determines his intention for hajj, umrah, or both collectively, and proclaims talbia, certain halal (permissible) things stand for him as haram; hence it is called ihram. This word is used figuratively for those sheets of cloth as well which are used by hajj pilgrims in the state of ihram.

Isha namaz: The Isha prayer is the fifth of the five daily prayers prescribed to be performed once the night settles until dawn.

Jahila: An Islamic concept of 'ignorance of divine guidance' or 'the state of ignorance of the guidance from God' referring to the condition in which Arabs found themselves in pre-Islamic Arabian society prior to the revelation of the Quran. By extension, it means the state of anyone not following Islam and the Quran.

Jamrah: This is the pillar at which the pilgrim throws pebbles. There are three Jamrah pillars at which pilgrims throw pebbles, viz. Jamrah Al-Ula, Jamara Al-Wusta and Jamrah Al-Aqabah.

Kalaam Majeed: Kalaam-e-majeed refers to the Holy Quran.

Karaat (qira'at): This means the recitation of the Quran.

Khalifa: The word Khalifa refers to the successor or representative of Prophet Mohammad or to one of his successors.

Khutba: This is a speech or sermon. It also refers to the sermon delivered inside a mosque, from a pulpit during the Friday congregational prayer.

Kufr: This means to show ungratefulness to Allah and not to believe in Him and His religion.

Labbaika: This is a call meaning 'Here I Come'. It is the Muslim's expression of answering the invitation of God to perform the hajj pilgrimage.

Labbaik Allahumma labbaik/ Labbaik la sharika laka labbaik/Innal hamda/ Wan-ni'mata/Laka walmulk/Laa sharika lak: O my Lord, here I am at Your service, here I am./There is no partner with You,/here I am./Truly the praise/ and the provisions are Yours,/and so is the dominion and sovereignty./There is no partner with You.

Marsiya: Marsiya is basically an elegiac poem that is recited to commemorate the martyrdom of Hazrat Imam Husain and his clan at Karbala in the then Iraq. Marsiya generally consists of six-line units, with a rhyming quatrain, and a couplet on a different rhyme. Actually Marsiya is an elegy on the death of a family member or close friend but in the course of history is has become synonymous with the martyrdom of Imam Husain. By 1830, the genre had emerged in Lucknow, at the hands of Mir Babur Ali Anis and Mirza Salamat Ali Dabir, in a form distinct from its earlier literary antecedents. Marsiya is extremely popular all over the world but some of the best exponents of Marsiya reside in Lucknow, the citadel of Shia Islam and capital of Uttar Pradesh. Shia Muslims regarded it an act of piety and religious duty to eulogies and bemoan the martyrs of Karbala. The sub-parts of Marsiya are called Noah and Soz which means lamentation and burning of heart respectively.

Masjid : Place of worship and *salaah* (prayer). It is called a mosque in English.

Naat: The dictionary meaning of '*naat*' is quality, praise, character of conduct. In a poetic term '*naat*' is an ode to and in praise of Prophet Mohammad (Peace be upon him) in which the character, qualities, conduct and inner and outer beauty of Prophet Mohammad are versified.

Quran Sharif: This means the Holy Quran.

Radhiallahu 'anhu: The meaning of this term is: 'May Allah be pleased with him'. This expression is used by Muslims whenever the name of a companion of the Prophet Mohammad is mentioned or used in writing.

Rabbana: This means: 'Our lord'.

Rabbana Lakal hamd: 'Our lord, praise is yours,' and it is said after rising from ruku in the namaz.

Rajab: Rajab is the seventh month of the Islamic calendar, which denotes 'the honoured month'. This month was held in great esteem by the pagan Arabs and like Muharram, it was a month during which fighting was forbidden.

Safar: Safar is the second month in the Islamic calendar.

Sadaqatul Fitr: This refers to the charity that is given on or prior to the day of Eid ul-Fitr.

Salaat: This literally means 'prayer'. It refers to a specific act in which one prays to Allah and is one of the five pillars of Islam.

Sallallahu 'alaihi wa sallam: 'May the blessings and the peace of Allah be upon him (Mohammad).'

Shariat: Islamic Law or the whole body of rules governing the life of Muslims which are derived from the Holy Quran and Sunna. It is also known as Sharia.

Sub'haanallah: 'Glory to Allah'.

Sunnat: In general, the word Sunnah means habit, practice, customary procedure, or action, norm and usage sanctioned by tradition. It refers to Prophet Mohammad's sayings, practices and living habits.

Sura: The Quran is composed of 114 chapters, each of which is called a sura. The plural of sura is called Suwar, which means chapters.

Sunni: This is a term referring to the Muslims who follow in the footsteps of Prophet Mohammad and who recognize the first four Khulafa as the rightful successors.

Tawaf-e-Qudoom: The first tawaf, observed by hajj pilgrims immediately after reaching Mecca, is called Tawaf-e-Qudoom or Tawaf-e-Tahiyya.

Tawaf-e-Sadr: The tawaf performed at the time of departure from Mecca is called Tawaf-e-Sadr or Tawaf-e-Wada.

Talbiyya: Proclaiming *Labbaik Allahumma labbaik* ..., and so on is called Talbiyya.

Wuzoo: It refers to the act of washing oneself before offering prayer. Muslims are required to perform wuzoo in preparation for ritual prayers and for handling and reading the Quran.

Yaum-e-Arafa: This refers to the ninth Zul Hijja, the day when hajj is performed and the pilgrims have to stay at Arafat.

Zakat: This literally means 'purity'. In Islam, it refers to alms-giving or charity of a stipulated amount. It is one of the five pillars of Islam.

Zumzum: This is the name of a well located in Masjid-e Haram near Baitullah in Mecca. It is a well to which Almighty Allah, out of his Divine power, made a spring of water to flow for the sake of His Prophet Hazrat Ismail and his mother. The water that comes out from this well is called zumzum water. Drinking of zumzum water is included in the rites of the hajj.

Urdu

Biryani: Biryani is a family of Middle Eastern and South Asian dishes made from a mixture of spices, rice, meat/ vegetables and yogurt.

Burqa: An enveloping outer garment worn for covering up the entire body. It is worn over the usual daily clothing (often a long dress or a shalwar kameez), and is removed when the woman returns to the sanctuary of the household.

Dars-e-Nizamiyya: Dars-e-Nizamiyya is a study curriculum used in a large number of madrasas in South Asia. It was standardized (and named after) Mullah Nizamuddin Sehalvi (d. 1748) at Firangi Mahal, a famous seminary of a family of Islamic scholars in Lucknow.

Dol: This is a round-shaped pitcher.

Dua: Muslims use this term and call out to God, and for Muslims, dua is the very essence of worship.

Dervish: The word 'dervish' refers to members of the Sufi Muslim ascetic religious *Tariqa,* known for their extreme poverty and austerity. The term is also used to refer to an unflappable or ascetic temperament.

Faqir: A fakir or faqir is a sufi, especially one who performs feats of endurance or apparent magic. When used to refer to sombre spiritual miracle-makers, the term fakir is applied primarily to a sufi, but also to Hindu ascetics.

Fatwa: This is an official decision taken by an Islamic religious leader or law-making body.

Gosht: Meat, usually mutton or beef.

Hajjat al-Wada: This signifies the Farewell Pilgrimage, when the Prophet bade farewell to his community (*ummah*).

Halq: Getting the hair of one's head shaven or shaving them on one's own is called halq. It releases one from the restrictions of ihram.

Hindi: Hindi also refers to 'Indian'. However, in modern times, this is specifically referred to as the Hindi language.

Hookah: A hookah is a single or multi-stemmed water pipe device for smoking. It originated in India but has gained popularity outside, especially in the Arab world. A hookah operates by water-filtration and indirect heat. It can be used for smoking many substances, such as herbal fruits and tobacco.

Hyderabadi biryani: The blending of Mughlai and Telangana cuisines in the kitchens of the Nizam (ruler of the historic Hyderabad State) resulted in the creation of Hyderabad biryani.

Iftar: *Iftar* refers to the breaking of the daily fast immediately after Maghrib (sunset) during the month of Ramazan. Iftar is often done as a community, with Muslims gathering in groups to break their fasts.

Ja-namaz: Prayer mat or prayer rug, also known as *musallah.* It is a piece of fabric used by Muslims during their five daily prayers.

Jama Masjid: Jama Masjid refers to the masjid in which Juma (Friday) prayer is offered. It is generally the main masjid in a town or city.

Lecture-baazi: It is literally the act of speaking at great length about something often in a boring way.

Loo: Loo is a strong, hot and dry wind, which blows during daytime in summer.

Maal: Maal means money or material.

Madrasa: Madrasa refers to an Islamic religious school that offers courses of study such as memorization of the Quran, *Tafsir* (Quranic interpretation), Sharia (Islamic law), Hadis (recorded sayings and deeds of Prophet Mohammad), *Mantiq* (logic) and Muslim history.

Mohalla: A term used to describe an area in the cities and towns of South Asia.

Moong dal: Moong bean, a type of a dal, also used in cuisine.

Mujawir: This refers to the caretaker of a Muslim dargah or shrine.

Mussalman: Mussalman is a synonym for Muslim.

Namaz: Namaz is a form of worship that Muslims are supposed to perform five times a day.

Nawab: In the Mughal Empire, a nawab was originally the subedar (provincial governor) or viceroy of a subah (province) or region.

Pathan: Member of a tribe living on the borders of Pakistan and Afghanistan.

Qazi: A qazi is a judge who is expert in Islamic law.

Qurbani: Qurbani (in Islam) refers to the ritual killing of animals during the Baqr Id festival.

Roza: This is the period of fasting observed by Muslims during the month of Ramazan.

Shurafa/Ashraf: Singular: Shareef. It refers to honourable or respectable men or families.

Sufi: This is a term used to refer to mystics or saints, also known as the *auliya* of Allah, (close friends of Allah), who have dedicated their entire lives in the submission of Allah.

Ziyarat: This literally means 'meeting'. The sites of pilgrimage include mosques, graves, battlefields, mountains and caves. Iranian Muslims use the word 'ziyarat' for both the hajj pilgrimage to Mecca and pilgrimages to other sites.

Bani Umayyah: The Umayyad dynasty, whose name is derived from Umayya ibn Abd Shams, the great-grandfather of Muawiyah I, was the first dynasty of the Muslim Khilafat, 660–750. Their capital was Damascus.

House of Saud: The House of Saud refers to the royal family of the Kingdom of Saudi Arabia. The modern nation of Saudi Arabia was established in 1932. Prior to the era of the Kingdom's founder, Abdul-Aziz ibn Saud, the family had ruled the Nejd and had had conflicts on several occasions with the Ottoman Empire, the Sharifs of Mecca, and the Al Rashid family of Ha'il.

Netherland Trading Company: This is the Dutch trading company, founded in 1621, mainly to carry on economic warfare against Spain and Portugal by striking at their colonies in the West Indies and South America, and on the west coast of Africa. The Dutch West India Company was much less successful than the Dutch East India Company, its counterpart in southeast Asia.

Royal Force: This refers to the naval military organization of the United Kingdom, charged with the national defence of the country at sea, protection of shipping, and fulfilment of international military agreements. The Royal Navy continued to be the world's most powerful navy well into the twentieth century.